Other Schiffer Books on Related Subjects:
Black College Football, 1892-1992: One Hundred Years of History, Education, & Pride, Michael Hurd, ISBN: 978-0-89865-882-8

Fighting for Fairness: The Life Story of Hall of Fame Sportswriter Sam Lacy, Sam Lacy, with Moses J. Newson, ISBN: 978-0-87033-512-9

Collectibles 101: Baseball, Don Raycraft, RC Raycraft, & Michael Raycraft, ISBN: 978-0-7643-0759-1

Library of Congress Control Number: 2017930639

Designed by Justin Watkinson
Cover design by John Cheek
Type set in Scala Sans/Minion Pro

ISBN: 978-0-7643-5284-3
Printed in China

Published by Schiffer Publishing, Ltd.
4880 Lower Valley Road
Atglen, PA 19310
Phone: (610) 593-1777; Fax: (610) 593-2002
E-mail: Info@schifferbooks.com
Web: www.schifferbooks.com

To the memory of Era Allen, who dreamed of a Hall of Fame induction for her son; to the memory of Terri Allen and to Richard Jr. and Heron, who are their father's greatest achievements in life; and to Howie Bedell, Mark Carfagno, Mike Schmidt, and Mike Tollin, who are determined to secure a bronze plaque in Cooperstown for their dear friend, Dick Allen.

TABLE OF CONTENTS

Foreword by Mike Schmidt 7
Preface 8

CHAPTER 1: Wampum 15
CHAPTER 2: Baptism by Fire 41
CHAPTER 3: Rookie of the Year 61
CHAPTER 4: Boo! 87
CHAPTER 5: Interlude 121
CHAPTER 6: Most Valuable Player 141
CHAPTER 7: Return to Philly 177
CHAPTER 8: Reconciliation 203
CHAPTER 9: Hall of Famer in Waiting 219

Appendices:
A: Dick Allen's Minor League Career Statistics 233
B: Dick Allen's Major League Career Statistics 235
C: Dick Allen's Honors and Career and
Single-Season Rankings 240

Notes 244
Bibliography............................284
Acknowledgments 286

Mike Schmidt, Philadelphia Phillies. *Artwork courtesy of Dick Perez*

FOREWORD

I remember standing at home plate at the stadium in Springfield, Illinois, back in 1970, with my best friend, Tom Smith. We were teammates on Ohio University's varsity baseball squad and happened to be killing some time. With no one else around, we began imitating Dick Allen.

Both of us had his unique batting stance and swing down perfectly—the closed stance, bat held low around the chest and cocked toward the pitcher; we recalled too his glasses, the old time batting helmet he wore on defense, his jersey unbuttoned at the top, and the white handball batting gloves. We were in awe of his game: a .300 hitter with power and speed.

It could be argued Dick was the best all-around player in the National League. As a black man playing in Philadelphia in the racially turbulent sixties, however, he was challenged with a life on and off the field that none of us today could imagine. He was booed unmercifully when his name was announced over the speakers at Connie Mack Stadium, often hit by objects thrown from the stands, and forced to live separately from his white teammates on the road because of the color of his skin.

Who could have imagined I would become his teammate a decade later when I began playing ball? In the mid-1970s, he shared his considerable knowledge of the game with me, something that allowed me to be the player I eventually became. He told me many times that I reminded him of himself when he was younger, and that he was, at age thirty-three, living the game through me. I now consider Dick one of my friends and mentors.

Dick Allen's story is *must* reading for all of today's players. Much like the stories of Curt Flood, Marvin Miller, and free agency, the plight of the black man, starting with Jackie Robinson in the 1940s and then Richie Allen in the sixties, is one we should all acknowledge.

William Kashatus has given us a clear view into the life and times of one of the greatest players in baseball history, but one who continues to be overlooked by baseball's Hall of Fame.

Mike Schmidt

Philadelphia Phillies' Hall of Fame third baseman

PREFACE

On Thursday, July 8, 1965, the Philadelphia Phillies were playing the San Francisco Giants at Connie Mack Stadium, their ramshackle ballpark at 21st and Lehigh Streets in North Philadelphia. It was the second game of a doubleheader. The Phils had already dropped the opener 10-2. With Jack Sanford—a seasoned veteran who once pitched for the Phillies—starting the second game for San Francisco, the Giants seemed primed for a sweep.

Ray Herbert, a journeyman pitcher, started the game for the Phillies and kept the Giants hitless in the first inning. In the bottom of the frame Johnny Briggs, the Phillies' speedy center fielder, led off and worked a walk. Second baseman Cookie Rojas followed with a bunt single, and right fielder Johnny Callison punched another single through the left side of the infield. With the bases loaded and no outs, Richie Allen, the Phils' young cleanup hitter, walked to the plate.

Allen, the Phillies' first African American star, was hitting .328 and had recently been named the starting third baseman for the National League's All-Star team. He won the coveted "Rookie of the Year" award the previous season when his hitting kept the Phils in the pennant race until the final day of the campaign.

Despite his success, Allen was treated with hostility by hometown fans. No sooner would his name be announced than the crowd would explode in a fusillade of boos and jeers. Some screamed "darkie" or "monkey" at him. Others were more hateful, shouting "Nigger!" at the top of their lungs. A white father seated behind the Phillies' dugout held his little boy in one arm and pointed at the beleaguered star with the other, teaching his son to boo.

Allen did not appear fazed by the maliciousness, but on this day he could feel the anger coursing through him. He stood in against Sanford and worked the count to two balls and one strike before tearing into a high-inside fastball for his twelfth home run of the season. It was also his first major league grand slam, a moon shot that easily cleared the left field roof of the stadium. Suddenly the boos turned into cheers as the 37,000-strong crowd took to their feet to give Allen a standing ovation. It was the "ultimate mind game," he would say after the Phillies' 4-2 victory.[1] Nor was it a solitary incident.

The schizophrenic treatment of Allen continued for the next four years. While the hometown fans appreciated his offensive prowess, they never really accepted Allen. Nor did they try to understand his difficult circumstances as a black superstar in a segregated city.

Between 1965 and 1969, when he was finally traded to the St. Louis Cardinals, Richie Allen found playing in Philadelphia to be an increasingly hellish experience. The city was in the throes of the Civil Rights movement. These were the years of a growing black activism. Cecil B. Moore, the militant local NAACP president, went head to head with the police commissioner Frank Rizzo, who had a well-earned reputation for brutality. Things became especially bad during the summer of '64, when a race riot broke out in North Philadelphia, not far from Connie Mack Stadium. It began on August 28 and continued for the next few days. None of the prominent black leaders could stop it. The neighborhood and local businesses were destroyed, resulting in three million dollars in damages. North Philadelphia never really recovered economically from the riot, which also had severe implications for the rest of the city. Fearing the worst, increasing numbers of white residents fled to the suburbs. Philadelphia became a city of minorities, the elderly, and the poor. Many whites who remained were resentful toward blacks, and those who were Phillies fans saw Allen as an easy target at which to express their resentment.[2]

It didn't matter that he was a regular .300 hitter who averaged thirty home runs and ninety RBIs each year.[3] Off the field Allen regularly received hate mail, some with death threats. Once he was sucker punched by a fan appearing to want to shake his hand. The front lawn of his Mount Airy home was strewn with trash, compliments of disgruntled fans.[4] On the ball diamond, Allen began wearing a batting helmet when he played the outfield to avoid injury from coins and beer cans that rained down on him from the bleachers. This idiosyncrasy earned him the nickname "Crash," a reference to a batting or crash helmet. At one point it got so bad some of his teammates urged the star to hire a bodyguard. But Allen took it in stride. "The fans are not the ones I want to beat," he said. "If I paid my money to see a ball game I guess I'd raise a little hell, too."[5]

At the same time, Allen fueled the conflict with his controversial behavior and inflammatory remarks to the press. He was a moody man whose closest friends were his black teammates, members of the clubhouse staff, and the grounds crew. When his repeated requests to be traded were denied by Phillies' ownership, Allen, who did not enjoy the luxury of free agency, tried to force a deal. He resorted to unexcused absences, arriving late to games, and scrawling words in the dirt around first base. It was during this period that Allen, claiming that his manhood was being disrespected, insisted he be referred to as "Dick" instead of the more boyish "Richie."[6]

Philadelphia's sportswriters were intrigued by Allen. They were in awe of his tremendous power and athletic ability, but wavered in their judgments of him as a person. Sometimes writers painted the beleaguered star as a malcontent who expected special treatment. Some even suggested Allen was playing on the racial tensions dividing the city at the time. On other occasions the city's baseball writers, especially the young ones, celebrated his rebelliousness as being consistent with the times.[7] For better, but mostly for worse, the Philadelphia sportswriters shaped and misshaped Richie Allen's public persona. In the end, Allen's rebellious behavior alienated him from many teammates, reinforced the negative stereotype the fans and the media imposed on him, and further inflamed the hostility toward him.

Whether you liked him or not, Allen forced Philadelphia's baseball fans to come to terms with the racism that existed in the city during the 1960s. He may not have done it with the same self discipline or tact as Jackie Robinson, but he exemplified the emerging independence of Major League Baseball players, as well as growing black consciousness. While his unexcused absences, candid opinions, and pre-game beer drinking earned him some of the harshest press in Philadelphia sports history, his tape measure home runs and exceptional speed gained him tremendous admiration from fellow players—black and white. That admiration continued after he left Philadelphia to play for the St. Louis Cardinals, Los Angeles Dodgers, and Chicago White Sox.

Allen's career also reflects the dynamic culture of the 1970s, with its changing fashions in clothing and hairstyles, the growth of Black Power, and the emphasis on antiheroes and nonconformists in American film and music. In fact, Allen was both a catalyst and product of '70s culture and its impact on the conservative baseball establishment. He was the first player to sprout an Afro and among the first to grow facial hair. He was the first player to be saddled with the reputation of "Baseball's Bad Boy." He was involved, albeit unintentionally, in Curt Flood's challenge to baseball's reserve clause. And he benefitted from the introduction of cookie-cutter, multipurpose stadiums with artificial turf during a decade when speed on the base paths became just as important as power hitting.[8]

Allen has always been a subject of endless fascination to me. I was in elementary school when he came up with the Phillies in the mid-1960s. He was known as "Richie" then. I attended a small, socially diverse Quaker school in northeast Philadelphia, and I quickly learned to appreciate the Society of Friends' strong commitment to civil rights. On more than one occasion my teachers pointed out the horrific treatment Allen received from Philadelphia's baseball fans as an example of the social injustice that was occurring in our city. The message was loud and clear: "Black people deserve the very same respect for human dignity given to white people, and if they're not receiving it we all have a responsibility to address the issue." Since that time I have found myself irresistibly drawn to baseball and civil rights, particularly those involving African Americans.

I was in high school when Dick Allen returned to the Phillies in the mid-1970s. Seated in the upper deck of Veterans Stadium, I eagerly anticipated a tape measure clout whenever he stepped to the plate. Together with Mike Schmidt, Allen inspired my fascination with the home run—what I believed to be the true measure of a hitter's brilliance. Thus, it is no coincidence that I adopted Allen as a personal hero, and later Schmidt, who was mentored by him.

Every kid needs a hero. Heroes represent the values a young person aspires to in life. No matter how public a hero becomes, he remains very personal to those who adopt him, because heroes help us define ourselves, our lives, and our ambitions, particularly during adolescence. "Class," "talent," and "strength"—these were the qualities I saw in Dick Allen, what I admired about him. When I grew older, I discovered that many others had also adopted him as their hero, but for quite different reasons.

Three books have been written about Allen: *Crash: The Life and Times of Dick Allen*, an autobiography he coauthored with Tim Whitaker in 1989; an earlier book I wrote titled *September Swoon: Richie Allen, the '64 Phillies, and Racial Integration*, which was published in 2004; and Mitch Nathanson's *God Almighty Hisself: The Life and Legacy of Dick Allen*, published in 2016.[9] *Crash* offers Allen's own perspective a little over a decade after he retired from professional baseball. The autobiography, written in a conversational tone, is a candid account, alternating between a "defense" and a "confession," which is not unusual for that genre. But the book was criticized by reviewers for "raising more questions than it answers" about Dick's career and for blaming Philadelphia sportswriters for creating an image of him as a malcontent. The reviewers were none other than Philadelphia sportswriters, who seem to have forgotten that Dick has a right to his own opinion about his career.[10]

September Swoon explores the Phillies' early efforts at racial integration through the lens of the 1964 team and explains why those efforts deteriorated into a living hell for Allen. What had begun as a promising effort to create Philadelphia's first truly integrated baseball team, as well as its first pennant winner in more than a decade, reached its high point on September 21, 1964, when the Phillies held a 6½ game lead over the St. Louis Cardinals and Cincinnati Reds, who were tied for second place. With just twelve games left to play, the Fightin' Phils dropped ten straight to finish one game behind the National League pennant-winning Cards. But the "swoon," considered the most heartbreaking event in Philadelphia sports history, was only the beginning of a self-destructive skid in team performance and racial integration. Ultimately, the two things that made those Phillies special threatened to tear them apart. An antagonistic press and contentious fans blamed Dick for the Phils' losing ways and accused him of dividing the team along racial lines. Allen, a victim of racism, manipulated the resulting controversy with the hope he would be traded, but in the process he unwittingly frayed further already tenuous relations.

I spent nearly a decade doing the research for and writing the book and was a beneficiary of two lengthy interviews with Allen, as well as more than a dozen more from his Phillies' teammates. As a result, I was overjoyed when *September Swoon* was extremely well received by the scholarly community, as well as by the popular press, and that *Elysian Fields Quarterly: The Baseball Review* presented it with their Dave Moore Award for "most important baseball book of 2004."[11]

Finally, *God Almighty Hisself* attempts to separate the myth from the reality of Allen's career and controversial behavior. The value of the book is Nathanson's successful effort to present Allen's life in the context of baseball's business shifts and ongoing desegregation process, which began in the mid-1940s when the Brooklyn Dodgers signed Jackie Robinson and continued into the mid-1970s. In addition, the depth and breadth of his research using primary source material regarding Allen's career is impressive.

Unfortunately, Dick refused to be interviewed for the book, forcing Nathanson to rely mostly on quotations from newspaper and magazine accounts.[12] The absence of this firsthand account is conspicuous, as is the author's failure to provide a definitive conclusion about Allen himself. Instead, Nathanson simply presents the alternating viewpoints of Allen's critics and his supporters throughout the work. Not until the epilogue does Nathanson suggest that the Phillies' first black superstar is a "tragedy." On one hand, he asserts that Allen was a "true rebel" who was ahead of his time, and that he "likely would have been embraced rather than caricatured if he played in the 1980s or 1990s." On the other hand, Nathanson writes that Allen, unlike other antiheroes who came in his wake, "refused to ask for forgiveness" for his controversial behavior, "so he has never received it," leaving the reader with the strong impression that Allen does not *deserve* forgiveness, either. The book is at best faint praise from a writer who doesn't know anything more about Allen than what he has read in the newspaper accounts of the 1960s and 1970s.[13]

On the contrary, I do not see Dick Allen as a tragedy. Instead, I view him as a genuinely good but complicated human being. Dick has a multifaceted personality: a son who worshipped his mother; an introverted and emotionally sensitive young black man who was forced into the national spotlight at a tumultuous period in baseball and American history; a devoted father who cares very deeply for his children; a teammate who guided younger players when they were struggling; an independent thinker who said and did as he pleased; a proud but humble man who refuses to campaign for the baseball immortality he so richly deserves; and a friend who quietly endears himself to others through simple acts of kindness.

Dick Allen: The Life and Times of a Baseball Immortal is a labor of love for my first childhood hero. It is based on contemporary newspaper and magazine accounts, interviews I recorded with Dick in 2001 and 2003, and more recent interviews with family members, friends, and teammates, as well as an in-depth analysis of his career statistics. The book is richly illustrated with the artwork of Dick Perez, Rob Larsen, and Charles Linnett, as well as photographs from *Sports Illustrated*, *Life Magazine*, *The Philadelphia Evening Bulletin*, Chicago Baseball Museum, Chicago White Sox Baseball Club, and the Allen family's private collection, which are published here for the first time.

Ultimately, this is the story of one of the finest players in the history of Major League Baseball and one who deserves to be enshrined in the National Baseball Hall of Fame.

William C. Kashatus

Philadelphia, Pennsylvania

August 2016

Note: Allen is referred to alternatively as "Richie," "Rich," or "Dick" throughout the book, depending on the time period and the team for which he played. During his early years with the Phillies, for example, teammates, coaches, the press, opposing ballplayers, and fans knew him as "Richie." When he played for the St. Louis Cardinals and Los Angeles Dodgers, he was generally referred to as "Rich" by those same groups. Still later, when he played for the Chicago White Sox, he was known as "Dick," the same name he was called by family members and childhood friends who were interviewed for the book.

Dick Allen was a standout basketball player for Wampum High School, leading the team to Pennsylvania state titles in 1958 and 1960.
Courtesy of James Santelli

CHAPTER 1:
WAMPUM

Wampum, Pennsylvania, is a sleepy little town forty miles north of Pittsburgh and ten miles east of the Ohio border. Founded in 1796 as a Kuskuskie Indian trading post, the settlement grew by leaps and bounds after 1870, when the Pennsylvania Railroad began transporting steel to the east coast from the neighboring towns of Ellwood City and Beaver Falls. By the 1940s, when Richie Allen was growing up there, Wampum's population was about 1,090. Residents were employed by the steel industry or other kinds of manufacturing, including Kastik Products, the Kohlman Bottling Company, and the Medusa Cement Company. Framed single-family dwellings were concentrated in one area of the town's four square miles. The town boasted one traffic light, four churches, two taverns, a two-story schoolhouse, one firehouse, and a hardware store along Main Street.

Wampum was also a picturesque community. The town, perched on a hill overlooking the Beaver River in scenic Lawrence County, was surrounded by a black hardwood forest where wildlife could be found, especially game birds and whitetail deer. From the dainty blossoms of springtime mountain laurel to the blazing colors of autumn, the region offered its residents some of the most breathtaking views in western Pennsylvania. Even in winter the contrast of dark green pine needles against the bright white of a new snowfall was inviting.

What was so special about Wampum in the post–World War II era were the people. They were friendly, humble, God-fearing folks. Neighbors took time to talk to each other, to protect each other and their children. After a hard day's work, shot-and-beer locals retreated to the town's two taverns, enjoyed a few Rolling Rocks, and discussed the recent fortunes of the Pirates or Steelers, both of whom played less than an hour away in Pittsburgh. There was a strong sense of community among the polyglot of whites descended from the original German and Scots-Irish settlers or the Russians, Italians, and Poles who followed, and the town's small African American population.[1] Regardless of ethnicity, Wampum's residents shared the same refreshingly innocent outlook toward life, one that was endemic to the small rural towns of western Pennsylvania.

Embracing the time-honored values of self-respect, personal industry, and a healthy cynicism toward outsiders, residents operated by the golden rule: if someone had a problem with a neighbor, they had an obligation to say their piece. Trust had to be earned; it was not freely given. Once earned, though, people were fiercely loyal

Era Allen, shown here in 1960, raised eight children and instilled a love of family, devotion to God, and self-respect in all of them. *Courtesy of the Allen Family*

to each other and the members of their family. In fact, an individual was defined by his family, especially his parents. If mom and dad were respected, the children were accepted by the community. Personal achievement was admired, as long as the individual remembered "where he came from" and didn't put on airs when he returned to acknowledge his past. It was an outlook held by a passionate people who, when they "liked" somebody, "liked 'em hard." But God help the person they did not like. And yet, for all of their ambivalence, the people of Wampum were genuinely good human beings who were generally optimistic about the future. Perhaps that is why there was no color line in the town. Race meant little in a community where everyone was struggling to make ends meet. Middle class, working class, or poor, it didn't matter. No one was wealthy. Everyone lived within modest means. But the residents also had a fierce sense of pride that often yielded to stubbornness. Charity was not accepted. If someone owed you money, it was paid back. If someone helped you out, you returned the favor.[2]

Era Allen epitomized these rural, small-town values. Born on January 23, 1907, in Enoree, South Carolina, Era was the fifth-born of James and Sallie (Whitmire) Rhodes's six children. Both parents had Native American and African American ancestry. James relocated his family to several northern cities in search of more lucrative employment. Sometime in the early 1920s, the family planted roots in Chewton, a small hamlet near Wampum, Pennsylvania, where James found permanent employment at the Medusa Cement plant.[3]

Era was an attractive woman whose Cherokee Indian ancestry was visible in her strong features. She and her younger sister, Cora, were inseparable. Like their mother, the two sisters joined the First Baptist Church and remained active members for the rest of their lives. In fact, Era, in her later years, was selected "Mother of the Church" by the congregation. In that role she was a mentor to many of the younger women.[4] In 1924, Era met and married Coy W. Allen, a mill worker at Medusa. She became pregnant with their first child soon after. Coy, fearing he was not ready for the responsibility of fatherhood, left his new bride and returned to his parents' 150-acre farm in King George, Virginia. Their separation would last nearly a decade.

A few years later Era met and married Wyatte Craine, who was also employed by Medusa. He was a good man who adored his wife, nicknaming her "Kitten." The couple had five children of their own—a son named Ceasar and four daughters, Helen, Dorothy, Iona, and Sarah—in addition to Era's son Coy Jr., who also took the surname Craine. When Wyatte died of pneumonia in 1931, Era was again on her own. For the next nine years she supported her family by working as a seamstress for various New Deal programs. "You just lived," she once explained. "You came through with scars, but you just thank God you made it."[5]

In 1940, Coy Allen Sr. returned to Wampum to reconcile with his wife. After meeting his son and namesake, he apologized to Era for leaving her and promised to do better by her if she agreed to take him back. Before she agreed, Era pointed out she now had five children—four by another man—and wanted to know whether Coy would accept them as his own family. "It doesn't matter," said Coy, "All those children would've been mine anyway if I hadn't left."

Coy began his own trucking business—an exceptional undertaking for a black man during the Great Depression —while Era stayed at home to take care of the family and continued as a seamstress for the New Deal's Works Progress Administration (WPA). The couple would eventually have three more sons: Hank, Dick, and Ronnie. Era and Coy shared a wonderful, earthy sense of humor, and made their home a place of happiness and joy for their family. Teasing and fun-loving wisecracks were a constant in the couple's ongoing repartee—a valued trait inherited by Dick, in particular. But there were also tensions in the marriage, as Era and Coy were strong-willed individuals. She did not like his beer drinking after a hard day's work and he did not appreciate her lectures on the evils of alcohol. Their differences were understandable.

Coy Allen Sr. with Cesar (left) and toddler Ronnie. Coy Sr. treated Wyatte Craine's children as if they were his own. *Courtesy of the Allen Family*

Sarah Craine holding baby brother Ronnie Allen. Era and Coy cultivated a strong sense of family loyalty among their children, regardless of the child's father. There was no such thing as a "stepchild" or "stepsibling"—all the children were well loved and treated equally. *Courtesy of the Allen Family*

Coy, like most men of the time, considered himself the "man of the house," and often felt as if he was being put down by his wife. On the other hand, Era's uncompromising dislike of alcohol came from the fact that her father and brother became argumentative when they imbibed. As a result, Coy never drank in excess, nor did he partake in the house; rather, he limited his drinking to the tavern. But when Era still expressed her displeasure over the habit and he could no longer tolerate it, Coy left the house for extended periods. Still, he always came back. Nor did either of them ever consider divorce.[6]

Whenever her husband left, Era went to greater lengths to make life happy for the children and to remind them they were her "pride and joy in life." She also found her own strength and happiness in them and in her Christian faith. "Family was extremely important to my mother," recalled Hank Allen. "We were all loving brothers and sisters, and we felt that way because my mother made it that way for us. She expected our family to sit down together every night for supper, no 'ifs,' 'ands,' or 'buts.' That made us close-knit, able to appreciate the things that were going on in each other's lives." Era also expected her children to be perfect ladies and gentlemen when they stepped outside her home. If she learned any of them misbehaved in school or in public, the offending child would be reprimanded sternly with the biting remark, "People are probably wondering what kind of a family you come from. Don't you ever embarrass yourself or this family again!" Applying guilt with the skillfulness of a seasoned judge, Era and her God-fearing ways instilled compassion and discipline in her children, as well as a fierce loyalty to each other. To be sure, Era Allen was the most influential person in the lives of her children, especially her fourth-born son Dick, who worshipped her.[7]

Born on March 8, 1942, Richard Anthony Allen was called "Dick" by his family because "Richard" sounded too stuffy and "Richie" too childish.[8] Friends nicknamed him "Sleepy" because an injury to his right eye left the eyelid slightly contorted, as if he was half asleep.[9] "We were poor, but we didn't realize it because Mom made us close," said Dick. "We were one of just fifteen black families in town. Most of them were white . . . Polish, Russian, a few Italians. But I never knew racism growing up. I ate and slept at white peoples' houses as a kid, and they ate and slept at ours."[10] Not that the Allen house had much to offer; it was an old frame structure with no indoor plumbing or furnace. "We had air conditioning, though," Dick would joke years later. "It was the kind that comes through the walls!"

To supplement groceries, the Allen family raised beans, okra, corn, rutabagas, and potatoes in their own garden, and each of the boys was expected to plant and pick vegetables. "My Mom could cook that stuff," recalled Dick. "Reach in there with a little smothered steak every now and then. Come in with that fried chicken on Sunday. Biscuits, greens, mashed potatoes . . . she could get down."[11]

On summer days Era sat on the porch of her old frame house sewing and watched her four sons play baseball on the WPA-constructed sandlot nearby.[12] "That ball field," she said, "helped me to raise my boys. It kept them out of trouble. They lived on the ball diamond 365 days a year, and I spent lots of days sitting on the porch watching them, and I'd have to call them in for dinner." Dick gave her the most trouble at dusk when it was time for supper. "I'd had to whip that boy to get him off the ball field," Era recalled. "If I didn't, he would never sleep or eat—just play ball."[13]

Walter Kubinski, the Allen's next door neighbor and grocery store owner, confirmed Era's observation. "What a kid!" he said. "Sleepy never wasted any daylight. If he could see, he'd play ball."[14]

Once Kubinski heard a continuous cracking sound against the back wall of his store. When he went outside to investigate he had to scramble to avoid being hit by a steady stream of pebbles flying overhead. But he immediately abandoned the investigation when he saw Sleepy picking up the small stones and whacking them in the direction of his store with a broom handle. At that moment the grocer realized Dick was determined to become a professional baseball player.[15]

Despite the "pebble whacking" incident, Kubinski insisted "Era Allen raised all her kids well." "None of 'em ever got into trouble," he explained, "because she always knew what was going on in their lives. She was a proud woman, too. Years ago I saved soup bones for Era, even gave her some credit. And every cent she ever owed me she paid back."[16]

Era was a strict disciplinarian to all the children. There were no exceptions. Accordingly, all of the Allen siblings attended church on Sundays; all of them had chores to do around the house; and all of them were expected to earn good grades. The day her children returned home from school with report cards for Era to sign, she waited at the front door to meet each one. There was no circumventing her, either. Hank discovered that sad reality when he was in seventh grade and tried to change the "F" on his mathematics grade to a "B" with a black ink pen. Era was not fooled, and she pulled him off the basketball team, a punishment all her sons considered worse than a good whipping.[17] As a result, Dick learned early on that if he wanted to play ball he had better do as his mother ordered, whether that be attending church services, doing his chores, or completing his homework before going on the playing field. "My mother didn't stand for any nonsense," he remembered. "The punishment for anything was a good whalin', and believe me, I took many of them." In fact, during his years in the majors, younger teammates would approach Dick and ask him to identify the toughest hitter he ever saw. "My mother," he replied, tongue in cheek.[18]

To be sure, Dick asserted his will more often than his siblings. Even his mother admitted he was "really strong-willed." "If he didn't like what I had to say, he would listen, then do what he pleased," she explained. "Yet he never sassed back."[19] That was an important distinction in the Allen household, where it was considered "disrespectful" to talk back, but simply "strong-willed" to disobey orders. Besides, Era secretly respected her young son's passion for baseball. "Dick kept his hat on in the house all the time," she said. "But because it was a baseball cap I let him wear it, except at meals and in bed. He'd be all dolled up in his Sunday best with that baseball cap on."[20] It was one of the very few concessions Era made because she knew how much her son loved the game.

Hank Allen, age five, drives a makeshift fire engine while younger brother Dick, age three, stands behind him. The two brothers were inseparable growing up. *Courtesy of the Allen Family*

When Dick was six or seven years old, he saw a baseball game on TV and told his mother, "I'm going to be a big leaguer someday. I'll play on TV, make a big salary and buy you a nice house."[21] When he told other youngsters about his plans they laughed at him, though he was accepted as "one of their own" because of his athletic prowess.[22] "Dick was a happy-go-lucky kid growing up," said his brother Hank. "Although he tended to be quiet and serious about certain things, he was also a cut-up and always kept us laughing."[23] Ultimately, Dick believed it did not matter what his peers thought. He was too much of an individual to care. Instead, the youngster marched to the beat of his own drum, a genuine nonconformist. And there was at least one adult in Wampum who believed Dick had the ability to

Dick, age four (right), with mother Era and baby brother Ronnie. *Courtesy of the Allen Family*

Dick, age five, is all smiles.
Courtesy of the Allen Family

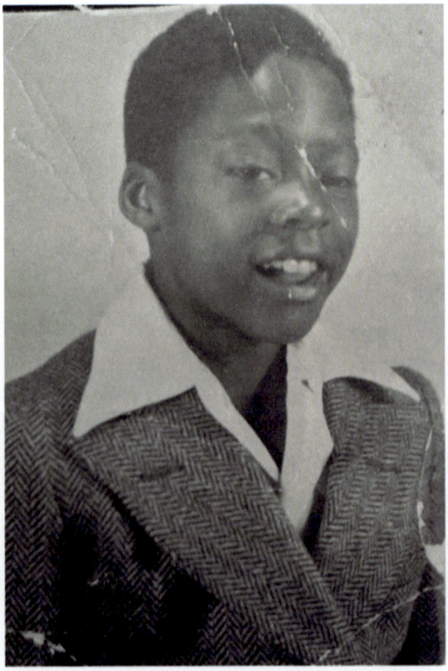

Dick, age six (1948), was always a fancy dresser.
Courtesy of the Allen Family

realize his baseball dreams: L. Butler Hennon, the principal at Wampum High School, who also doubled as a little league coach and varsity basketball coach.

"Once Dick literally knocked the cover off a baseball when he was nine years old," recalled Hennon. "He hit that ball so hard it went over a row of pines and it hit a willow, and when we found it the cover was off."[24] The next day Hennon told Era about the incident and predicted "someday that boy's going to play in the big leagues."[25]

"Sports was all I had," Dick admitted years later. "My biggest fear growing up was that I'd end up working in the steel mills or some other kind of factory job. I didn't want that—working ten- or twelve-hour days, only to go home and sit in front of the television with a beer. That possibility scared the hell out of me."[26]

Despite his gift for sports—or perhaps because of it —Dick was not given a free pass. Like his siblings, he earned money by delivering newspapers and working at Carvelli's vegetable store in addition to the chores his mother gave him. The jobs were meant to inculcate a sense of responsibility, and perhaps were negative incentive to leave the depressed area after high school.

While Dick was raised primarily by his mother, his father was still a constant in his life until age fifteen, when his parents separated for good. Even then Coy Sr. continued to have a relationship with his sons. "My brothers and I got our love of horses from our father," said Hank in a recent interview. "On Sundays Dad would hitch up his horse 'Jack' to a buggy and take Dick, Ronnie, and me for a long ride out in the country." Coy Sr. also taught his sons how to care for the animal.

Nicknamed "Sleepy" by friends because of a drooping left eyelid that made him appear as if he was half asleep, Dick, by his senior year of high school, was a reserved individual with tremendous athletic ability. *Courtesy of James Santelli*

He had another horse named "Ginger" who was suffering from distemper. To heal him, Coy devised a concoction of chicken feathers, pine tar, and sulfur, spread it across a blanket, and placed the blanket over the horse's head. After a few treatments the horse not only regained its health, but was one of the finest looking animals in Lawrence County. Dick spent hours with his father, "working with the horses and exercising them," which is how he "developed his own love for breeding thoroughbreds."[27] Richard Jr. believes the arrangement also allowed Dick to maintain a relationship with his father even after Coy Sr. relocated to Coreopolis thirty miles away.[28]

Interestingly, no one in Wampum expected Dick to make a name for himself in baseball, but rather in basketball. One of only five African Americans in a class of forty students at Wampum High School, Dick, following in the footsteps of his older brothers, excelled at the sport. "Sleepy was much better known for basketball around here," said Wendell Allen (no relation), who operated a gas station in the town. "Wampum was the smallest high school in Pennsylvania—only forty-six boys. Sleepy sparked our school to eighty-two straight victories and two championships. He was one of the best basketball players ever to come out of these parts."[29] It was high praise for a player who hailed from a basketball powerhouse.

Under the tutelage of head coach L. Butler Hennon—also the school principal and history teacher—Wampum High School's varsity basketball team put the tiny town on the map, achieving a reputation for incredible success on the hardwood floor. Between 1942 and 1962, the Wampum High Indians won a total of sixteen

Wampum High School. *Courtesy of James Santelli*

Wampum High School today. *Author photo*

Western Pennsylvania Interscholastic Athletic League (WPIAL) Section 20 championships and three Class B state titles. The 1950s were an especially fruitful period for Hennon's Indians, who won twelve straight WPIAL Section 20 championships and three state titles. Although Wampum was so small it had a Class C affiliation, it regularly played much larger Class B schools and defeated them. The Indians achieved their first Class B state championship game in early 1953, but lost a heartbreaker (71-70) to Irwin, a larger high school near McKeesport. Not to be denied, Wampum, led by senior sensation Donnie Hennon, the coach's son, posted an incredible 31-0 record and won their first Class B state title in 1955. The team also went undefeated in league play the following season, but unfortunately bowed out in the WPIAL finals.[30]

L. Butler Hennon was the principal of Wampum High School, as well as a history teacher and the schools' basketball and baseball coach. *Courtesy of James Santelli*

Although Wampum High was such a small school, Butler Hennon was blessed with some special talent, including Dick and his brothers—Coy Jr., Ceasar, Hank, and Ronnie—as well as Hennon's own son Donnie, who would go on to star at the University of Pittsburgh and later pass up a career in the National Basketball Association to become a physician. "I think Coy Jr. set the standard for the rest of us," explained Hank:

> We called him "Sonny," and he graduated from high school in 1943, so Dick, Ronnie and I never saw him play high school ball. But we knew from the stories everyone in town told us he was an amazing basketball

Coy Allen Jr., the first of the Allen brothers to play for Coach Hennon, set an example of hard work and a team-first attitude for his younger siblings. *Courtesy of the Allen Family*

Harold "Hank" Allen was the captain and leading scorer of Wampum High School's state championship basketball team in 1957–58. *Courtesy of the Allen Family*

> player and one of the top five scorers in the school's history.
>
> Sonny used to get up at 6:00 in the morning and practice his free throws, layups, and outside shots for more than an hour before school started. He was a hard worker and a team player, too. It's no coincidence that Dick and I followed his example. We idolized Sonny. In fact, when I was in grade school I used to page through a scrapbook full of newspaper articles on his [high school] basketball career and dream of being just like him. That's why I took his uniform No. 7 when I played.[31]

Just as much credit for the Indians' success belonged to the coach. Known as "Hook" to his players because of his hook-shaped nose, Hennon, a Wampum High and Geneva College graduate, used some unusual practice techniques. It was not uncommon for his players to practice wearing weighted jackets, heavy gloves, thick boots, and special glasses to improve their skills.[32] "Hook was a very innovative basketball coach," said Jim Santelli, who played on Wampum's 1960 state championship basketball team:

Dick, like his brothers before him, practiced his free throws and outside shots an hour before school began every morning. *Courtesy of James Santelli*

Younger brother Ronnie joined Dick on the varsity basketball team as a sophomore. Ronnie would later accept a basketball scholarship to Youngstown State University. *Courtesy of the Allen Family*

> He wasn't like most coaches who yelled at their players. He rarely yelled at us. But he would make you practice with boots on, or juggle balls, things like that, and the players would do it, too. Anything he said we'd do. Hook was the kind of coach who'd make you want to go out and practice on your own. You could do that, too, because he made sure the gym was always open and the balls were left out for us.[33]

Hennon's unusual practice techniques and inspirational influence produced the desired effect of winning.

The high point for Wampum High School basketball came between 1957 and 1960. Led by Hank and Dick "Sleepy" Allen, the small, Class C school dominated the local competition while competing against larger Class B schools like Union, Shenango, New Wilmington, Laurel, and Bessemer, and even larger Class A schools like Ellwood City, New Castle, and Zelienople. The Indians recorded several lengthy unbeaten streaks, including an amazing eighty-two-game win streak. In 1957–58, the Indians defeated a much taller Avonworth team in the WPIAL semifinals (77-52) to advance to the District 7 title game. Hank was the leading scorer in that game

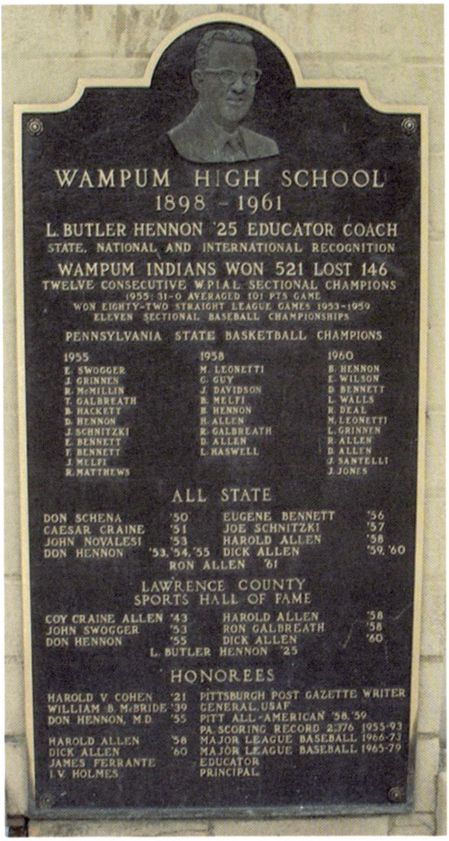

Wampum High School's honor roll included the Allen brothers. *Author photo*

with eighteen points, while Dick added another fourteen points.[34] In the title game against Bethlehem Dick scored eighteen and Harold fifteen to pace the Indians to a 69-57 victory, allowing the team to advance to the first round of the Class B Pennsylvania Interscholastic Athletic Association's (PIAA's) playoffs.[35]

Hank was unstoppable against Renovo—the Indians' opponent in the first round of the PIAA—leading the team with twenty-two points and twenty-eight rebounds; Hank paced Wampum to a 77-35 blowout victory.[36] In round two Wampum faced Fredonia, who led by seventeen points at halftime. Hennon used a full-court press in the second half to shut down Fredonia's offense while the Allen brothers went to work at both ends of the court. At game's end, the Indians had pulled out a 63-60 squeaker. Hank scored twenty points and pulled down twenty-six rebounds, while Dick contributed sixteen points and fourteen rebounds to advance the Indians to the state championship game.[37]

On March 28, 1958, more than 6,000 spectators packed the Hershey Arena to see the Indians take on Columbia for the state Class B basketball title. Hank scored the first two points for Wampum in the opening minute, and they never trailed the rest of the game. Hank (twenty-one points) and Dick (sixteen points) led the attack. Shooting 50%, the Indians walked off with the title 82-64. Wampum also captured national attention in January when the team was featured in a cover story in *Life Magazine*.[38]

Although Wampum lost to Snowden of Allegheny County for the WPIAL title in 1958–59, the Indians posted an impressive 20-2 record.[39] The team set a national scoring record when it defeated Neshannock 154-54 and broke a WPIAL record in stringing together eighty-two straight victories in Section 20 play dating back to 1957. Wampum's only losses came to Philadelphia's Overbrook High School and Union in the season finale. It was also a good year for Dick, who was joined on the

Wampum High School Indians, 1958 Pennsylvania state champions. Seated (left to right): Bill Hennon, Hank Allen, Ronald Galbreath, Dick Allen, and Larry Haswell. Standing (left to right): Coach L. B. Hennon, Mike Leonetti, Gary Guy, Jack Davidson, and Bill Melfi. *Courtesy of James Santelli*

team by his younger brother Ronnie. Sleepy topped all scorers with 536 points in twenty-two games, averaging more than twenty-four points per game.[40]

By the beginning of the 1969–70 school year Dick, a senior, was getting bored with his studies. He would occasionally pass the time by getting into mischief with a classmate. More often than not Dick did not instigate the prank; he simply got caught in the act and was punished for it. Fortunately, Principal Hennon was looking out for him, though not in a way he might have appreciated. "If Sleeper did something wrong in school," recalled Jim Santelli,

> Mrs. Allen knew about it immediately because Hook would go and tell her.
>
> It's not like that today when a kid misbehaves and the school disciplines him for it. Then the parents go complain to the principal and take their kid's side. Growing up in Wampum in the mid- to late 1950s, you couldn't get away with anything because the parents and the school were on the same page. That had its advantages, too.
>
> Hook was beloved in Wampum because he always communicated with the parents and stayed on top of their kids. That created a tight knit community. For Sleepy, Hennon was like a second father. If Hook said something Sleeper might not have liked it, but he listened. It was the same with his mother.[41]

In his senior year Dick became the undisputed star of the team. As captain and starting guard he led all Indian scorers with 445 points that season; his single-game high was thirty-nine in an 86-61 victory over Union on February 23.[42] Unlike many of today's exceptionally talented high school players, Dick possessed a genuine sense of humility that would not allow him to show up an opposing player or team.

"Sleepy had this thing against dunking the ball," recalled teammate Jim Santelli. "It's not that he couldn't do it, either. But we grew up as country boys, and country boys don't like to showboat."[43] Instead, Allen was so graceful on the court that others believed the game came easy to him. On the contrary, he worked hard to be successful. "I'll never forget Sleepy's hustle," said a former teammate Larry Craven. "He worked hard all the time. It didn't matter if it was a game or practice. And he took losses like a death in the family."[44] In fact, Dick tried hard to hide his true feelings, as if his performance, whether it was exceptional or poor, did not faze him.

Dick, shown here with Coach Hennon, was the captain and leading scorer for Wampum High School's 1960 state champion basketball team. At the end of his three-year varsity career, Dick had tallied a total 1,125 points and was being offered basketball scholarships from several colleges, including Tennessee State University. *Courtesy of James Santelli*

"People didn't know Dick," explained Hennon:

> He liked everyone to think he doesn't care, that he doesn't take the game seriously. That's all a put on. Many times he'd try to make us think he wasn't practicing. But then I'd see him in the gym at 7:00 a.m. working out all by himself so no one would see him.[45]

In fact, Dick was simply following the examples of his older brothers Coy Jr. and Hank, who also practiced their shooting on a daily basis an hour before school started. He passed down that same example to his younger brother Ronnie. Still, there was more to Dick's tendency to practice basketball in isolation than simply following the example of his brothers. It was more in keeping with his shy, introverted personality. Dick was a loner by nature, someone who could get along well with teammates but generally preferred to be by himself.

Wampum High School Indians, 1960 Pennsylvania state champions. Seated (left to right): Michael Leonetti, Lynn Grinnen, Dick Allen, Ronald Allen, Jim Santelli, and Jack Jones. Standing (left to right): Bill Hennon, Eugene Wilson, Duane Bennett, Larry Walls, Ralph Deal, and Coach L. B. Hennon. *Courtesy of James Santelli*

In the 1960 WPIAL Class B quarterfinals, Dick scored nineteen points to lead the Indians to a 63-44 victory.[46] He contributed another twenty-two points in a semifinal victory over West Newton (77-49), and seventeen more in Wampum's 47-27 victory over Etna to clinch the WPIAL Class B title on March 14.[47] Dick continued his scoring mastery in the PIAA state tournament, scoring twenty-seven points in Wampum's 71-41 win over Laurel Valley in the first round; fourteen in the Indians' 51-37 victory over West Middlesex in the semifinal; and fifteen in Wampum's state championship title clincher against Montrose, 57-51.[48] It was the school's second state championship in three years, and Dick had the distinction of contributing significantly to both of them.

At the end of his three-year varsity career, Dick had tallied 1,125 points and was being offered basketball scholarships from several colleges, including Tennessee State University.[49] Selected as the WPIAL Section 20 Most Valuable Player for 1959–60, and the only Class B player to be chosen for the Associated Press's "All-State Team," Allen was lauded by Hennon for his selflessness. "I've held him back most of the year," admitted the Indians' coach.

> You don't know what the boy can really do. He can shoot from anywhere and put the ball in from almost any spot. And some of his shots are amazing. But he is also an unselfish player. When Wampum had a big lead, which was often, he'd ask to be taken out of the game because he wanted to see the other boys get a chance.[50]

Dick was just as good a rebounder as he was a scorer. *Courtesy of James Santelli*

The sportswriter Thad Bukowski of the *New Castle (PA) News* was also highly impressed by Dick, calling him a "great rebounder and a smooth, agile performer" who plays "aggressively on defense" and "steals many a ball from careless ball handlers." In Bukowski's estimation, Allen was "one of the most polished performers to come out of Section 20 play in a long time."[51]

Dick was such a gifted high school athlete, as well as one of the rare ones who worked hard to improve himself, that he probably would have excelled at any sport he chose. "Sleeper could've played in the NBA," insisted teammate Jim Santelli. "He was just that good because of his sheer athleticism. I even think he loved basketball more than baseball. If our school had a football team I'm sure Sleeper would have excelled at that sport, too, but we didn't."[52] Instead baseball became Dick's sport of choice and the one where his prospects were brightest.

"The high school baseball team was good," said Guy Demaio, who coached Wampum's American Legion team, "but not as successful as basketball. Part of the reason for that is because Hennon, who coached both teams, was more relaxed when

The court where Dick practiced his basketball magic looks the same today as it did in 1960. *Author photo*

it came to baseball. After coming off a highly competitive basketball season he just didn't have the same fire about baseball." In addition, there were no state playoffs or championship games in baseball, so there was not much at stake. The furthest a team could advance was to the county level, and Wampum made it to three Lawrence County championships during Allen's time at the school. Since the school was so small, with no more than forty students in a class, Hennon found himself with multiple responsibilities.[53] Although his primary role was principal, he also taught history, and as was the case with many small rural high schools, those who coached often did so for more than one sport.

Hennon, who played baseball at Geneva College, used some unorthodox methods, just as he did in basketball. "If you were on first base and he wanted you to steal second, for example, he'd just hold up two fingers," recalled Demaio. "If you were on second and he wanted you to steal third, it'd be three fingers. So the opponent knew exactly what was coming. It really wasn't difficult to figure out."[54]

American Legion baseball was much more competitive. Wampum's Legion team often played opponents from much larger towns. Sometimes they found themselves in a "David and Goliath" situation. "I'll never forget when we were supposed to play New Castle," said Demaio.

> They were one of the best Legion teams in western Pennsylvania, so good they actually played on a minor league field.
>
> I usually drove Sleeper, Harold, and Ronnie to away games. Once when I went to their house to pick 'em up, their mother told me they couldn't go because they

First Baptist Church of Chewton, where Era Allen and her family worshipped on Sunday mornings. If any of her sons skipped church, she punished them by refusing to let them play sports. *Author photo*

> skipped church. She was a strict disciplinarian and a very religious woman, so that didn't sit too well with her.
>
> Well, I begged her to reconsider. I told her that there was no sense in going unless her three boys were in the line up. I also suggested that it was like punishing the rest of the team to keep her sons from playing. I promised I'd do anything for her. She finally decided to let them go. Thank God she did because Harold won the game for us with a two-run homer over the left field fence. The victory was like beating the Pittsburgh Pirates.[55]

Demaio claimed that all three of the Allen brothers could "slug the ball." But he knew Dick was "something special" because of "one of the most impressive hitting performances he put on" during the summer between his junior and senior years in high school. On that occasion Allen slammed a pitch deep to right center field at Wampum's Recreation Park:

Chewton Eagles Softball Team, 1959 Pennsylvania State Champions. Front (left to right): Bug Jones, Ken Tillia, Hank Allen, Dick Kosher, Wendal Goatley, Sonny Baker, and Chuck Dombeck. Standing (left to right): Eugene Oakridge, Sonny King, Gary Guy, Henry Highjack, Clarence Freer, Dave Kozar, Ron Allen, Jim Ciro, Bill Campbell, Manager Dick Allen, Sleepy Allen, Hardy Barrett, and Louis Kozar. Note: Manager Dick Allen was no relation to the Allen brothers. Dick is listed as "Sleepy" in this caption. *Courtesy of the Allen Family*

> There was a light pole in right center that was 403 feet away from home plate, I measured it personally. Sleeper hit the ball over that pole and it kept going over the railroad tracks beyond it. That ball easily went some 450 feet. I knew then that the scouts were going to be coming after him. Sure enough, the following summer the Phillies signed him.[56]

Dick played softball for the Chewton Eagles and Legion ball for Wampum in 1959, the summer before his senior year of high school. Semipro baseball had died out by that time, and slow-pitch softball had become the sport of choice in the summers. The Eagles were sponsored by the Medusa Cement Company and was comprised of employees—mostly in their early to mid-twenties—and high school players in their late teens. All three Allen brothers played on the team, but Hank was the star.

"We were good enough to play in the world championship tournament at Cleveland in 1959," recalled Sonny King, who worked for Medusa and played with the team in the evenings:

> The highlight was playing in Municipal Stadium, home of the Cleveland Indians. We lost the championship game there to a team from Gastonia, North Carolina. But Hank hit a ball into the light standards in left field, which was some 450 feet from home plate. Of course I'd seen Dick hit some pretty impressive home runs that summer, too.[57]

Playing for Wampum's American Legion team in the spring of his senior year, Dick captured the attention of John Ogden, a gruff, no-nonsense, sixty-six-year-old scout for the Philadelphia Phillies. Ogden, who read nearly two dozen newspapers each day in search of amateur talent, came across a story in the *New Castle (PA) News* that discussed Dick's basketball prowess. Scanning down to the last paragraph, the scout noted the youngster was a shortstop who hit twenty-two home runs between his high school and Legion seasons the previous year. Power-hitting shortstops were rare in professional baseball, so he tore out the article and made plans to see the prospect from Wampum.

The following week Ogden traveled to the small hamlet in western Pennsylvania. He located the baseball field in Wampum's public park across from the high school and watched Dick play. "First time I saw Richie he struck out twice," recalled Ogden:

> Then he hit two home runs. One of 'em was 525 feet, the other 550, according to the tape measure we brought with us. Now I've scouted 90,000 players in my lifetime and Allen was the greatest I ever saw. I'd been looking thirty years for a kid like this and I wasn't going to lose him.[58]

John Ogden, a former major league pitcher with the St. Louis Browns, was the scout who signed Dick to his first professional baseball contract with the Philadelphia Phillies. *Courtesy of the National Baseball Hall of Fame and Library, Cooperstown, NY*

Over the next few months the scout was dogged in his determination to sign Dick to a Phillies contract.

Ogden was rare among major league scouts. In the early 1920s, he pitched for the International League Baltimore Orioles under Jack Dunn, the manager who discovered Babe Ruth. Ogden went on to a six-year career in the majors with the New York Giants, St. Louis Browns, and Cincinnati Reds. He often said the highlight of his career came in a 1928 game against the New York Yankees when he pitched to Babe Ruth and "Murderer's Row," though he never revealed the outcome.[59] In fact, one of the reasons Ogden was so impressed by Allen was because Dick was "the only player he ever saw who hit a ball as hard as Babe Ruth in his prime."[60]

But what distinguished Ogden from other scouts was his integrity. A member of the Religious Society of Friends (Quakers) and a graduate of Swarthmore College, his intellect was surpassed only by his ability to earn the trust of a young prospect. Whether it was his Quaker faith or his genuine humanity, the veteran scout refused to judge a prospect by his skin color. Talent and personal character were the defining measures of the athletes he pursued. For Ogden, ability was less difficult to judge than character, which could be determined only by how the prospect handled himself off the playing field. Dick was clearly a "can't miss" prospect in terms of talent, but Ogden was just as impressed with the deference and respect he showed his mother. In short, Dick was a dream come true. "He was a smiling, muscled kid who didn't smoke, drink, cuss, or hit any home run under 500 feet," said the Phillies scout. "He had it all."[61]

Ogden wanted to sign the "Wampum Walloper" so desperately he courted not only Dick but also the Allen family. Dick's older brother Coy Jr. handled the negotiations. Having played with the Homestead Grays of the Negro Leagues, Coy had more experience with professional baseball than anyone else in the family. He was also selfless, placing the interests of his brothers above his own. Era, who knew nothing about baseball, naturally relied on her eldest son for help.

On Ogden's initial visit to the Allen home in April 1960, he made sure to be accompanied by the former Negro League great William "Judy" Johnson, who had recently joined the Phillies' scouting ranks. Johnson was brought to break the ice. After the scouts announced their intentions to sign Dick, Era was adamant that her son complete his high school education. "Wild horses wouldn't keep Dick from baseball," she admitted. "He was dead set on quitting high school his senior year to play ball."

"Oh no, you don't," said Era, when she learned of her son's idea.

"Well, I won't study then," countered Dick, who could be just as strong-willed.[62]

When Ogden suggested he could return to sign Dick after graduation, Era refused again, insisting her son was going to accept one of the many college basketball scholarships he had been offered. But Ogden would not quit. Instead, he turned his attention to Dick's brother Hank, who was already attending Baldwin College on a basketball scholarship and playing semipro baseball in the summers. Without invitation, the Phillies' scout began negotiations to sign the other Allen brother.

"At first Mr. Ogden offered me $300 a month, but Sonny said 'no,'" recalled Hank,

> So he upped the offer to $450 a month. That sounded great to me, because I was washing cars during the summer months and making nowhere near that kind of money. But I couldn't say anything because my mother taught us not to intercede in an adult conversation unless we were being addressed directly.

> Sonny eventually talked Mr. Ogden up to $650 a month and then asked my mother. She still said "no" because she wanted me to finish college.
>
> Finally Mr. Ogden turned to me and asked, "Can you make the major leagues?"
>
> "Of course," I said.

Satisfied with the response, Ogden promised that if Hank signed with the Phillies, he would add an incentive clause to the contract that would award him a $10,000 bonus plus $650 a month. The clause would kick in when Hank was promoted to the majors. But even that did not persuade Era.

"Mr. Ogden," she said, "my children are the most important thing in my life, and I don't want them to be used by anybody."

Ogden said he certainly understood her feelings and promised he would take care of Hank.

"Let me ask you a question," Era continued. "Say I came into your house and said I wanted to take your son away from home. What you would you do?"

There was silence. Then tears began to well up in the scout's eyes. Soon they were streaming down his face.

"Mrs. Allen, my only son was killed in Korea," he replied, trying to choke back the tears.

Era felt terrible. She walked over to the scout, apologized, and wrapped her arms around him. Not only did she allow Hank to sign with the Phillies, but she agreed to let Ogden return to discuss Dick's future.

"After that, my mother and Mr. Ogden got along well," said Hank. "They developed a very close relationship."[63]

Ogden returned the following month, but Era continued to insist that Dick go to college.[64] As a result, the Phillies' scout did everything in his power to win over Era and Coy Jr., who continued to serve as the family's negotiator. Ogden sat down to supper with the family and listened to their concerns. He hired Coy Jr. as a scout and promised to sign the youngest brother, Ron.[65]

Throughout the courtship Sleepy sat on the windowsill in the family parlor, "just smiling and listening to us talk." "I don't think he knew one club from another," said Ogden. "He just wanted to play."[66]

"I don't think there was a greater scout in the game than Mr. Ogden at the time," Dick said years later. "The thing that appealed to me most about him was his honesty. Everything he promised to me or to my mother he delivered. Nothing had to be written. His handshake was as good as his word."[67]

Ogden, impressed by Allen's character as well as his potential as a power-hitting shortstop, finally signed him in June 1960 for $70,000, the highest bonus ever paid to an African American ballplayer at the time.[68] After he received the money, the first thing Dick did was purchase a new brick ranch house for his mother in Wampum. When asked about the purchase he said, "That's my job—to take care of my mom. Even if I make a million dollars playing baseball, it wouldn't be enough to repay her for all the things she did for me."[69]

The next week Dick left home for the Phillies' short-season club at Elmira, New York. Little did he know what the future would bring.

Richie Allen as an Arkansas Traveler, 1963.
Courtesy of the Allen Family

CHAPTER 2:
BAPTISM BY FIRE

Before the 1960s, the Philadelphia Phillies was a racially segregated team in a racially segregated city. During Jackie Robinson's quest to break the color barrier in 1947, the Phillies front office phoned the Dodgers president Branch Rickey before the two teams met and told him "not to bring that nigger here."[1] When Rickey refused, Robinson paid a horrific price. Led by Manager Ben Chapman, the Phillies treated

In 1947, the Phillies manager Ben Chapman led his team in a racist verbal attack against Jackie Robinson, who was making a quest to break baseball's color barrier. When ordered to pose for a conciliatory photograph Chapman grudgingly agreed, but he refused to shake Robinson's hand. *Courtesy of Temple University Urban Archives, Philadelphia, PA*

the Dodgers' black rookie the worst of any National League team. Pitchers threw at his head, infielders purposely spiked him on the base paths, and in one of the lowest moments in baseball history, the Phils humiliated Robinson by standing on the steps of their dugout, pointing their bats at him, and making gunshot sounds.[2]

The Phillies were also the last team in the National League to integrate. They did not field an African American player until 1957, when John Kennedy appeared in five games for the Phils at third base—a full decade after Robinson broke the color line.[3] Even then the Phillies maintained segregated spring training facilities, a practice that was finally abandoned in 1962.[4]

Like their major league baseball team, the city was also struggling with racism.

During the early 1960s, Philadelphia was experiencing middle-class "white flight" to the suburbs. Whites were escaping the crime, drugs, and gang warfare of north and west Philadelphia, where the black population had relocated from the old-time ghettos. While whites made their new homes in the outlying suburbs of Merion, Abington, Haverford, Malvern, Swarthmore, and Bucks County, poor blacks who migrated from the rural South and other low-salaried city dwellers came to dominate the city's diminishing tax base. As expenses increased the city was forced to make decisions on questions of education, employment, and public welfare, for which it was ill prepared. The "race factor" often became a rhetorical device for greater state and federal funding to meet those needs. In fact, the hope of the city rested with upwardly mobile black families whose wage earners were employed in banks, insurance companies, law offices, and government agencies, and who lived in sections of the city like Germantown, Mount Airy, Queen Village, and Fairmount.[5] But it was still a struggle for them.

The mayor James Tate, a conservative Democrat, favored the white working class and distanced himself from the downtown business and liberal communities. His tenure was riddled by a succession of scandals and political quarrels. Charges of zoning concessions, extortion, and conflicts of interest brought a series of resignations in high places. Pressing social concerns were largely ignored, while a growing protest movement focused on civil rights for blacks erupted on the city's streets. Together with Philadelphia's rising crime rate, black protest accelerated white flight to the suburbs. To his credit, Tate realized the widespread unrest was fueled by idealism as well as resentment, and he responded with a two-pronged approach.[6]

To stem the tide of protest, Tate appointed Charles Bowser, a young black lawyer, to head the Anti-Poverty Action Committee, an organization inspired by President Lyndon B. Johnson's "War on Poverty." The appointment curried favor with the black community, as Bowser worked hard to ensure local community participation on public welfare issues. At the same time, Tate appointed Frank Rizzo as police commissioner in order to address the pressing need for crime control. Unfortunately, Rizzo's streetwise, shoot-from-the-hip, tough-cop style became synonymous with the public image of Philadelphia—and it was not a good one. The new police commissioner antagonized the black community with his outspoken comments on race, voicing sentiments previously unspeakable among responsible public officials. Just as disturbing, Rizzo couched his remarks in a rhetoric of physical intimidation. The size of his charisma and personality inspired unreasoned loyalty among whites and fear, as well as violent opposition, among blacks. During Rizzo's tenure as police commissioner, "crime control" became a euphemism for "anti-black movements."[7]

Ironically, the Phillies were one of the few rays of hope for a city in racial turmoil. By the 1960s, it had become clear that the best days of the 1950 pennant-winning Whiz Kids were behind them. Robin Roberts—the ace of that team—and Richie Ashburn, the sparkplug and center fielder, were nearing the end of their Hall of Fame-worthy careers. Age had also caught up with shortstop Granny Hamner and Willie Jones, who were hampered by injuries. Other Whiz Kids had become lackadaisical, and it showed in the team's performance. The Phillies had not finished higher than fourth place since 1953.[8] It was time to rebuild. There were also clear indications that the Phillies were making an earnest effort to distance themselves from a racist reputation.

Connie Mack Stadium—the Phillies' ballpark—was in North Philadelphia, where racial demographics were changing. At Twenty-first Street and Lehigh Avenue, Connie Mack, opened in 1909, was once a handsome structure highlighted by Federal-style windows along either side of a domed tower entrance. It gave the appearance of a French Renaissance castle from the outside. But by the mid-1960s, the ballpark looked as sullied and rundown as the surrounding row homes. Once a white, working-class neighborhood, the area was now integrated. African Americans and Hispanics were arriving in increasing numbers, inhabiting row houses vacated by the Irish, Polish, and Germans.[9] The Phillies were making an effort to court this more socially diverse fan base. It was good business as well as common sense to sign black and Hispanic players who would appeal to the minority groups moving into the neighborhood, though the team's owner Robert R. M. Carpenter Jr. was unwilling to admit it.

Carpenter, who purchased the club in 1943, poured his family's fortune into giving dignity to what had traditionally been a losing franchise. Although he did not expect to realize huge profits from the Phillies, Carpenter was a tough-minded businessman who used his family connections with the mammoth DuPont Company to build a winner. Throughout the late 1940s and 1950s, when other National League clubs were scouting and signing black and Latin American players, the Phillies remained reluctant to do so, only serving to further the organization's segregationist past. Carpenter insisted he was not "opposed to Negro players," but he was not "going to hire a player of any color or nationality just to have him on the team."[10] But his actions spoke louder than his words.

In 1960, Carpenter hired Gene Mauch, a little-known thirty-four-year-old manager and journeyman infielder of the American Association's Minneapolis Millers to replace Eddie Sawyer as the Phillies' manager. Mauch was ideally suited for the rebuilding process. He was a young disciplinarian who had come up through the Brooklyn Dodgers organization in the late 1940s. Having played for Branch Rickey, he experienced firsthand the process of integration and learned to respect the abilities of his black teammates. At the same time, Mauch's career batting average of .239 underscored the fact that the game had not come easy to him. He was a better tactician than a player, and one who studied the game with exceptional attention to detail, a trait that would later earn him the moniker "Little General." On good days he was able to steal a victory by manipulating his roster to be one step ahead of the opposing manager. On bad days he would overmanage, costing his team a victory that had been in easy reach. But no one could deny that Mauch had the temperament to manage. He was surly and sharp-witted, and he refused to back down from anyone, regardless of their size or authority. Sportswriters loved him for the ease with which he conducted postgame interviews, serving up some of the most colorful—if not unprintable—quotes imaginable.[11]

By the late 1950s, the Phillies' owner Robert R. M. Carpenter Jr., an heir to the DuPont fortune, realized he could not build a winning team without African American and Latino players and reluctantly began to sign them. *Courtesy of the Allen Family*

When he became the Phillies' manager in spring 1960, Mauch immediately set a new tone. In a closed-door clubhouse meeting he criticized the players' off-field behavior and set a strict curfew. "I want my players to realize that Baseball is their livelihood—not a way to have fun," he declared. "My ultimate goal is to get this ball club to a point where it won't need rules. But now they take privileges that good players on other clubs have to ask for. I think if a player doesn't have respect for himself he'll have a hard time getting respect from someone else."[12]

Mauch, who was also known to use racially inflammatory language, may not have been color blind, but he, like the new general manager John Quinn, certainly seemed to be "color neutral" when it came to judging a player's abilities. Scouting reports indicate the number of African American players in the Phillies farm system—consisting of approximately 200 players on ten teams—jumped from three in 1958 to thirty-four in 1961, and steadily increased through the mid-1960s.[13] Among the more talented black players were the outfielders Johnny Briggs, Richard and Robert Haines, Alex Johnson, Larry Hisle, and Ted Savage; the pitchers Grant Jackson and Ferguson Jenkins; and of course the Phillies' first black superstar, Richie Allen. Nor did the Phillies spare much expense in signing that talent. With the exception of Jackson, who signed for a $1,500 bonus, the others each received a bonus of $8,000 or more. Briggs and Jenkins received $8,000 each; Savage signed for $17,500; Johnson for $18,000; the Haines brothers for $40,000 each; Hisle $50,000; and Allen for an unprecedented $70,000.[14] Similar white talent signed during the 1960s received lower bonuses. For example, Rick Wise, who would become the most consistent Phillies pitcher in the late 1960s before he was traded to St. Louis for Steve Carlton, signed for $12,000 in 1963. Similarly, Larry Bowa, who would go on to play shortstop for the pennant-contending Phillies teams of the mid- to late 1970s, as well as for the 1980 world champions, received just $2,000 for signing in 1965. Hispanic players were the least expensive to sign —they were given little to no bonus money.[15] If there was a racial bias in the Phillies' signing of prospects, it certainly seemed to favor the black players. Indeed, integration was a conscious process for the organization.

General manager John Quinn, hired by the Phillies in 1959, also enhanced the racial composition of the team through trades. Some of his earliest deals involved two white players who would eventually become some of the greatest names in Phillies' history: Jim Bunning, a future Hall of Fame pitcher who came from the Detroit Tigers in a trade for Don Demeter; and Johnny Callison, who, along with Allen, combined for most of the Phillies' home runs and RBIs in the 1960s. Callison came from the Chicago White Sox for Gene Freese. Other African American players were added, including Wes Covington from the Kansas City Athletics and Bill White from the St. Louis Cardinals. An increasing number of Hispanic players rounded out the roster, including Tony Gonzalez and Cookie Rojas from the Cincinnati Reds, Ruben Amaro from the Cardinals, and the fan favorite Tony Taylor from the Chicago Cubs.[16] But Allen, who would be renamed "Richie," was the most gifted prospect in the organization and one who quickly became the centerpiece of the rebuilding process.

Allen broke into professional baseball in 1960 at Elmira, New York, with the Phillies' Class D farm club. The Elmira Pioneers played in the New York–Penn League, which was a short-season circuit mostly for those prospects signed out of high school. He was just eighteen years old, a shy, hesitant country kid who had never been away from home. At least he enjoyed the company of his older brother Hank, who was the Pioneers' starting first baseman. "I'll never forget Dick's first season at Elmira," recalled Hank.

The Phillies' team logo 1960s. *Courtesy of the Philadelphia Phillies Baseball Club*

Gene Mauch, a journeyman ballplayer who began his career with the Brooklyn Dodgers, had experienced the process of integration. He was also a disciplinarian with a keen knowledge of baseball strategy, and he emphasized the fundamentals—assets that were imperative to develop young talent. *Courtesy of the National Baseball Hall of Fame and Library, Cooperstown, NY*

The Phillies general manager John Quinn seemed to be "color neutral" when signing prospects, but he was a tough negotiator when it came to player salaries. *Courtesy of the Allen Family*

> It was either "feast or famine." His first game we were playing Geneva, a team that included future Hall of Famers Pete Rose and Tony Perez. Dick played short[stop] and batted third. First time up, he hits a home run.
>
> A few weeks later we're playing a double header against Wellsboro. We beat them 20-0 in the first game, and everyone got a hit except Dick. We're beating them 18-0 in the second game, but again Dick is hitless. So in his last at bat he tries to bunt for a base hit. He fouled off the first pitch, fouled off the second, and the pitcher drilled him in the head with the third pitch. Hit him straight in the left eye.
>
> Of course, the pitcher thought the Pioneers' shortstop was trying to show him up with an 18-0 lead, and the [unwritten] code [governing baseball] demands that a hitter like that gets drilled, but he didn't have to hit him in the head. I was furious and charged the mound.[17]

Allen spent his first season in professional baseball at Class D Elmira in the New York–Penn League. Although he committed forty-eight errors at shortstop, the youngster demonstrated great offensive promise. In eighty-eight games Richie hit .281, with eight home runs and forty-two RBIs — exceptional statistics for a middle infielder. *Courtesy of the National Baseball Hall of Fame and Library, Cooperstown, NY*

Richie was immediately taken to the hospital. Although Hank wanted to accompany his brother, Jack Philips, the Pioneers' manager, ordered him back on the field to finish the game. That was the first of many mistakes the Phillies organization made with their first black superstar, who still believes his brother's attempt to defend him led to their separation the following year.[18]

Philips, jealous over Richie's $70,000 signing bonus, did not permit him to steal bases at his own discretion and insisted he change his batting stance. Within a week's time Allen's average plummeted and Philips allowed him to return to his old form. Still, Richie managed to have an impressive debut. He hit .281 in eighty-eight

Hank Allen (as a Washington Senator) played with Dick at Elmira in 1960. *Courtesy of the Allen Family*

games, with eight home runs, forty-two RBIs, nineteen doubles, ten triples, and an on-base percentage of .389.[19]

The following season Allen played for the Phillies' Magic Valley, Idaho, club, a member of the Class C Pioneer League. Since Hank had been promoted to Class B Des Moines in the Tri-I League, Richie was on his own. To make matters worse, Philips, his manager at Elmira, was reassigned to Magic Valley and continued to goad him. Richie became so homesick he ran up a $400 phone bill calling his mother. When John Ogden learned of his prospect's desperation, he flew to Idaho to deliver a pep talk. "Don't expect anyone to help you in this game," he said. "You help yourself, and I know you'll make me proud!"[20]

Although Allen showed marked improvement offensively—hitting .317 with twenty-one homers, ninety-four RBIs, and an on-base percentage of .401—the Phillies were so dissatisfied with his fielding at shortstop that they switched him to second base and later offered him to the National League's two new franchises, the Houston Colt 45s and the New York Mets. Fortunately for the Phillies, neither expansion team wanted him.[21]

In 1962, Allen was promoted to Class A Williamsport of the Eastern League. The season proved to be one of the happier ones of his professional baseball career. Williamsport's Bowman Field was a cozy little ballpark where residents congregated on summer evenings to socialize and watch the hometown Grays. Fans got to know the players, some striking up friendships that lasted well beyond the season or two the ballplayer spent in the central Pennsylvania town. Such was the case between Jimmy Moore and Richie, who befriended the local teenager.

Moore's father Boyd was a huge Grays fan who attended all the team's home games. Nicknamed "Bucket" during his playing days because he had a bad habit of putting his "foot in the bucket" whenever he hit, Boyd Moore was so impressed with Allen's power hitting that he boasted about it to his twenty-year-old daughter, Barbara. One night Bucket was sitting in the parlor with Barbara when Jimmy walked in with Richie in tow. "That's the kid I'm talking about!" he boomed, jumping out of his chair to introduce himself. Allen charmed the family with his polite manners and delightful personality. He also became smitten with Barbara, and a romance was born.[22] Things were going just as well for Richie at the ballpark.

On his first trip to Bowman Field he met the clubhouse manager Pete Cera, who would become a life-long friend. "Where's my locker?" Allen asked Cera, a short, stocky man holding three nails in his mouth and a hammer in his hand.

"You're right here by me," Cera replied as he pounded one of the nails into the wall. "Hang your clothes on that," he added. "You're not going to be here [in Williamsport] long."[23]

Cera, a World War II veteran who hailed from the anthracite coal region of northeastern Pennsylvania, began working for the Phillies in 1953 and had seen many prospects as they made their way through the farm system. He also knew talent when he saw it, and when Richie Allen entered the minors in 1960, he was one of the most gifted ballplayers Cera had ever seen. Cera quickly became a surrogate parent to Richie, making sure he attended church on Sundays and checking to see whether he made curfew. Allen considered the small but stocky clubhouse manager his "best friend," and would later insist Cera was "a great influence on [him] through tough segregated times" when the two of them were promoted to Philadelphia in 1964.[24]

The Williamsport team enjoyed its best season since the championship team of 1924. Under manager Frank Lucchesi, the Grays got off to a remarkable start and never looked back. By June 14, they had an eleven-game lead over second-place Charleston and extended it to twenty games by early August. During the interim, the Grays enjoyed thirteen-game and ten-game winning streaks. The '62 Grays had all the necessary elements of a contender: consistent and timely hitting, scrappy fielding, excellent speed, and outstanding pitching. Richie Allen led the offensive attack along with the outfielder Bobby Sanders, who batted .310 and led the Eastern League in runs scored with ninety-eight. Ray Culp was the pitching ace, with a 13-8 record and 185 strikeouts, while Gary Kroll was a solid number two starter with a superb 12-2 record. Bob "Gunner" Gontkosky and Harry Oliver rounded out the starting rotation and were every bit as reliable. Finishing the season eleven games in front of second-place Elmira, the Grays compiled a stellar 83-57 record and an all-time best record of 49-22 at Bowman Field.

The 1962 Williamsport Grays. Front row (left to right): Bob "Gunner" Gontkosky, Ray Culp, Dick Teed (player coach), Frank Lucchesi, Gary Kroll, and Harry Oliver. Second row (left to right): Jack McCracken, Bob Bubash, Bruce Gruber, Jim Ponceroff, Dave Getz, Ed Lunsford, Ferguson Jenkins, and Pete Cera (trainer). Third row (left to right): John Mustion, Bill Sorrell, Jerry Griffin, John Shockley, Bobby Sanders, Tommy Norwood, Larry Cutright, and Ed Kenders. Back row (left to right): Bill Pickelner (Grays club official), Curtis Johnson (bat boy), Dick Edwards, Richie Allen, Joe Johnson (bat boy), Joe Mosser (Grays president), and Otto Stradley (Grays club official). *Courtesy of the* Williamsport Sun-Gazette

Richie with the pitcher Ray Culp. Allen and Culp were key in the Williamsport Grays' victory over the parent club Philadelphia Phillies on July 31, 1962. *Courtesy of the* Williamsport Sun-Gazette

Richie Allen, Rankin Johnson (Eastern League president), and Pat Corrales. Allen is seen receiving a wristwatch for Topps Player of the Month in May 1962; Pat Corrales is receiving an award for being a Class B All Star. *Courtesy of the* Williamsport Sun-Gazette

Williamsport defeated Springfield in the first round of the Eastern League playoffs, capturing the best-of-three-game series. In the pivotal second game, Bob "Gunner" Gontkosky struck out eight and limited Springfield to just three runs in the Grays' 7-3 victory. He received all the help he needed from Allen, Bill Sorrell, and Jerry Griffin, who smacked home runs. But the Grays lost the final round, three games to one against Elmira. Their only victory came in the third game, when Allen powered Williamsport to a 7-2 victory with a home run, a double, and four RBIs.[25]

Richie exceeded the Phillies' expectations at Williamsport, despite being converted to a new position. He hit Eastern League pitching at a .332 clip with twenty home runs, 109 RBIs, and a .409 on-base percentage while learning to play center field.[26] Allen just missed capturing the league batting title on the final day of the season, being edged out by Jim Ray Hart, who would later become the San Francisco Giants' third baseman.[27] But his exceptional performance helped the Williamsport Grays capture the Eastern League title with a 83-57 record.[28] It seemed as though the majors were on his horizon.

Allen realized the Phillies already had a strong outfield with Covington, Gonzalez, and Callison, but he still believed they could use his bat and intended to win a spot on their roster in 1963. Invited to spring training, Allen hit nine home runs, the most on the club. But at the end of camp he was told he needed more seasoning, and this time the Phillies sent him to their Triple A club in Little Rock, Arkansas. Richie pleaded with Quinn and Mauch to give him a shot at the majors, but they refused. Quinn might have been put off by the black prospect's request for a $50 raise as a symbolic reward for his impressive performance at Triple A, interpreting it as a demand by an ungrateful young man who had already been given the opportunity of a professional baseball career.[29] If so, the general manager's liberalism had its limits, and Allen had exceeded them. But Allen believed the Phillies were using him to break the color barrier in Arkansas, that the front office viewed him as Philadelphia's own "Jackie Robinson," and that his presence in Little Rock would be the club's first step toward dismantling its infamous reputation as a racist organization.

"Sixty-three was the first season for Triple-A ball down there," Allen recalled in his 1989 autobiography *Crash*:

> It was the first season with the Phillies as the parent club—and no blacks. They had no choice but to bust it. I didn't know anything about the race issue in Arkansas and really didn't care. Maybe if the Phillies had called me in, man to man, like the Dodgers had done with Jackie Robinson, and said, "Dick, this is what we have in mind. It's going to be very difficult, but we're with you"—at least I would have been prepared. I'm not saying I would have liked it. But I would have known what to expect.[30]

Before reporting to Little Rock Allen married Barbara Moore. Although he planned to bring his new wife with him, he deferred to his mother's judgement that "it would be a better idea to leave Barbara at home" because of the racial turmoil caused by the 1957 integration of Little Rock High School. "Instead I was on my own down there," he recalled.[31]

Allen was just twenty years old when he was sent to Little Rock. As he moved through the Phillies farm system, he was respected for his extraordinary athletic abilities but kept at a distance because of his race. But in Arkansas he encountered a heightened awareness of race, one that he had never experienced before. He was unfamiliar with Southern culture or the manner in which the city's blacks navigated the racial discrimination they experienced on a daily basis. As the first African American ballplayer in Arkansas history, Allen was immersed in a racist environment that operated on the stereotype of blacks as "ignorant laborers," "troublemakers," and "criminals." His emotional response was anger, confusion, and alienation.

The fact that the Little Rock sportswriters made little to no effort to prepare the fans for Allen's presence on the team made matters worse. They made only passing reference to Richie's race as they wrote about the upcoming season. That he would be the first African American player on the Travelers was never reported. Jim Bailey, a baseball writer for the *Arkansas Gazette*, confirmed years later that the newspaper's editors told their sportswriters not to mention that crucial fact, probably because

Despite constant racial discrimination while playing at Triple A Arkansas, Richie Allen managed to hit International League pitching at a .289 clip, with thirty-three home runs and ninety-seven RBIs. *Courtesy of the Butler Center for Arkansas Studies, Central Arkansas Library System*

many readers boycotted the *Gazette* after it supported the desegregation of Little Rock's Central High School just six years earlier. "The editors decided we'd be better off not getting things all stirred up again," Bailey said. "So we didn't make a big deal out of Allen being the first black Traveler."[32] The *Arkansas Democrat* adopted a similar approach. In pre-season articles Dick's race was mentioned occasionally, but not his being the Travelers' first black player.[33]

Amis Guthridge, the president of the Capital Citizens' Council of Little Rock, and members of the white supremacist organization became suspicious. To ascertain

CONSPIRACY AT LITTLE ROCK TO NEGRO-IZE TRAVELERS BASEBALL TEAM

Censorship and news suppression by the Little Rock Press Media, kept the following news from you. BELOW ARE THE "CHAMPIONS" OF THE SO-CALLED "FREE PRESS" WHO STAGED A NEWS "blackout" on the apparent plan to integrate our Travelers Baseball Team, Travelers Field, our Hotels and Coffee Shops.

UNITED PRESS INTERNATIONAL
ARKANSAS DEMOCRAT
ARKANSAS GAZETTE
COMMERCIAL APPEAL
HERBIE BYRD, KLRA
ASSOCIATED PRESS
KARK-TV
KTHV

(Each of the above received a copy of this letter as a news release nearly two weeks ago—But "Killed" IT.)

October 13, 1962

Mr. Ray Winder
General Manager
Little Rock Baseball Company
Travelers Field
Little Rock, Arkansas

Dear Mr. Winder:

A group of baseball fans who have always assisted in the advance ticket sales for the Little Rock Travelers asked me to inquire of you about certain aspects of our baseball club being in the American Association next season.

1. Do the American Association teams have negro players?
2. If so, will the Little Rock Travelers employ negro players?
3. If so, will the grandstand, as well as the bleachers, be race-mixed?
4. If so, will rest room facilities be race-mixed?
5. If so, will "Ladies Night" activities be co-mingled?
6. If you bring race-mixed baseball to Arkansas' capital city, will the negro players room and eat at the Albert Pike and LaFayette Hotels as the Southern Association teams have done in the past?

In addition to requesting an immediate, forthright answer to each of the above questions, the baseball fans for whom I am speaking are interested also since you are asking our voters to elect you November 6, to the highest governing body of Little Rock, the City Board of Directors.

I have taken the liberty of sending a copy of this letter to all press media, as the questions are of great public interest not only in Little Rock, but to people everywhere who support the Travelers and patronize or work in our hotels.

Yours very truly,

Amis Guthridge
President
CAPITAL CITIZENS' COUNCIL

AG/jt

P.S. To this date Mr. Winder has not answered this letter but he stated over the telephone Definitely and Emphatically to a Little Rock Minister that he was bringing NEGRO BASEBALL to Little Rock.

Published and Distributed by the Capital Citizens' Council, P. O. Box 1977, Little Rock, Ark.
Amis Guthridge, President

Flier circulated by the Capitol Citizens' Council of Little Rock, Arkansas, opposing the integration of the hometown Travelers baseball club. *Courtesy of the Butler Center for Arkansas Studies, Central Arkansas Library System*

the intentions of Travelers' management, Guthridge sent the following letter to Ray Winder, the club's general manager, dated October 13, 1962:[34]

Dear Mr. Winder:

A group of baseball fans who have always assisted in the advance ticket sales for the Little Rock Travelers asked me to inquire of you about certain aspects of our baseball club being in the American Association next season.

Do the American Association teams have negro players?

If so, will the Little Rock Travelers employ negro players?

If so, will the grandstand, as well as the bleachers, be race-mixed?

If so, will rest room facilities be race-mixed?

If so, will "Ladies Night" activities be co-mingled?

If you bring race-mixed baseball to Arkansas' capital city, will the negro players room and eat at the Albert Pike and Lafayette Hotels as the Southern Association teams have done in the past?

In addition to requesting an immediate, forthright answer to each of the above questions, the baseball fans for whom I am speaking are interested also since you are asking our voters to elect you November 6, to the highest governing body of Little Rock, the City Board of Directors.

I have taken the liberty of sending a copy of this letter to all press media, as the questions are of great public interest not only in Little Rock, but to people everywhere who support the Travelers and patronize or work in our hotels.

Yours very truly,
Amis Guthridge, President
CAPITAL CITIZENS' COUNCIL

Winder never responded to the letter, but he reportedly told a Little Rock minister he intended to integrate the Travelers. Nor did any of the local newspapers acknowledge receipt of the letter, or whether the ball club had definitive plans to integrate the team.[35] Even after the regular season began, the sportswriters limited their reporting to game coverage. That is, with the exception of an April 21, 1963, column in the *Gazette* by Orville Henry, who observed that "in manner and speech Allen shows good background and a measure of sophistication," and that he performed "with the typical loose all-out exuberance of his race."[36] It was a strange remark, almost as if Henry was a sociologist and Richie an object of anthropological curiosity. In the North such an observation would be considered demeaning.

Predictably, Allen's arrival was received by fans with a mix of emotions, including hostility, begrudging acceptance, and confusion.

On opening night, a capacity crowd of 7,000 fans packed Little Rock's Ray Winder Stadium to see history in the making. Outside the ballpark, marchers, led by Guthridge, handed out fliers titled, "Conspiracy at Little Rock to Negro-ize Travelers Baseball Team" and bearing the unanswered letter the white supremacist leader had sent to the team's general manager. Others picketed the ballpark, carrying signs that read, "DON'T NEGRO-IZE BASEBALL" and "NIGGER GO HOME."[37]

Inside the ballpark sat Governor Orval Faubus, best known for his unsuccessful attempt to bar black students from Little Rock's Central High School. Faubus was waiting to throw the ceremonial first pitch.[38] Allen was terrified.

Starting in left field for the Travelers that night, he botched the very first ball hit to him. "It was a lazy fly," he recalled. "I just froze, then I took a few steps in and the ball flew over my head. I missed that ball because I was scared, and I don't mind saying it."[39] Bailey, who was covering the game for the *Gazette*, recalled that the fans' reaction was immediate and unmistakable. "It sounded like somebody had swatted a gigantic beehive with a baseball bat," recalled the Little Rock sportswriter.[40] Later in the game Allen atoned for his miscue by hitting two doubles. The second one set up the Travelers' game-winning rally.

After the game, Allen purposely waited until the clubhouse cleared before walking to the parking lot. "When I got to my car," he said,

> I found a note on the windshield. It said, "DON'T COME BACK AGAIN, NIGGER." I felt scared and alone, and what's worse, my car was the last one in the parking lot. There might be something more terrifying than being black and holding a note that says "NIGGER" in an empty parking lot in Little Rock, Arkansas, in 1963, but if there is, it certainly hasn't crossed my path yet.[41]

Things only seemed to get worse as the season unfolded. Allen did not live in the same hotel as his teammates, but with a family at 1121 Cross Street, on the black side of town. He could not be served in a restaurant unless accompanied by a white player. He was stopped routinely by local police for no apparent reason, he received threatening phone calls, and he was forced to endure the epithets of racist fans. "There were fans who got off on racial intimidation," Allen recalled.

> When I came in from the outfield to the dugout between innings I would hear the voices—"Hey, Chocolate Drop" or "Watch your back, nigger." I would look up, but I could never find the guy who made the remark. I would have loved to go a round or two with one of those racist cowards. I think a slugfest would have given me the release I needed.[42]

Initially Allen felt sorry for himself and wanted to return home to Wampum. But his mother Era quickly dashed that idea. "Early on, I called my Mom and asked to come home," Dick remembered.

> If I was looking for sympathy, I wasn't going to get it from her. "You listen to me, boy," she said. "God gave you a gift and a place to show it. If you don't do that you're not only being disobedient to me, but you're being disobedient to God."
>
> Well, I didn't have much choice. I went back to the home where I was staying, laid down on the bed, and just cried like a baby. Then I got to thinking, "Well, maybe she's right."[43]

Still concerned that his younger brother might abandon his big league dream, Coy Jr. flew to Little Rock with the Phillies' general manager John Quinn and John Ogden, the scout who signed Richie. They discovered an angry young man left on his own without any support from an organization that refused to protect him. "Up to that point, the Phillies had no interest in how Dick was making out down there," said Coy in a 1989 interview:

> They were either totally unaware of the situation or they just didn't care. All they cared about were his home run production and batting average, but not how he was making out in an all-white Deep South environment. When he told them he was thinking of going home to Wampum, *then* they cared.

Coy managed to convince Dick there was no future for him if he left pro ball. If he returned to Wampum, he would have to get a job either in the steel mill or the cement factory, employments Dick swore he would never enter. After that conversation, Dick decided to stick it out with the Travelers.[44] To ease his burden, his new bride Barbara joined him in Little Rock. The couple rarely went out on the town, believing it was best to stay at home. "I heard the word 'nigger' a lot that summer," said Barbara in her husband's 1989 autobiography:

> It was never someone coming up and saying it right to my face. It was more like the word was around me all the time, especially when Dick came up to bat.
>
> I also had to learn how to act down there. I learned to always make sure to go to the bathroom before going to see Dick play at the ballpark. I would never go to the refreshment stand. It was best to stay in my seat, out in the open."[45]

In a recent interview, Barbara confirmed that she "really didn't have many problems in Little Rock" because she quickly learned how to navigate the racial politics. But she also admitted that "Dick had it much worse than [I] did."[46]

Most of Allen's Traveler teammates kept their distance during the first half of the season. A few, like Lee Elia and Pat Corrales, would offer him encouragement, but neither of them could relate with his situation. Manager Frank Lucchesi, who had also been promoted from Williamsport in 1963, treated Dick just like any other ballplayer. "I had a lot of confidence in Richie," said Lucchesi in a recent interview. "Sure, he was treated poorly when he first came to Little Rock. But by the end of the season Richie had won over the fans. They voted him Most Valuable Player of the team that year. Do fans who hate a player vote him MVP? I don't think so."[47] It was a rather naïve statement from a man who made little attempt to soften the discrimination Allen faced that season.

"Frank Lucchesi didn't understand me as a person," Dick insisted after his playing career ended:

> What did he know about racial abuse? He never bothered to understand my situation, either. Not that I felt he owed me anything but a fair opportunity to show what I could do on the playing field. But while I was in bed listening to gunshots he was eating at the best restaurants in Little Rock. Frank only had one thing in mind: managing in the majors.[48]

Ruly Carpenter, son of the owner and an administrator in the low minors in the 1960s, believes it was not that the Phillies *refused* to protect Allen as much as they *didn't know how*. "Little Rock was a hotbed of racial unrest in the 1960s," he said.

> It wasn't a great place to be for a black ballplayer, and it was unfortunate that the Phillies had the Triple A club down there. But we did, and we were under contract to be there. It didn't make any sense to keep Richie at [Double A] Williamsport. He wouldn't have gotten the kind of playing experience he needed there, and he wasn't ready for the majors yet. We had no choice.[49]

Although the Phillies might not have protected their prized outfielder, Frank Lucchesi was right about one thing: Allen did win over the Traveler fans in 1963. He had an outstanding season, batting .289 and leading the International League in home runs (33), RBIs (97), and triples (12).[50] "There were fans in Little Rock who truly loved the game," Dick admitted later. "For some of them, color didn't matter. Those were the fans I gathered my strength from. They kept me going through the bad times."[51]

At the end of the minor league season, Allen was promoted to Philadelphia, where he proceeded to hit major league pitching at a .292 clip.[52] The September call up and the experience of those ten games with the Phillies showed him that "baseball is baseball, regardless of the level of competition," and that he "had the ability to move up and play in the major leagues."[53] But the discrimination he faced in Little Rock left Allen bitter and distrustful of the Phillies organization. In his 1989 autobiography *Crash*, Allen wrote that his season in Little Rock taught him two sets of rules existed: "one set for the white players and one set for Dick Allen, the black outfielder." "From that time on," vowed Allen, "I decided that if there were ever a double standard again, I would be the beneficiary."[54]

Ruly Carpenter, son of the Phillies' owner, worked in the organization's minor league system. He still believes the Phillies had no choice but to promote Allen to Triple A Arkansas in 1963 because it was the only place where he could gain the experience needed to make the Phillies the following season. *Courtesy of the National Baseball Hall of Fame and Library, Cooperstown, NY*

Richie Allen watches one of the twenty-nine home runs he hit in his rookie year leave the ballpark.
Artwork courtesy of Dick Perez

CHAPTER 3:
ROOKIE OF THE YEAR

When Richie Allen was promoted to the Philadelphia Phillies in spring 1964, he quickly became the right ballplayer in the right place at the right time. Perennial losers, the Phils had not finished higher than fourth place since 1953. The team hit rock bottom in 1961, when they suffered a twenty-three-game losing streak—a major league record that still stands today.[1] Thus, it came as no surprise that the Fightin' Phils were a long shot to capture the pennant in 1964. But for Allen—the most gifted of a nucleus of talented young players—the Phillies' dismal fortunes offered him an opportunity to shine.

Although there was no place for Allen in the outfield—Wes Covington, Tony Gonzalez, and Johnny Callison had become fixtures there—there was room in the infield. The Phillies had traded Don Demeter, a veteran third baseman, to the Detroit Tigers for Jim Bunning, a side-arming right hander who they hoped would provide some sorely needed pitching. As a result, the competition for third base fell to Allen and Don Hoak, an aging veteran. Mauch made no attempt to hide his choice.

Going into spring training, the Phils' skipper told the sportswriters that his lineup was loaded with left-handed hitters and he needed a right-handed bat. While Allen and Hoak hit right-handed, Mauch stated he had "real high hopes" for the black rookie, and that

> any player good enough to be considered a prospect at shortstop should be able to play anywhere in the infield.
>
> I'm sure he can play third good enough to get by. He has good reactions and good hands and third isn't as demanding a spot as shortstop where he began his career. Besides, I know that Allen's bat has to help us. He can drive the ball a mile to right center.[2]

Ordering Allen to report early to spring training, Mauch told the muscular rookie, "Third base is yours until you play yourself out of it."[3] When Allen was given the directive he was ecstatic. "I love it!" he told the Philadelphia press:

> I've been waiting to get back in the infield. In high school I was a shortstop for four years. But when the Phillies signed me I was moved into the outfield, where I became confused. It's good to be back where I belong.[4]

Of course, Hoak was much less enthusiastic. In the course of a single year, Hoak had gone from being Mauch's team captain to trade bait. Nagging injuries and a .231 batting average made the thirty-six-year-old veteran expendable. He even considered retiring after the 1963 campaign, but his never-say-die attitude forced him to return for another season. Realizing his fate rested less with his own performance than with Allen's, Hoak spent most of spring training playing in B games, brooding about an uncertain future and scrutinizing Allen's every move. When asked by the sportswriters why he seemed to be paying so much attention to his twenty-two-year-old competitor, Hoak replied "I just want to see what he can do. I like to know what every ballplayer can do. You never know when the information will come in handy. Whether I'm with this club or another club, it's good to know all you can."[5]

Allen wasn't fazed by the attention. "If he were in my shoes, would he be bothered?" said the highly touted prospect. "Look, there's nothing he can do that I can't do. The only edge he has on me is experience. That's all."[6] When told of the remark, Hoak insisted he held no animosity toward Richie. "Why should I?" he said.

> My chance will come, then it's up to me. This is my eighteenth year in the game, and I've never been impressed by anyone who hits well in spring training. But if I were, I'd have to say that Allen is one hell of a prospect.[7]

Hoak would soon be out of a job. Richie had a tremendous spring, hitting nine home runs and twenty-five RBIs; his most impressive shot came on March 24 against the Cincinnati Reds at Tampa's Al Lopez Field.[8] The baseball historian Bill Jenkinson, who spent more than thirty years researching tape measure home runs in Major League Baseball, noted that Allen's four-bagger was "unanimously described by witnesses as a rising line drive that struck the top of the light pole beyond the left field fence." "The light pole was ninety-six feet high and 358 feet from home plate when the ball was interrupted in mid-flight," he added. "In fact many, including Phillies manager Gene Mauch, swear the ball was still ascending on impact."[9] Allen's offensive performance earned him the starting job at third.

After the team headed north, the rookie power hitter carried the Phillies from the very beginning of the regular season. During the first three weeks of April, the Phils were in first place. Richie was on fire, hitting .430 with five homers, and Hoak was given his unconditional release.[10]

By mid-May, the Phillies were locked in a see-saw battle with the hard-charging San Francisco Giants for first place in the National League.

Willie Mays, who was hitting at a .490 clip, and the pitching ace Juan Marichal, who entered the month with a perfect 4-0 record, kept the Giants in hot pursuit. But the Phillies, who won fifteen of their first twenty-four games, refused to let up.[11] Allen, Covington, and Callison were fueling the offense. In one of the most memorable slugging performances—a May 9 game at Philadelphia's Connie Mack Stadium against the Cincinnati Reds—Covington hit a mammoth home run to the far side of the Longines clock atop the sixty-four-foot-high scoreboard in right center. He also collected two singles and five RBIs in the game, while Callison contributed two triples, a double, and a single in the 11-3 rout.[12] A week later, the Phillies defeated Marichal and the Giants at San Francisco's Candlestick Park (7-2), a loss that dropped the Giants to second place and eight percentage points behind the Phils. Once again, Callison made the difference in the game, going five for five with a home run and five RBIs.[13] Callison, a fan favorite once dubbed "the next Mickey Mantle" as a rookie with the Chicago White Sox, finally seemed to be realizing his enormous potential.

Allen's 1964 Topps rookie card. *Courtesy of The Topps Company, Inc.*

Allen was even more prodigious. Through May, the rookie third baseman led the Phils in every major offensive category, with a .431 batting average, seven home runs, and thirteen RBIs.[14] "There's just no telling how good this kid can be," Mauch boasted:

> He's got great hands and a very quick, very short swing. But what impresses me most about him is his professional approach to the game. He doesn't get way up when things are going good, or way down when things are going bad. And that's the best approach to any professional sport.[15]

Allen's numbers were so impressive for a rookie that the Pittsburgh Pirates hosted a "Richie Allen Night" two weeks later at Forbes Field to honor the local product.[16] By that time the Phils were a half game in front of the Giants and 1½ games in front of the Milwaukee Braves, who were tied for third with the St. Louis Cardinals. The Pirates were in fourth and only two games out.[17]

Phils pitching was anchored by Jim Bunning, a six-time All Star who won more than 100 games in the American League. The Tigers believed Bunning's best days were behind him and traded him to the Phillies, where the slender Kentuckian was a workhorse with a competitive fire that burned white hot when he was on the mound. After winning his first National League start against the New York Mets (4-1), Bunning threw a six-hit shutout against the Chicago Cubs, striking out nine batsmen. In his third start, he held the Braves scoreless for eight innings before Chris Short and the newly acquired reliever Ed Roebuck finished them off for a 5-3 victory. In those three starts, Bunning surrendered just one earned run in a total of 25⅔ innings of work.[18] He was even better in May, when he flirted with no-hitters on two occasions.[19] Bunning would go on to win nineteen games that season and strike out 219 batters.[20] While some of his success was because none of the other teams had faced him before, Bunning's competitiveness and experience gave him an edge over his opponents. "I just try to pitch like it's 1-0 every time I go out there," he explained, entering the month of June with a perfect 5-0 record.[21] The lefthander Chris Short, used by Mauch as a starter and a reliever, was also extremely valuable. During the first three months of the season, Short sported a very impressive earned run average of 2.20 or lower. He would go on to win seventeen games and strike out 181 hitters that season.[22]

Fans both black and white were getting excited about the Phillies, and with good reason. The Phils entered June with a 25-15 record and a .625 winning percentage.

The 1964 Philadelphia Phillies. Front row (left to right): Jim Bunning, Dennis Bennett, Johnny Callison, Bob Oldis, Peanuts Lowery (coach), Gene Mauch (manager), George Myatt (coach), Al Widmar (coach), Art Mahaffey, John Boozer, and Tony Gonzalez. Second row (left to right): Joe Liscio (trainer), Richie Allen, Bobby Shantz, Ray Culp, Johnny Briggs, Frank Thomas, Rick Wise, Alex Johnson, Jack Baldschun, Danny Cater, and Cookie Rojas. Top row (left to right): Clay Dalrymple, Ruben Amaro, Bobby Wine, Gus Triandos, Wes Covington, Ed Roebuck, Roy Sievers, Vic Power, and Chris Short. Bat boys (left to right): Charley Bauer and Ken Bush. *Courtesy of The Topps Company, Inc.*

They were locked in a tight pennant race with San Francisco, which was a half game out, and playing some of the most exciting baseball the city had witnessed in years.[23]

To be sure, Allen, Callison, Bunning, and Short were carrying the Phillies. The supporting cast was solid but not nearly as talented as the four-member core. It was also Philadelphia's first truly integrated baseball team. Latin American players like the infielders Ruben Amaro, Cookie Rojas, and Tony Taylor, and the centerfielder Tony Gonzalez, provided speed on the base paths and a steady defense. Black players like Johnny Briggs, Wes Covington, and Alex Johnson added some power to the offense. Whites dominated the pitching staff. Chris Short, Dennis Bennett, Art Mahaffey, Ray Culp, and the rookie Rick Wise were the other starters. Jack Baldschun, Ed Roebuck, and Bobby Shantz were in the bullpen, and Clay Dalrymple and Gus Triandos split the catching duties.[24] What's more, a special chemistry was developing among the players that spring. Most of them were in their early to mid-twenties and had already weathered the adversity of being perennial cellar dwellers, including a twenty-three-game losing streak. They could see that the future looked much brighter. They pulled for one another on the field and enjoyed a loose camaraderie off the field.

Contrary to the portrayal of those Phillies by *Philadelphia Daily News* as divided along racial lines, the players insisted there was no animosity, racial or otherwise, among them. "There was no racism I could see," said pitcher Dennis Bennett. "We all liked each other and joked around with each other. It was one of the tightest group[s] of guys I ever played with."[25] Although Bennett, who was traded the next year, was speaking strictly of the 1964 team, other players who remained with the club throughout the 1960s agreed there was *never* any race problem on the Phillies.

The 1964 Phillies were Philadelphia's first truly integrated baseball team, with Hispanic players like Cookie Rojas (left), whites like Johnny Callison (second from left), and African Americans like Richie Allen. Gene Mauch (right) was the ideal manager for the team, having experienced the integration process as a player with the Brooklyn Dodgers in the late 1940s. *Courtesy of the Allen Family*

Tony Taylor, another Latino, was one of the most popular players on the team. *Courtesy of the National Baseball Hall of Fame and Library, Cooperstown, NY*

Wes Covington, obtained from the Milwaukee Braves, was a veteran outfielder who added power to the Phillies' lineup. *Courtesy of the National Baseball Hall of Fame and Library, Cooperstown, NY*

Tony Taylor, the Latino second baseman, credited Gene Mauch with "keeping all the players together, to function as a team." "He had already been through integration as a player in the Dodger organization," said Taylor. "Gene knew the importance of team chemistry on an integrated club. So there was a great chemistry between the Hispanic, black, and white players on the team."[26] Tony Gonzalez, the team's Hispanic center fielder, also believed the players "got along all right." "Sure, players kidded around with each other," he said:

> One of my teammates called me a "Cuban monkey." But that didn't bother me because that kind of stuff went on in all clubhouses back then. Besides, he didn't mean anything by it because he was one of my best friends on the club. Everybody—white players, black players, Hispanic players—got along fine.[27]

In today's politically correct atmosphere, baseball players are much more hesitant to use racial vocabulary as terms of endearment, but that was certainly not the case in the 1960s. Racist language was a natural part of clubhouse culture throughout the majors. In Philadelphia, white veterans often used the term *nigger* to demonstrate their acceptance of an exceptional black player. "Richie Allen and I were very close friends," explained Clay Dalrymple, a white catcher.

> We'd walk down the street with our arms around each other's shoulders. I'd call him "nigger," he'd call me "white trash," and we'd be laughing like sons-of-bitches. But he trusted me because I was Pat Corrales's roommate, and Pat [a Hispanic player] was one of his closest friends on the team.[28]

If there was any divisiveness, the players certainly did not see it. Most of them still consider their time with the club as a highlight of their baseball career. In so many ways, 1964 looked to be an enchanting season for the Phillies, their fans, and even the sportswriters, who had grown accustomed to counting out the hometown team at the end of spring. What's more, the fun was just beginning.

On Father's Day, June 21, Jim Bunning threw a perfect game against the Mets in the first game of a doubleheader at New York's Shea Stadium. The Mets' biggest threat came in the fifth inning, when Jesse Gonder, their left-handed hitting catcher, smacked a hard shot into the hole between first and second. But Tony Taylor, diving to his left, somehow managed to spear the ball and throw him out. Bunning was unstoppable after that, going on to secure the perfect 6-0 victory.[29] Two weeks later, on July 7, Johnny Callison would capture the national spotlight—again at Shea Stadium, where the All-Star Game was played that season. Selected as a reserve player along with Bunning and Chris Short, Callison entered the game in the bottom of the ninth, with the American League clinging to a 4-3 lead. With two outs and two runners on base, the Phils' slugging outfielder drove the ball into the right field grandstand for a climactic three-run homer, and the National League walked off the field with a 7-4 come-from-behind victory.[30]

Jim Bunning, who hurled a perfect game against the Mets on Father's Day 1964, was the ace of the Phillies. *Courtesy of the National Baseball Hall of Fame and Library, Cooperstown, NY*

Allen's bat proved to be the deciding factor in many games, but his defense was a liability; he averaged seven errors per month through June. "It really didn't matter how many errors Richie made at third base," admitted catcher Clay Dalrymple,

> because his offense more than made up for it. He was lanky, but he had strong hands and forearms that allowed him to drive the ball a distance. In fact, Richie hit a baseball harder than anyone else I ever played with. He could pull the ball as well as hit opposite field, and he *always* hit the ball hard. That's why he was such a dangerous hitter.[31]

By mid-season, his swing was being compared with that of Cincinnati's Frank Robinson and his hitting with that of Hank Aaron of the Braves. The *Philadelphia Daily News* sportswriter Larry Merchant, in an unusually generous column, wrote: "There is no way that Richie Allen can have anything but a big year." Comparing the rookie third baseman's start with the debuts of such legendary sluggers as Frank Robinson, Orlando Cepeda, and Mickey Mantle, Merchant predicted Allen would hit "around .300" and "drive in and score 100 runs, get 190 to 200 base hits with 30-35 home runs, 35-40 doubles, and 10 triples." Of course Merchant also predicted Allen would "strike out 160 times." Never one to give much credit to management, the *Daily News* columnist attributed the rookie's success to the fact the Phillies coaches "leave him alone and let him play ball."[32]

If Richie was letting his success go to his head, he certainly did not show it. His mother made sure of it. "All this [success] is nice," Era told her son, "but being a baseball player isn't everything. I want you to do right, to be a right kind of man."[33] Allen, who purchased a new house for his mother shortly after he signed with the Phillies, paid close attention to her advice:

> If I made a million dollars in baseball and gave it all to her, it wouldn't be enough to repay my mother for what she did for me. If you wanted to play ball at our house growing up, you had to get up before daybreak and do your homework. She didn't stand for any nonsense. Outside of baseball, I think she was the best hitter I ever saw![34]

To honor his mother's wishes, Allen tried hard to be the "right kind of man." He became a valued mentor to other young African American players who were promoted to the Phillies during the season. Grant Jackson remembers being called up to the big club with Ferguson Jenkins late in the 1964 campaign. "Richie looked out for us because we weren't making much money," he said. "He and his wife Barb invited me to stay at their house in Germantown and they refused to take any rent. They even let me use their car."[35] Similarly, Allen took Johnny Briggs and Alex Johnson under his wing.[36] Briggs was genuinely liked by teammates and ownership, and he relied on Richie's encouragement to realize his own potential. Johnson was more difficult to understand or like. "Alex called everybody "dickhead," recalled Allen.

> To him, baseball was a whole world of dickheads. Teammates, managers, general managers, owners. Everybody was a dickhead to him. That was just his way. But the front office types took it personally. They said he was surly. But Alex was also the kind of guy who would come over to my house and play with my kids, or jump into his car and drive out to the Schuylkill Expressway to help a clubhouse attendant fix his broken-down car. People just didn't understand him. All Alex wanted to do was be left alone to play ball.[37]

Interestingly, the same could have been said about Richie Allen years later when his relationship with the Phillies organization had soured. While he "just wanted to be left alone to play ball," he was still the kind of person who would, and did, "jump into his car and drive out to the Schuylkill Expressway to help a clubhouse attendant fix his broken-down car." Similarly, Richie remained loyal to his teammates, regardless of their skin color. In one of the unwritten rules of baseball, pitchers retaliate when an opposing hurler throws at a teammate. Often the benches clear after a knockdown pitch in a show of loyalty to either the victim or the offender. In his rookie year, Allen made it clear to all the Phillies pitchers that he would be the first to protect them in such cases, and he followed through on his promise whenever such an incident occurred.[38]

Richie Allen was a dream come true, not only for Philadelphia's growing pool of African American baseball fans but also for Phillies management, who appreciated

Allen committed forty-one errors as a third baseman in 1964, but his twenty-nine home runs, ninety-one RBIs, and .939 OPS made up for it. *Courtesy of the Allen Family*

Allen at the plate. *Artwork courtesy of Rob Larsen*

his exceptional maturity on and off the playing field. Perhaps as a show of their appreciation, the organization signed Dick's brother, Ron, a twenty-year-old catcher, who was assigned to Bakersfield and converted to first base. With Harold Allen already playing at Chattanooga in the Southern League, the Phillies had both of Richie's brothers playing in their farm system by season's end.[39]

Richie was a public relations dream come true for the Phillies in 1964. His power hitting and speed on the base paths drew fans to the ballpark, and his loyalty to teammates was unmatched. *Courtesy of the National Baseball Hall of Fame and Library, Cooperstown, NY*

When the Phillies returned home from a difficult West Coast trip on July 24, more than 5,000 fans turned out to greet them at Philadelphia International Airport. Placards and bumper stickers with the words "GO PHILLIES GO" began to surface throughout the city. With the Phillies in first place by a full game over the second-place Giants, pennant fever was raging in Philadelphia for the first time in more than a decade.[40] But Mauch knew better than to take his club's first-place standing for granted.

The Phillies managed to hold on to first by beating the National League's weaker teams. Their cumulative record against the Houston Colts, Mets, Cubs, and Dodgers at that point in the season was 30-11. The Phillies had been less successful against the Reds, who had taken six of eleven games from them, and the Cardinals, who had won nine of the sixteen contests between the two teams. Both of these teams were sending left-handers to the mound against the Phillies, whose only power-hitting right-handed hitter was Allen.[41] If the Phils were to contend in the second half of the season, they would have to have more success against the stronger teams and trade for a right-handed power hitter. Roy Sievers tried to convince Mauch he could fill the void, but the thirty-seven-year-old first baseman was hitting just .183, with four homers and sixteen RBIs through early August. Instead, Quinn acquired power-hitting first baseman Frank Thomas from the New York Mets for the rookie pitcher Gary Kroll, a minor leaguer, and cash.[42]

Thomas, a strapping six-foot-three-inch, two-hundred-pound slugger, was a three-time All Star who up to that point had hit 272 home runs in an eleven-year career with the Pirates, Reds, Cubs, Braves, and Mets. A dead pull hitter who crowded

Allen playing third base. *Artwork courtesy of Rob Larsen*

the plate, Thomas attracted Quinn's attention in 1962, when he hit thirty-four homers and ninety-four RBIs for the expansion Mets.[43] Thomas carried the Phillies for his first two weeks with the club, hitting .302, with seven homers and twenty-six RBIs. He became so popular that WFIL Radio gave him a morning show in which he would play the most recent hit records and talk baseball.[44]

With Thomas in the lineup, Allen and Callison became even more dangerous at the plate. By mid-August, both players were tied for the club lead in home runs with twenty each, while Callison led the Phillies in RBIs with seventy to Allen's sixty-one. Both players were leading candidates for Most Valuable Player, with Allen favored to capture the National League's Rookie of the Year Award.[45]

Having been in contention since opening day, the Phillies were favored to capture the flag. Heading into mid-August, they were getting excellent pitching from Bunning, Bennett, and Short. Jack Baldscun was an extremely effective closer, with Roebuck as another consistent reliever. Quinn added depth to the bullpen by acquiring veteran left-hander Bobby Shantz from the Chicago Cubs.[46] After defeating Milwaukee (6-1) on August 26, the Phillies held a commanding 7½ game lead over San Francisco, with a hot Cincinnati club in third—eight games behind—and the Cardinals in

Although he was better known for his power hitting, Richie was an excellent base runner who stole an average of ten bases a season during his early years with the Phillies. *Courtesy of the Allen Family*

Richie Allen, 1964. *Artwork courtesy of Rob Larsen*

fourth at ten games out.[47] Their enchanting summer had continued through the dog days—a make-or-break period for most contenders. But when the team returned home from the Midwest on August 28 to face the Pirates at Connie Mack Stadium, they were confronted by one of the most devastating race riots of the civil rights era.

Earlier that night a black police officer approached a black woman whose car had stalled at the intersection of Columbia Avenue and Twenty-second Street in North Philadelphia, just a few blocks from the ballpark. Refusing to move her car, the motorist and her passenger husband stepped outside the car to confront the officer. The couple were intoxicated. Tempers flared. Suddenly the woman slapped the police officer and shoved him out of her way. A crowd gathered as the police officer radioed for support. As the disorderly motorist was being arrested, the police were attacked by a hailstorm of bricks and bottles. By 10:30 p.m., the incident had erupted into a full-fledged riot, with as many as 2,000 people looting, destroying storefronts, and setting fires.

Just before dawn 600 policemen converged on the North Penn District, but the looters continued their rampage. Nothing worked until 9:00 a.m., when Mayor Tate arrived to announce a curfew on a 410-block square of North Philadelphia. Accompanied by another 600 police officers, Tate finally managed to restore some semblance of order.[48]

The game between the Phillies and Pirates went on before a near-empty stadium that night. Allen tripled and hit his twenty-fourth home run, knocking in four runs, while Callison hit his twenty-third homer and collected three RBIs. Art Mahaffey, who enjoyed a 10-0 lead, was knocked out in the eighth when the Bucs rallied for four runs. The reliever John Boozer replaced him but surrendered another four runs before Baldschun could finish the game, a narrow 10-8 victory.[49] During the game, the mob resumed its rampage, ignoring Tate's curfew. Marching west on Columbia Avenue, the rioters destroyed white-owned businesses one by one. The rioting continued all day Sunday as the Pirates humbled the Phillies 10-2 at Connie Mack. Not until Monday evening, after all the stores on Columbia Avenue had been looted, did the riot end. When it was over, two people were dead and 339 were wounded, including 100 police officers. Another 300 people were arrested and more than 600 businesses, many owned by white Jewish merchants, were destroyed, with damages estimated at $3 million. North Philadelphia's neighborhoods were now blocked off from the rest of the city by police barricades.

The fans stayed away from Connie Mack Stadium for days after the riot. Black rage had increased the fears of the whites who lived in the North Penn District, hastening their flight to the suburbs. It also increased police presence around the ballpark. Between fifty and sixty officers surrounded the stadium, an additional 100 patrolled the neighborhood, and another 1,000 could be found across North Philadelphia.[50]

Like African Americans across the nation, Philadelphia's blacks were becoming more race conscious. They had grown tired of being second-class citizens, demanding integration into the American mainstream. Blacks resented white dominance of the businesses in a neighborhood that was increasingly populated by African Americans. In North Philadelphia, the Phillies were one of those white-owned businesses. "The only thing I regret about the riot," said one black resident, speaking on condition of anonymity,

> was that we didn't burn down that goddamn stadium. They had it surrounded by cops and we couldn't get to it. I just wish we could've burned it down and wiped away its history that tells me I'm nothing but a nigger.[51]

North Philadelphia's residents were not the only ones awakened by the black rage sweeping across their neighborhoods. Richie Allen also became acutely aware of the fact that he was a black superstar on a team that had never been accepted by the city's African Americans and, as such, became a symbol of the racial unrest that was consuming Philadelphia. "Racial tensions were at the boiling point," recalled Allen years later:

> The neighborhood around Connie Mack looked like a bomb had just hit it. The streets were empty. People stayed indoors. Police cars patrolled the streets. Stores were boarded up. And whites blamed blacks for that. I guess being the star black player for the Phillies also made me a threat to white people, especially since I said what was on my mind. They weren't used to a black athlete like that.[52]

On September 1, the Phillies held a 5½-game lead over the second-place Cincinnati Reds and seemed to be on their way to the World Series.[53] On September 7 (Labor Day), the Phillies split a doubleheader with the Dodgers in Los Angeles, while the Reds lost two games to the St. Louis Cardinals, increasing the Phillies' lead to 6½ games, with twenty-five left to play. Then things began to go wrong. The first sign of trouble was a string of injuries to key players. Frank Thomas broke his right thumb sliding into second base on September 8 and was out for the season. Ray Culp, the number four starter in the pitching rotation, suffered problems with his right elbow, while Dennis Bennett, the number three starter, struggled with a sore arm. Art Mahaffey inexplicably developed control problems.[54]

Things seemed to settle down on September 13, when ace Jim Bunning beat the Giants for his seventeenth victory of the season, and Short and Bennett followed up with wins over Houston. On September 16, Bunning took the mound again after Culp was scratched because of a sore elbow. Pitching on just two days' rest, Bunning surrendered a two-run home run by Rusty Staub and lasted only 4⅓ innings. He was much better in his next start on September 20, when he beat the Dodgers 3-2, throwing a five-hitter.[55] It would be the Phillies' last win in September.

When they returned to Philadelphia on September 21, the Phils enjoyed a 6½-game lead over St. Louis and Cincinnati, both of whom were tied for second, with just twelves games left to play in the season. Over the next week, the Phils lost every game they played, while the Cards and Reds won all of theirs. Mauch panicked, relying on Bunning and Short to get them out of the fix. On three separate occasions during that stretch, the Phillies' skipper pitched his two top hurlers, each with only two days' rest. The collapse began September 21, when the Phillies opened a three-game series against the Reds. Mahaffey started the first game, his first appearance since a 9-1 loss to the Giants on the twelfth. It was a pitchers' duel between Mahaffey and the Reds' John Tsitouris until the sixth inning, when Cincinnati's Chico Ruiz singled and was advanced to third on a liner by Vada Pinson. Frank Robinson came to the plate next. He swung and missed for strike one on Mahaffey's first offering. Ruiz, on third, noted that Mahaffey had not checked him before the pitch and broke for home on the next delivery. Surprised, Mahaffey threw high and wild over the outstretched arm of the Phillies' catcher Clay Dalrymple, and the ball bounced off the screen. Ruiz's successful steal of home gave the Reds the lead and the game's only run. "It was the play that broke our humps," Allen would say later.[56]

The following night Chris Short took the mound but didn't make it through the fifth, when Frank Robinson smashed a two-run homer. The Phillies lost 9-2, and their lead was down to 4½ games. September 23 was "Richie Allen Night" at Connie Mack Stadium. Organized by the local business community, the special night was opposed by the Phillies front office, which did not believe in honoring rookies. Nevertheless, Allen, the presumptive "Rookie of the Year," was presented with a television, snow tires, luggage, a stereo, and a $1,000 scholarship for his infant daughter's education. The rookie third baseman was noticeably moved by his mother's presence. After the pregame ceremonies, he posed with her for a photograph and joked, "I guess all of those years of cutting class at Wampum High to play ball have finally paid off."[57] Of course Era Allen did not find the remark very amusing, but she was

The lefthander Chris Short pitched on less than two days' rest down the stretch. *Courtesy of the National Baseball Hall of Fame and Library, Cooperstown, NY*

extremely proud of her son. Dennis Bennett pitched that night, lasting six innings with a sore arm before the Phils went down in a 6-4 defeat. Their lead was now down to 3½ games.[58]

Milwaukee came in next, and Bunning was the starter in the opener, which the Phils lost 5-3. Then Chris Short pitched on two days' rest in the next game—the Phillies lost—and the losing streak was at five, with the lead now down to a game and a half. On September 26, the Phils' advantage over the Reds was reduced to just half a game as the reliever Bobby Shantz squandered a 4-0 lead, losing to Milwaukee 6-4. Bunning tried to salvage the final game of the series with the Braves, again pitching on two days' rest, and lasted three innings in a 14-8 loss. With the fourth loss against the Braves and the seventh loss in a row, the Phillies dropped to second and the Reds, having swept a doubleheader, took first place by one full game. The Cardinals were right behind them, 1½ games out.[59]

On September 23, 1964, Philadelphia's business community held a "Richie Allen Night" to honor the presumptive "Rookie of the Year." *Courtesy of Temple University Urban Archives, Philadelphia, PA*

The "ghost" program the Phillies ordered in anticipation of clinching the National League pennant in 1964 is a sad reminder of the worst collapse in the history of major league baseball. *Courtesy of the Philadelphia Phillies Baseball Club*

Unfortunately, Mauch seemed to destroy the very chemistry he had worked so hard to build the longer his team was mired in the slump. "Mauch was only 38 years old and he wanted to win so badly," explained Allen:

> He would have done anything to win. But somewhere along the line in '64, he forgot the most elementary rule of baseball: to have fun. Once we started to skid, he'd become a wild man. After losses he would close the clubhouse door and start dressing us down, throwing things around. All we really needed was for him to pat us on the fanny and say, "Thanks fellas, good effort, we'll get 'em tomorrow." Instead we got ranting and raving and all that did was make us feel more tired than we already were.[60]

One of the best experiences for Richie Allen in 1964 was the birth of his daughter, Terri, here held by her mother Barbara. *Courtesy of the Allen Family*

Richie poses with Tony Oliva of the Minnesota Twins, the American League's 1964 Rookie of the Year, at the postseason Topps award banquet. *Courtesy of the Allen Family*

Having lost every game of their last home stand, the now second-place Phillies traveled to St. Louis for a crucial three-game set against the Cardinals. They dropped the first game of the series to Bob Gibson, 5-1. It was their eighth loss in a row, dropping them to third place. The Cardinals would sweep all three games and assume first place for good. The Phillies' losing streak finally ended in Cincinnati during the last two games of the season, with wins of 4-3 and 10-0 over the Reds. There were no playoffs in 1964, and the Phillies ended the season at 92-70, tied for second place with the Reds.[61] Today the "Swoon"—as the ten-game losing streak would come to be known—is one of the most notable collapses in sports history.

Richie Allen's 1965 Topps baseball card. The gold trophy acknowledges the honor of being selected for the 1964 Topps All-Star Team. *Courtesy of The Topps Company, Inc.*

Watching the pennant slip through their grasp was devastating for the Phillies. The organization had already printed World Series programs and tickets. In the minds of the players, the fans, and the front office, the pennant had already been clinched. Yet the season wasn't without its successes.

The Phillies were a close-knit team, comprising young players who genuinely liked each other on and off the field. They were Philadelphia's first truly integrated baseball club, with blacks, Hispanics, and whites. They were a good, solid team who had a *great* season through 150 games, but just did not have the playoff experience to clinch the pennant down the stretch. And in Richie Allen they had one of the premier players in Major League Baseball.

Allen enjoyed one of the greatest rookie seasons in major league history, batting .318, with twenty-nine home runs and ninety-one RBIs. He led the National League in multiple offensive categories, including runs scored (125), triples (13), extra base hits (80), and total bases (352), and he won the National League Rookie of the Year award.[62] To be sure, Allen did have some flaws in his play—he led the league with 138 strikeouts and a whopping forty-one errors at third base.[63] He also received a lot of criticism for the Phillies' historic collapse, though it was unjustified. Allen batted .341 in the final month of the season, with a .618 slugging percentage. He hit five home runs, and his seventy-six total bases were far greater than his total in any other month. The rookie third baseman even turned his play up in the final twelve games of the season, hitting .438 with three home runs, eleven RBIs, and seventeen hits.[64]

"I never enjoyed a player more than I enjoyed Richie Allen in 1964," Mauch said later. "We both had a lot of fun. It just wasn't so much fun at the end."[65] That season Mauch had come the closest he had ever been to being a pennant winner, and he watched it slip away before his eyes. Afterward, he would become more distant from his players. His relationship with Allen in particular would vacillate between a protector and an antagonist. In the end, Gene Mauch would be jealous but respectful of his young slugger's exceptional talent, and their relationship would end in a nasty divorce.

Manager Gene Mauch's relationship with Allen would vacillate between "protector" and "antagonist" over the next four years. *Artwork courtesy of Rob Larsen*

Richie Allen's 26 longest home runs at Philadelphia's Connie Mack Stadium, 1964–1969

Courtesy of Bill Jenkinson, "Dick Allen's HR Log"

HOME RUN	DATE	OPPONENT	PITCHER	EST. HR DISTANCE (FEET)	WINNER / SCORE
A	May 31, 1964	Houston Colt 45s	Jim Owens	450+	Phillies / 4-1
B	June 12, 1964	New York Mets	Tracy Stallard	450+	Mets / 11-3
C	June 14, 1964	New York Mets	Galen Cisco	450	Phillies / 9-5
D	August 22, 1964	Pittsburgh Pirates	Frank Bork	450+	Pirates / 9-4
E	May 12, 1965	Cincinnati Reds	Sammy Ellis	420–450	Reds / 4-3
F	May 29, 1965	Chicago Cubs	Larry Jackson	529	Phillies / 4-2
G	June 10, 1965	Los Angeles Dodgers	Johnny Podres	510	Phillies / 4-0
H	July 8, 1965	San Francisco Giants	Jack Sanford	450+	Phillies / 4-2
I	June 1, 1966	Chicago Cubs (Game 2)	Bob Hendley	448	Phillies / 4-3
J	July 4, 1966	New York Mets	Gerry Arrigo	450+	Mets / 9-6
K	August 17, 1966	Chicago Cubs	Ken Holtzman	420–450	Cubs / 5-3
L	August 19, 1966	New York Mets	Bob Friend	500+	Phillies / 5-4
M	April 16, 1967	New York Mets	Bill Denehy	450+	Phillies / 2-0
N	June 6, 1967	Chicago Cubs	Joe Niekro	550+	Phillies / 8-6
O	June 16, 1967	Pittsburgh Pirates	Vern Law	450+	Phillies / 5-3
P	July 9, 1967	St. Louis Cardinals	Nelson Briles	500+	Phillies / 4-3
Q	August 20, 1967	Chicago Cubs	Ken Holtzman	500+	Cubs / 6-1
R	April 21, 1968	Houston Astros	Wade Blasingame	450+	Phillies / 8-0
S	May 22, 1968	New York Mets	Don Cardwell	450+	Phillies / 8-0
T	June 18, 1968	San Francisco Giants	Gaylord Perry	450+	Phillies / 9-1
U	April 14, 1969	New York Mets	Jim McAndrew	500+	Phillies / 5-1
V	May 8, 1969	Houston Astros	Tom Griffin	450+	Astros / 9-7
W	May 15, 1969	Cincinnati Reds	John Noriega	500+	Phillies / 7-0
X	June 17, 1969	New York Mets (Game 2)	Don Cardwell	500	Phillies / 7-3
Y	June 21, 1969	Pittsburgh Pirates	Bob Veale	500	Pirates / 8-2
Z	August 5, 1969	San Francisco Giants	Mike McCormick	420–450	Giants / 5-3

Richie Allen's Historic Home Runs at Connie Mack Stadium, 1964–1969. *Courtesy of Greg Sgambato, Choice Sports Cards*

Richie Allen's image as baseball's "bad boy" was reinforced by this photo that appeared in the August 22, 1969, issue of *Life Magazine*. After that, it was difficult for him to shed the infamous reputation, even though it no longer applied after he left Philadelphia. *Photo by Charles Bonnan,* Life Magazine/*Getty Images*

CHAPTER 4:
BOO!

In 1965, the Phillies were determined to capture the pennant that should have been theirs the year before. Desperate to land the veterans who could make the difference, their general manager John Quinn acquired Dick Stuart, a power-hitting first baseman, and Bo Belinsky, a free-spirited pitcher with a lively arm. But it didn't work. Stuart was inconsistent at the plate and his wacky defense earned him the nickname "Dr. Strangeglove." Belinsky's social life was livelier than his pitching. He won only four of thirteen decisions and argued constantly with Mauch. Also, a few veterans were on the downside of their careers. Frank Thomas and Vic Power added punch to the Phillies' lineup as part-time players in '64, but were struggling to keep their jobs in '65. Nor was the Phillies' pitching nearly as good as the previous season. Not surprisingly, the Phillies struggled to play .500 ball for most of 1965.[1] Allen, on the other hand, picked up where he left off in '64. At the end of June, Richie was hitting .348, with eleven home runs and forty-nine RBIs, and had been named to the National League All-Star team. Then, on July 3, his season went into a freefall.

Frank Thomas, a power-hitting first baseman acquired by the Phillies from the New York Mets in 1964, struggled at the plate the following season. He also became the center of controversy in 1965, when he struck Allen with a bat before a July 3 game against the Cincinnati Reds. *Courtesy of the National Baseball Hall of Fame, Cooperstown, NY*

Allen was fielding ground balls at third base before that night's game against the Cincinnati Reds while Frank Thomas was in the cage taking his cuts. Thomas, a thirty-six-year-old veteran, was the kind of slugger who could carry the team when he was hitting well, but he was in a slump, batting .250 with no homers in seventy-six plate appearances, and he had recently lost his job in the outfield. Although he was popular with the fans, Thomas, who was white, antagonized his teammates with clubhouse pranks and racially inflammatory language. The veteran liked to bully Johnny Briggs, a younger black teammate who replaced him in the outfield. Thomas constantly called him "boy," considered a racial epithet by blacks. On another occasion he pretended to offer Briggs a soul shake and when the younger player offered his hand in return Thomas grabbed his thumb and bent it back, causing it to swell.[2]

The outfielder Johnny Briggs was one of the talented African American players promoted to the Phillies in 1964 and Richie Allen's close friend. *Courtesy of the National Baseball Hall of Fame, Cooperstown, NY*

Briggs was Allen's best friend, and he did not appreciate the abuse Thomas was doling out. Richie could relate with the twenty-one-year-old outfielder because they both experienced the same alienation playing minor league ball in Arkansas. Allen also knew the Phillies were expecting too much too soon from Briggs. After an impressive start at Class A Bakersfield, where Briggs hit .297, with twenty-one home runs and eighty-three RBIs, the Phillies rushed him through their farm system. Playing fewer than two hundred games in the minors, Briggs, a speedy base runner who played the outfield with an exceptional instinct, was promoted to the Phillies for the '64 pennant race. He played so effectively for twenty games the Phillies decided to keep him on the roster in '65. It was a mistake.

Briggs platooned center field with Tony Gonzalez and was also made the lead-off hitter. He struggled to hit .230 for most of the season and never really felt comfortable with his role on the team. In fact, he expressed a preference for returning to Little Rock just to play on an everyday basis.[3]

Ironically, the Phillies found themselves in a no-win situation. While Briggs was a part of their earnest attempt to integrate the team, the Phillies only damaged his self confidence by not sending him back to the minors. Perhaps their decision was based on potential, or simply a genuine desire to protect a young black player from even more discrimination at the hands of the Little Rock fans. Regardless, the Phillies failed on both counts, and Allen knew it. As a result, he was especially protective of Briggs.

While Thomas was struggling to make contact in the batting cage, the outfielder Johnny Callison stopped by to visit Allen at third base. Looking to make mischief, Callison suggested they taunt Thomas for his poor showing at the plate in the previous night's game. Both players had been the object of Thomas's ridicule several times before and they were ready to get even.[4]

Down in the cage Thomas took a big swing and missed. "Hey Donkey!" yelled Callison, referring to the veteran by his nickname, "Why don't you try bunting?" Instead of responding to Callison, Thomas glared down the third base line at Allen and shouted: "What are you trying to be, another Muhammad Clay, always running your mouth off?" Insulted by the comparison to Cassius Clay, the colorful but controversial heavyweight boxing champion who had recently changed his name to Muhammad Ali, Allen charged the cage and the two players went at each other. Allen hit Thomas with a left hook to the jaw, sending him to the ground. When Thomas got to his feet he was wielding his bat and connected with Allen's left shoulder, breaking one of the most fundamental rules in the game—*never* hit another player with a bat. In seconds the rest of the team was at home plate frantically trying to restrain the two players.[5]

"Richie was under control until Thomas took that swing at him with the bat," recalled Callison, who retreated to the safety of the dugout when the fight broke out. "After that it took five guys to keep Allen off Thomas."[6]

After the dust settled, the Phillies went on to lose to the Reds 10-8. Despite a throbbing shoulder, Allen hit two triples: one a 400-foot shot off the Ballantine Beer scoreboard in right center field in the seventh. Thomas, still steaming from the fight, slammed his first homer of the season the next inning. It was too little, too late.[7] After the game, Thomas was waived to Houston and Mauch threatened Allen with a $2,000 fine if he discussed the incident with the press. Richie pleaded with the "Little General" to spare Thomas, who had a large family to support. "I begged Gene to release me instead of Thomas," recalled Allen in his 1989 autobiography, *Crash*. "But Mauch refused. He said, 'What? Are you kidding? We get a hitter like you once

Johnny Callison and Richie Allen sharing a joke, something that led to the July 1965 brawl between Allen and the white veteran Frank Thomas. *Courtesy of the Allen Family*

Manager Gene Mauch. *Artwork courtesy of Rob Larsen*

in a lifetime!' So I asked him why we couldn't tell the truth, but he just looked at me like I was crazy."[8]

When the press asked the Phillies' skipper about the decision, Mauch replied: "I had to choose between a thirty-six-year-old veteran who was hitting .250 and a twenty-three-year-old power hitter who was batting .348, the kind of player you see once in a lifetime."[9] It was the worst thing he could have said.

Thomas took his case to the press, exploiting the role of victim. "I've always liked Richie," he insisted. "I've always tried to help him. I guess certain guys can dish it out but can't take it."[10]

The view was different in the Phillies clubhouse. "Thomas rubbed a lot of people the wrong way," said Johnny Callison.[11] "In fact, Mauch wanted him gone, and the fight gave him an excuse. Thomas got himself fired." Eleven years later, Mauch admitted that Thomas "was going to go anyway." "I should have shipped him sooner," he conceded. "If I had the town wouldn't have come down on Richie's head."[12]

Phillies fans, known for being tough on hometown players even in the best of times, never forgave Allen. The rest of the season proved to be a nightmare. Initially the abuse was verbal, mostly obscenities. Racial epithets soon followed. Allen vividly recalls being sucker punched by one fan, others screaming "darkie" or "monkey" at him, and one especially painful memory of a man "holding his little boy up in the air with one hand and pointing at me with the other, teaching his son to boo."[13] Eventually Allen was showered with garbage, coins, and even flashlight batteries when he took the field. To protect himself Richie began wearing a batting helmet when he played defense. The idiosyncrasy gave rise to another nickname "Crash Helmet," shortened to "Crash."[14] The press could be even more malicious.

Larry Merchant, Stan Hochman, and Bill Conlin of the *Philadelphia Daily News* led the media's assault. Unwilling to forgive the team or its young superstar for the "'64 Swoon," these sportswriters represented a new, adversarial breed who celebrated controversy and discouraged heroism among players, especially when the team was not winning. After the Allen-Thomas brawl, Merchant, Hochman, and Conlin became contentious, choosing to emphasize racial discord in the clubhouse and in the players' personal lives, which were once considered "off limits" by the press. For the rest of Allen's early career in Philadelphia, they often portrayed him as a malcontent or "prima donna" who expected special treatment.[15] "The press made a much bigger thing out of the fight than it really was," said second baseman Tony Taylor, Allen's roommate.

> They knew that Thomas liked to intimidate young players, but he was also a popular veteran brought here to help win the pennant. Dick, on the other hand, was still a young player trying to make a name for himself. Everybody on the team liked him. But the press gave him the label of "troublemaker." It just wasn't fair.[16]

After the Thomas incident, Allen began to wear a batting helmet whenever he played the outfield to protect himself from the coins, batteries, and bottle caps thrown at him from the stands. *Courtesy of the National Baseball Hall of Fame and Library, Cooperstown, NY*

Butler Hennon, the principal and legendary basketball coach at Wampum High School, was horrified by what he had read about his former student athlete. "I just can't understand it," he told a sportswriter for the local *Pittsburgh Press*. "Rich was a good kid. He never gave me any trouble in all the years I knew him, and that goes back to his days in little league." But when Hennon learned that Johnny Callison was responsible for antagonizing Thomas and that Allen, who was simply standing by, was accused of provoking the fight, the Wampum principal admitted Allen was "easily led." "Rich always seemed to take the blame for another mischief maker," he explained.[17] Hennon's suggestion that Allen was vulnerable to being made a scapegoat had much validity.

In many ways the Allen-Thomas fight reinforced, in the minds of white Philadelphians, the racial stereotyping of African Americans as "troublemakers." Whites pointed to the rise of the Black Mafia, a street gang based around Twentieth and Carpenter Streets, as justification for the stereotype. Led by Benjamin Coxson and "Big Sam" Christian, this organized band of black gangsters controlled gambling, prostitution, and drug dealing in the city's African American neighborhoods. Gangs like these gradually displaced the traditional "Pop system," where older black men who were respected members of the community mentored black youth, encouraging clean living and education as the keys to success. Instead, the black gangs that were sprouting up across the city in the 1960s offered a quick and illegal way to make money.[18] For white city dwellers, the gangs also colored their perception of the civil rights movement. African Americans were protesting their inability to gain access to politically connected unions. Black moderates, intent on brokering a compromise with the white Democrats who controlled city hall, jousted with the local NAACP, which had become more aggressive under the leadership of president Cecil B. Moore. Crime, poverty, and gang warfare increased as black youth were denied employment. Working class and middle-class whites took exception to black self-determination. Those who could leave the city for the more affluent suburbs did, resulting in a steady "white flight." Those who could not stayed behind, voicing negative and condescending remarks about the "colored."

As the 1960s unfolded, *colored* was often replaced with *nigger*, and the remarks reflected greater hatred and intensity than ever before. In a declining manufacturing center like Philadelphia, blacks and whites were fighting over a limited supply of pride—blacks trying to attain it and whites desperate not to lose it. Police Commissioner Frank Rizzo worsened the situation by making crime control synonymous with an arbitrary crackdown on the black community. Allen's early baseball career coincided with the racial unrest, often providing the city's white baseball fans with an easy target for their racial hostility.[19]

In Philadelphia's racially charged atmosphere, Allen's own situation was inevitably distorted, not only by the press, but also by the city's baseball fans. The abuse eventually took its toll on the young slugger. "After the Thomas fight I started playing angry baseball," he confessed:

> It seemed the whole city of Philadelphia blamed me for what happened. They hung banners from the bleachers supporting Thomas. I began getting hate mail and lots of it. Most of the letters started off with "nigger."

The front lawn of his Mount Airy home was strewn with trash, compliments of disgruntled fans. The abuse became so bad that some of Allen's friends urged him to hire a bodyguard.[20]

In fact, the intrusive sportswriters from the *Philadelphia Daily News* and bigoted fans made life miserable for the Allen family. "We lived on a corner property in Mount Airy, right off Wissahickon Avenue," recalled Richie's wife, Barbara.

Allen's prolific home run swing. *Artwork courtesy of Rob Larsen*

> It was a nice neighborhood, but you couldn't control others who found out where we lived. So we had to watch Terri and Dickie Jr. [the couple's children] whenever they went out to play.
>
> I felt bad for Dick and the children because he enjoyed taking them to the ballpark for games and they just loved to go with their father. But as his situation with the Phillies became worse he stopped that, too.[21]

Allen's performance was inevitably affected by the abuse, along with his badly bruised left shoulder. After the fight he hit only .271, but sometimes his anger produced impressive results. On July 8, 1965, Allen, in a game against the San Francisco Giants at Connie Mack Stadium, rocketed a Jack Sanford fastball over the Longines' clock that topped the gigantic, seventy-five-foot-high scoreboard in right center field. The moon shot was estimated at well over 450 feet.[22] In an August 19, 1966, game against the New York Mets, Allen launched an estimated 500-foot blast that sailed over the right field wall and cleared the row houses on the other side of North Twentieth Street.[23] In still another game on June 6, 1967, against the Chicago Cubs, the Wampum Walloper nailed a Joe Niekro delivery an estimated 550 feet, rocketing over the Philco sign in left center field.[24] In addition, Allen hit at least eighteen other homers that landed on or over the roof of the two-deck grandstand in left field.[25]

Allen also occasionally called his own shot, especially if he felt the pitcher had shown him up and he was angry. On July 7, 1967, the Phils were playing St. Louis at Connie Mack. Losing 3-2 in the bottom of the eighth, the Cards brought in the hard-throwing right-hander Nelson Briles to close out the game. There was a runner at first with two outs, and Allen was due to hit. Before stepping to the plate, Richie turned to Tony Taylor and said, "This will be our last at bat." Then he turned to the batboy Kenny Bush and told him to "put all the equipment away" because the Phils "won't need it in the ninth." True to his word, Allen blasted a 1-1 fastball 500 feet over the roof in center field, stealing a 4-3 win for the Phillies.[26]

On September 29, 1968, the Phillies were playing the New York Mets in the season finale at Shea Stadium. Tom Seaver was pitching for New York. He walked Allen in the top of the second and struck him out looking in the fourth. When he got back to the dugout, Allen sat down next to Taylor and said, "I feel comfortable now. Next time up I am going to hit one out. If I get two or three more chances, I'll hit more."

Teammates who overheard the remark looked at Dick as if he were crazy. Taylor, his closest friend on the team, asked, "How can you feel comfortable when you just stood there looking at strike three?"

Allen just sat there and smiled.

Richie stepped to the plate again with one out and one on in the top of the sixth. By that time Seaver had already recorded nine strikeouts. "Okay boys, here we go!" he said, standing in the on-deck circle.

Allen proceeded to smash Seaver's second offering some 550 feet over the fence just right of dead center. Stunned, his teammates just sat in the dugout shaking their heads in disbelief as Allen circled the bases, nodding his head as if to say, "There you go!" But Richie wasn't quite finished.

In the top of the eighth, with the Phillies holding a 4-3 lead, Allen blasted a Calvin Koonce breaking ball over the center field backdrop for a solo home run. The Wampum Walloper stepped to the plate again in the top of the ninth, with the Phils leading 6-3. This time the bases were loaded and Richie slammed Ron Taylor's first pitch over the left center field fence for a 485-foot grand slam.[27]

Perhaps Allen's most amusing home run occurred on May 15, 1969. The Phils were beating the Cincinnati Reds 6-0 at Connie Mack Stadium. In the bottom of the eighth, John Noriega entered the game to mop up. His first pitch was a fastball at Richie's head. Allen hit the dirt, and when he got back on his feet he was fuming.

Undaunted, Noriega kept his eyes fixed on Richie as if he were trying to intimidate him. When Allen stepped back into the batter's box, still infuriated, he dug in, spit on the ground, and deposited the next pitch more than 500 feet over the roof in left center field. As Richie was rounding the bases, his teammates could hear him cursing at Noriega, something Allen rarely, if ever, did.

Fans' reactions to Richie vacillated from admiration for his offensive prowess to resentment for his outspokenness on race relations. When they were not pelting the Phillies' black superstar with objects, the bleacher bums made banners acknowledging the prodigious distance of his home runs. *Courtesy of Temple University Urban Archives, Philadelphia, PA*

When he got back to the dugout the catcher Pat Corrales asked, "Why are you so mad?"

"Didn't you see what happened?" Allen replied, astounded by the question. "First he threw at my head. Then he stood there staring at me funny like he was daring me to come out and fight him."

Corrales began laughing. "Noriega wasn't staring at you," he explained. "He was probably just trying to find the plate. He's blind in one eye!"

Everyone on the bench was laughing hysterically. Allen had to admit it was pretty funny, but he felt bad and later found Noriega outside the visitors' clubhouse and apologized for cussing him out while circling the bases.[28]

Nevertheless, Allen's tape measure home runs intimidated even the toughest pitchers, including the future Hall of Famer Tom Seaver, who admitted Dick was the hitter who "scared him the most." The prodigious blasts also inspired Willie Stargell of the Pirates to say, "Now I know why they [the Phillies fans] boo Richie all the time. When he hits a home run there's no souvenir."[29]

Teammates and opponents were in awe of Allen's forty-ounce bat, the biggest in the National League and the heaviest since the days of Babe Ruth. Dick also had a body built for baseball, with a thin waist, broad shoulders, quick wrists, massive forearms, and sprinter's legs. Together with a natural combination of power, torque, and heavy lumber, Allen's physical strength produced shots that rivaled those of Jimmie Foxx, another Philadelphia legend. Despite all the turmoil, Allen still finished the '65 season with a very respectable .302 average, twenty home runs, and eighty-five RBIs.[30] Over the next four years he did even better, averaging .300, thirty homers, and ninety RBIs during that span.[31] But it was not enough for the sportswriters or the fans.

As the losing seasons mounted, Mauch began to overmanage his young team. Frustrated with the results, he traded away the Phillies' future for proven veterans from other teams, few of whom panned out. The more the Phillies lost, the more Allen became the target of abuse from the fans and the press because of his tremendous potential and the unfulfilled expectations they had for him and the team. Initially, Richie found release in riding his quarter horse, "Old Blaze," in Philadelphia's Fairmount Park. Despite his powerful physique, Allen dreamed of being a jockey. "I'm one of those guys who would like to weigh about 115 pounds for a couple of hours in the afternoon and then go back to my own size about 5 o'clock," he mused.[32] But eventually even the horseback rides failed to provide the release he so desperately needed, and he turned to the bottle.

On July 8, 1967, Allen arrived late to Connie Mack Stadium, unable to walk a straight line or talk without slurring his words, and he was sent home by Coach George Myatt. Mauch awkwardly announced a "late fine," claiming that Allen went home because he was "too late to play." Eleven days later he was slapped with another fine, this time because his "car broke down." Allen admitted that drinking was the only way he could deal with his problems. "Instead of going straight to the ballpark, I started making regular stops at watering holes along the way," he admitted years later. "Whenever Mauch would smell booze on my breath he'd throw a tantrum and then fine me. I told 'em I expect to pay when I mess up. Let him put an envelope in my box, but don't call me in for no lectures."[33]

In today's game, Allen would most likely be treated with counseling or with a substance abuse program, but no such thing existed forty years ago. Instead, he was considered a bum.

Mauch was trying to protect his prized slugger, but Allen made it increasingly difficult for him to do so. The press had already labeled him "lazy" and a "troublemaker." Even honest mistakes were treated with deep cynicism. On August 24, Richie sustained a career-threatening injury while trying to push his stalled car up the driveway of his home in northwest Philadelphia. In the process his right hand slipped and broke through the headlight, severing two tendons and the ulnar nerve in his right wrist. After a five-hour operation, doctors gave him just a fifty-fifty chance of making a comeback. Immediately, rumors spread that Allen was knifed in a bar fight, or jumped through a window after being caught sleeping with a teammate's wife.[34] "The reporters go after Dick like a hound goes after a stray bird," complained Era when she learned of the rumors that had been published in the *Philadelphia Daily*

Richie rides "Blaze," the first horse he ever purchased, in Philadelphia's Fairmount Park. *Photo by George D. McDowell,* Philadelphia Evening Bulletin. *Courtesy of Temple University Libraries, Philadelphia, PA*

Allen pitches to his son, Dickie Jr., during spring training of 1967 in Clearwater, Florida. *Courtesy of the Allen Family*

News. "They don't know anything about my son. The nasty things they are writing about him just aren't true. I didn't raise him that way."[35]

Anger and resentment eventually took control of the Phillies slugger. "I'd been hearing that I was a bum for so long that I began to think that maybe that's just what I was," he explained.[36] By 1968, Allen desperately wanted out of Philadelphia, and he did not have the luxury of free agency to achieve that goal. Having asked repeatedly for a trade —and being denied repeatedly by owner Bob Carpenter —Allen, as a last resort, forced his own departure. Curfew violations, beer-drinking episodes, and excessive lateness to games became commonplace. Fines were no deterrent. Allen paid them, realizing his lucrative contracts would more than make up for it. In the process, Allen and the Phillies developed a mutual distrust of each other.

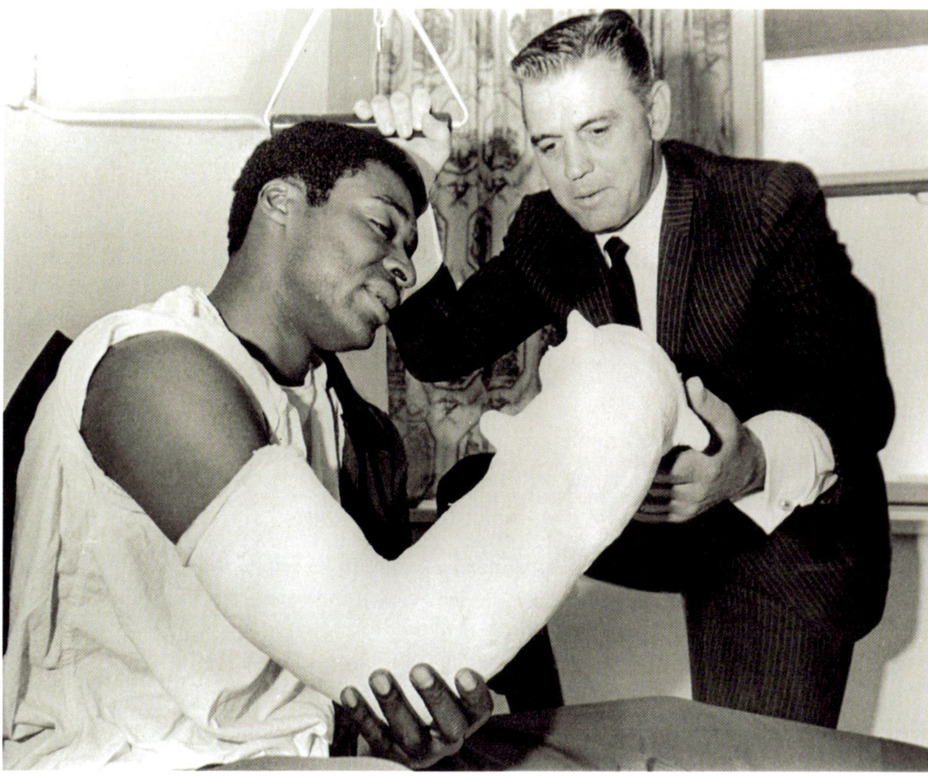

Manager Gene Mauch visits Richie at Temple University Hospital on August 27, 1967, after the slugger severed tendons in his hand trying to push his stalled car up the driveway of his Mount Airy home. *Courtesy of Temple University Urban Archives, Philadelphia, PA*

On May 26, Mauch fined Allen for failing to hustle on the base paths, and the following night Richie reported to the ballpark with alcohol on his breath. Mauch sent him home, telling the press the slugger was out with a groin injury. In fact, Allen was hit with a two-week suspension. When he finally returned to the team in June, Richie announced a "sit down strike" and refused to play. "Hell, how can they suspend me until they hear my side of the story?" he asked the Philadelphia press. Shortly after, Allen was given that opportunity by the sportscaster Al Meltzer in a candid television interview. Registering his "deep disappointment with the behavior of the fans," Allen insisted that he be "left alone off the field" and that he be "judged solely on his playing abilities."[37] Bob Carpenter had heard enough. In a closed-door meeting, Allen agreed to a truce, telling the owner he had been "ready to play all along." When Mauch was informed of the response, he supposedly gave Carpenter a "me or him" ultimatum, asking, "Do you want me to call him a liar?" Finally, on June 15, the Phillies skipper was dismissed.[38] Allen's plan had backfired.

1966 Topps card. *Courtesy of The Topps Company, Inc.*

To be sure, Allen's behavior was not the only reason for Mauch's firing. The Phillies were going nowhere in 1968. Having traded the thirty-six-year-old Jim Bunning to Pittsburgh, they were pinning their hopes on a new ace, Chris Short, and on Larry Jackson, a thirty-seven-year-old veteran acquired from the Chicago Cubs. Short missed several stretches early in the season because of a knee injury, and Jackson was ineffective. The youngsters Rick Wise and Grant Jackson were too inexperienced to pick up the slack and the pitching staff collapsed, ending the season with a 3.36 ERA, the third worst in the National League. What is worse, the team's top two hitters were trying to recover from serious injuries. Allen was still hampered by the damaged nerve in his right wrist, and the aging first baseman Bill White, acquired from the St. Louis Cardinals, was recovering from a severed Achilles tendon.[39]

As long as the Phillies fielded a contender, Mauch's job had been safe. The Little General did not have the patience to wait for younger players to develop, though. Besides, he had just a year left on his contract. General manager John Quinn was

1967 Topps card. *Courtesy of The Topps Company, Inc.*

1967 Topps "Hurlers Beware" card. *Courtesy of The Topps Company, Inc.*

just as impatient. He was so driven to achieve immediate success that he acquired the aging Larry Jackson from the Cubs by trading away a promising hurler in Fergie Jenkins, who went on to have a Hall of Fame career with Chicago. As the Phillies dropped lower in the standings, it became clear that a change had to be made.

While Quinn admitted the "Allen problem was a factor" in the decision to fire Mauch, he insisted it was *not* the "entire reason."[40] Mauch's wife had been recently hospitalized with a serious illness and the Phillies questioned whether he would be able to manage with the added pressure. Four days after his firing, Mauch absolved Carpenter and Quinn for the decision. "Something had to be done," he admitted. "They made the best decision under the circumstances. They couldn't foresee Nina Lee getting sick. It was a terribly tough situation. Besides, if someone had told me that I would be managing the Phillies for nine years, I'd have to say they were nuts. I didn't get a raw deal." When asked about the difficulty of managing Allen, Mauch insisted that he wasn't "going to knock Richie." "That son-of-a-gun gave me many a thrill," he added. "There was nothing personal in my handling of Allen. It was objective. When I jump on a player it is to make him better."[41]

1968 Topps card. *Courtesy of The Topps Company, Inc.*

1969 Topps card. *Courtesy of The Topps Company, Inc.*

Mauch's response was calculated. He knew that Major League Baseball was expanding to Montreal the next season and that he would be the most eligible candidate for a managerial post there as long as he took the moral high ground. The press would do the rest. And they did.

Stan Hochman of the *Philadelphia Daily News* speculated that Allen had become so intolerable for Mauch that the Phillies' skipper wanted to be released from his contract and gave the general manager John Quinn an ultimatum: either trade Allen or he quits. "Unable to trade the enigmatic slugger to the Giants for Jim Ray Hart, or to Houston for Jimmy Wynn," asserted Hochman, "the Phillies fired Mauch, whose only concern was to win."[42] News of Mauch's firing played just as big in New York as it did in Philadelphia. Arthur Daley of *The New York Times* made Mauch into a martyr, attributing his dismissal almost solely to "disciplinary problems with Richie Allen, a superstar with built-in distaste for discipline." Daley registered his admiration for the Little General's repeated public defense of Allen whenever Richie broke team policy. "But no manager can permit an athlete to erode the morale of an entire ball

Allen stands near third base as a smoke bomb is thrown in his direction from the stands during an August 18, 1967, game. *Photo by George D. McDowell,* Philadelphia Evening Bulletin. *Courtesy of Temple University Libraries, Philadelphia, PA*

club by disregarding the rules that others faithfully observe," he added. "Richie has done the damndest things. Yet Gene might have survived if he had bowed his neck ever so slightly to Allen, another guy with an unbowable neck."[43]

"I often wondered how successful the Phillies would've been if Richie had become the leader of the team like Mauch wanted him to be," mused Clay Dalrymple, long after his playing career ended:

> I once asked Richie why he didn't accept the leadership role. It was right there for him to take if he wanted it. "All you have to do is learn how to talk with the press," I told him. "I'd rather let my bat do my talking and be a team player," he told me. Well, that was typical Richie. He never wanted to tell others what to do, probably because he didn't like to be told what to do.[44]

Baseball was changing, and Allen was a catalyst for that change. In the past, controversy was handled discreetly by the press, but in the 1960s, when television made on-stage celebrities of baseball players, the sportswriters began to change the rules of player coverage. They believed that drinking, drugs, promiscuity, and deviant behavior in general gave the game a greater appeal among Baby Boomers who indulged in the same kinds of vices themselves. In that atmosphere, Richie Allen became a hero—or antihero—for a generation of rebellious youth. His insistence on being called "Dick" instead of "Richie" was part of that independence. "People who call me 'Richie,'" he explained, "are people who don't want to see me as anything but a baseball player. They don't want to see me as a complex man, to take me seriously."[45] Out of spite, the Philadelphia press began to refer to him as Dick "Don't Call Me Richie" Allen.

The role of the manager was also changing. Before Mauch's firing, a manager could threaten a player with a demotion no matter how talented he was. But Allen was a highly paid superstar, and one who was coveted by the team's owner. Mauch could demean him, fine him, and suspend him, but Carpenter certainly would not allow his black superstar to be demoted or traded. Allen did not see it that way, though.

"Hell, I didn't want Mauch fired," he insisted in his 1989 autobiography *Crash*, written with Tim Whitaker. "I liked him. He was tough, but mostly he was fair. I wanted to get myself traded instead." In fact, Allen had gone to Bob Carpenter as many as five times earlier and asked to be traded. But the owner refused every time, telling the beleaguered slugger that things would change for the better. Allen didn't buy it. "The fans were no longer just booing me, it was open warfare," he explained. "My family was scared and unhappy. And the Phillies were a lousy team. I had my mind on only one thing: getting the hell out of Philadelphia."[46] Ironically, Allen's efforts to force a trade for himself resulted in the forty-two-year-old manager's firing.

Richie returns a pen to an autograph-seeking fan during an August 2, 1969, game. *Photo by George D. McDowell,* Philadelphia Evening Bulletin. *Courtesy of Temple University Libraries, Philadelphia, PA*

The Phillies replaced Mauch with Bob Skinner, a soft-spoken thirty-six-year-old who managed San Diego of the Pacific Coast League. When asked about the possibility of having one set of rules for Allen and another for the other twenty-four players on the roster, Skinner told the press that he "anticipated no trouble" with Allen and that he would have "one set of rules" for all of the players.[47] Allen responded to Skinner's hiring by going on a tear. After the All-Star Game he led the Phils on a seven-game winning streak, banging out fifteen hits in thirty trips to the plate, including five homers and fifteen RBIs. By mid-July, he was hitting at a .314 clip. In an equally impressive performance, Allen, whose wife Barbara had just given birth to another son, Heron, celebrated by hitting two homers, a double, and two singles, leading the Phillies to a doubleheader sweep against the San Francisco Giants, 10-2 and 9-1.[48]

Bob Skinner replaced Gene Mauch as the Phillies' manager near the end of the 1968 season. *Courtesy of the Allen Family*

Despite Allen's offensive prowess, the Phillies continued to lose. As the team dropped lower in the standings, the fans became more abusive of him. "The fans were brutal to Richie," said his teammate Howie Bedell, who was also signed by John Ogden:

> I remember watching him shag fly balls during batting practice and wearing a batting helmet out there to protect himself from the batteries and coins the fans would throw at him. One day he said to me, "C'mon, Howie, let's go shag some flies. You're a white guy. If you go out there, they won't throw anything at me."[49]

The remark was made only half in jest. By 1968, throwing projectiles at Allen had become such a popular pastime among the Boo-Birds that teammates gave him the nickname "Crash" for the trademark batting helmet he routinely wore in the outfield to protect himself. Still, Allen never knocked the fans and even accepted some of the blame for their negative behavior. "It was sad," said Bedell. "Richie really was a genuinely good person. My eight-year-old son, Greg, adored him. One night we got home from the game and Greg was crying. When I asked him what was wrong, he said, 'I don't like it when they boo Mr. Allen, Dad.'" Greg also expressed his wish that his father return to Double A Reading because he didn't want him to be treated the same way by the Boo-Birds.

"I was very moved by that," admitted Bedell. "My son, as young as he was, was sensitive to Dick's feelings, as well as the possibility that I might be treated the same way."[50] His son got his wish. Three weeks after his father was promoted to Philadelphia, the team sent him back down to the minors, but not before ending Don Drysdale's record string of scoreless innings at 58⅔ with a long sacrifice fly that knocked in teammate Tony Taylor in a 5-3 loss to the Dodgers.[51]

While he finished the season with a .263 average, Allen was among the National League's leaders in home runs (33) and RBIs (90).[52] Still, the Phillies finished in seventh place with a 76-86 record, twenty-one games behind the pennant-winning Cardinals. It was their worst performance since 1961, and the fans had registered their disapproval. Only 664,546 turned out to see the Phillies that season, though it took about 950,000 to break even at the gate.[53]

Howie Bedell befriended Allen during his early years with the Phillies. Both players were signed by John Ogden. *Courtesy of Howie Bedell*

"One way or another, you'll see a new team out on the field in 1969," vowed Bob Carpenter, who planned to rebuild. "I feel we'll bounce back next year with four or five kids to excite people. Even Allen's not untouchable. I'm disappointed in his production. I think he should give us a .300 average and 120 RBI."[54] It seemed Richie would get his wish to be traded. In fact, Carpenter even directed Quinn to explore possibilities to trade Allen to the New York Mets or Cleveland Indians during the off-season. The Phillies' asking price proved to be too high in both cases.[55]

During the off-season, Allen, who sang professionally with a doo-wop group called "The Ebonsistics," did the Philadelphia nightclub circuit. Audiences enjoyed his high, delicate tenor and the selection of rhythm and blues and Motown songs he sang. Allen even gained lasting praise for a recording on the Groovy Grooves label titled, "Echoes of November." But put him before a sports crowd and it could be ugly.

Once that winter, the Phillies slugger entertained a crowd during halftime of a Philadelphia 76ers basketball game. Dressed in a flowered shirt with a six-inch tie and hip-hugging, bell-bottomed pants, Allen walked out onto the court at the Spectrum before a crowd of 9,557 fans. Predictably, he was booed. Two songs later the fans, impressed with his singing, began to cheer almost as warmly as they did when he was a rookie in 1964.[56] It was perhaps the last pleasant memory Allen would have of his stormy early tenure in the city.

Richie returned to Philadelphia in '69, this time as a full-time first baseman. He also intended to reduce his number of strikeouts after finishing second in the National League in that category with 161 the previous year. During spring training, Allen, in a rare batting practice appearance, stepped into the cage against coach George Myatt and said, "I struck out too many times last season, so it's time to makes a change."

Assuming a left-hander's batting stance, Richie, a natural right-hander, proceeded to smash pitch after pitch over the outfield wall. Stump Merrill, who was catching the batting practice, had a bird's eye view of the spectacle. "Richie must've hit at least a dozen balls out of the park," Merrill said in a recent interview. "Unless I saw it for myself I wouldn't have believed it."[57]

Although Allen never did hit left-handed that season, the incident still raises the question of how good he could have been if he had chosen to switch hit. It would not be the only time Richie inspired awe among his teammates by achieving a near impossible feat seemingly at will. For all his success in Philadelphia, Allen was more intent than ever to force a trade.

In early May Richie missed a flight to St. Louis, then missed the same flight the next morning. As a result, he missed one complete game and part of another against the Cardinals. Skinner was furious and fined him $1,000. "I definitely need to get out of Philadelphia," Allen told the press. "Bob Carpenter has been real good to me, but I've got to play somewhere else." When asked to explain the reasons for his frustration with Philadelphia Richie pointed to the press:

> "I get along great with my teammates," he insisted. "But you fellas have created an atmosphere where people who've never met me hate me. Sometimes I get so disgusted.
>
> "I don't care if you knock me, but when you don't come to me and ask about a situation and instead take someone else's word and write it as fact, then I got to cut you loose. I really do love to play the game, but the writers take all the fun out of it."[58]

In mid-June, the reserve infielder Cookie Rojas called a clubhouse meeting and tore into Allen. Rojas told him that the team "resented his coming and going as he pleased," as well as his "lack of hustle on the field." The team, which had previously been supportive, was now divided in its opinion of Richie. "When Carpenter gave him that $85,000 contract everybody lost authority over him," said one disgruntled white veteran. "Nobody that age deserves that kind of money. He doesn't hustle and he has his own set of rules. He's letting us down." But another white player suggested, "it might just look like he doesn't care, the way he never changes his expression when he strikes out. Maybe we're jealous of his talent and expect too much of him."

When he learned of his teammates' remarks, Richie was "hurt by them." "I just started to say, 'The hell with it,'" he admitted.[59]

On June 24, Allen missed a twi-night doubleheader against the New York Mets at Shea Stadium, choosing to remain at a horse race in New Jersey. He claimed he tried to phone Skinner when he realized he would be late. On his way to the stadium, he learned over the radio that the manager had suspended him. Instead of going to the game, Allen went to his hotel room. "I sat there all night and got madder and madder. I really thought Skinner had been treating me fairly. He said he'd never take any action until he heard my side of the story." Fined $2,500 and slapped with an indefinite suspension, Allen could have returned to the team at any time, but he chose to stay away from the game for twenty-six days, claiming he would "never again play for the Phillies."[60]

Allen with his wife Barbara and his agent Clem Capozzoli at Philadelphia's Liberty Bell Race Track in 1969.
Courtesy of the Allen Family

At the urging of owner Bob Carpenter and Clem Capozzoli, a sales manager for the American Baking Company who served as Allen's agent, Richie agreed to be reinstated on the condition that the Phillies would trade him at the end of the year. "I can play anywhere," he told the sportswriters in one of his more infamous quips. "First, third, left field . . . anywhere but Philadelphia." The fans registered their disapproval by refusing to vote Allen to the National League All-Star squad, though he was among the league leaders in homers and RBIs.[61]

At a White House press reception before the All-Star Game, President Richard Nixon, an avid baseball fan, approached the Phillies' lone representative on the National League squad, the pitcher Grant Jackson, and said:

> You tell Richie Allen to get back on the job. You tell him that he's not going to get as good a job if he quits baseball. You tell Richie that it's not for the good of the Phillies, or the good of the fans, but for the good of Richie Allen that he get back.

"You tell him, Mr. President," Jackson replied with a smile. "He's making more money than the both of us."[62]

Humor aside, Nixon was airing the very same feelings of the baseball establishment, where conformity was the rule. Any exhibition of individualism was a threat to the establishment, and Allen was testing its operating principle. The fact he was African American at a time of growing black consciousness accentuated that threat. Even his physical appearance challenged the status quo. Allen wore an Afro, mutton-chop sideburns, and a mustache before they were generally acceptable in baseball. His wardrobe of Edwardian suits, six-inch ties, bright shirts with ruffled cuffs, and bell-bottomed trousers was described as "new-hipster."[63]

"Basically, he's just a 'regular brother,'" wrote Lacy J. Banks of *Ebony*, a popular African American magazine. "He's hipped out with all the jive-time routines of coolness, arrogance, and happy-go-lucky attitude."[64] While the

Pitcher Grant Jackson, an All Star in 1969, was asked by President Richard Nixon to tell Richie Allen to end his holdout. *Courtesy of the National Baseball Hall of Fame and Library*

"hip" image attracted many young blacks and whites, especially those in the throes of adolescent rebellion, it did not sit well with the Philadelphia press or the city's white middle-aged and elderly baseball fans.

Philadelphia was an old fashioned city, one of the last bastions of Victorian life in America. In the 1960s, the City of Brotherly Love disdained controversy and banned anything or anyone who created it. In Philadelphia, Allen was an affront to the status quo because he challenged it, repeatedly. His tremendous talent gave him a much larger spotlight, and *that* earned him the infamous national reputation of "baseball's bad boy," the quintessential antihero. Had the Phillies won a World Series, all might have been forgiven. Winning has a way of mending differences between players and ownership, softening the criticism of the sportswriters, and earning forgiveness from the fans. But the Phillies had not won anything during Allen's six years with the organization. He was an easy target for anyone who wanted to blame him for the Phillies' failure to capture a pennant and much more.

A week before he was to play in his first post-suspension game, Allen removed his belongings from the clubhouse and set up his own private dressing room in a storage area near the manager's office at Connie Mack Stadium. When the press asked why he "relocated," he said, only half in jest, "To keep the writers away." In fact, Allen told Skinner that his reputation as "baseball's bad boy, the bad ass of the National League" could have a negative effect on his closest friends, like Johnny Briggs, Larry Hisle, and Grant Jackson, so he decided to remove himself from "the clubhouse controversy."[65] Skinner, infuriated, ordered Allen's belongings returned to the clubhouse. "I don't care if he sits in that closet," he told the press, "but he'll dress with everyone else!"[66]

There is some truth to Allen's explanation, though. Richie was protective of the younger black players in the organization. He was especially close to Briggs and Hisle, both of whom credited the veteran first baseman with intensive hitting instruction. "I'm a late swinger," said Hisle. "My power's always been to right and right center. Rich showed me how I could turn that power the other way by keeping the bat head out in front and swinging down on the ball." Similarly, Allen could be found almost any night next to the batting cage, studying Briggs's practice cuts and giving him constructive criticism.

Richie's concern even extended to up-and-coming superstars from other teams, like Reggie Jackson of the Oakland A's, whom he befriended over the winter. Jackson credited Allen with being a major factor responsible for his emergence as one of the brightest young sluggers in the game. "Rich and I got together before spring training," said the Oakland power hitter:

> We started talking hitting and we didn't stop for three days. I never knew that Rich had so much scientific knowledge about hitting. He convinced me that I should

> throw my bat out front and down on the ball to get distance, instead of swinging up on it. It's a big reason why I'm hitting so many homers.[67]

Back in Wampum, Butler Hennon was "puzzled" when he learned about the dispute with Skinner. "I spoke with Dick not long ago and he seemed happy," Hennon told a sportswriter from the *Pittsburgh Press*. "He told me he liked Bob Skinner and that he was pleased with the way the team was coming along." When the reporter informed Hennon that Allen had removed his things from the clubhouse and his teammates were complaining about his lack of hustle, the high school coach insisted Allen "likes everyone to think he doesn't care, that he doesn't take the game seriously." "That's all a put on," insisted Hennon. "He cared more than anyone else who's ever played for me. I'd come to school at 7:00 a.m. and find him practicing in the gym all by himself so no one would see him." When asked why Allen was distancing himself from his teammates, though, the only explanation Hennon could offer was, "Rich must still be hurting underneath from that Thomas fight." "In our last conversation, Dick also told me that he'd wished [the fight] never happened and that the fans will never forgive him for it."[68]

But few understood that Richie Allen was at heart a reserved young man from rural western Pennsylvania who simply wanted to be left alone to play the game. The sportswriter Ray Kelly of the *Philadelphia Evening Bulletin* was one of the few who did understand the enigmatic slugger. "He's had nothing but trouble his whole career," Kelly explained to Myron Cope of *Sport Magazine*. "Actually, he's a good guy who would give you $500 if you needed it and he had it. Hell, he's still a kid from Wampum. [Mickey] Mantle was a country boy, too. But the writers and the fans cut him some slack."[69] Still, the more Skinner tried to discipline Allen, the more he rebelled.

Skinner tried to assert his authority with fines. When Allen failed to hustle on the base paths, he was slapped with a $500 penalty. If he missed batting practice, the Phils manager imposed another $500 fine. By the end of July, Richie was being fined several times a week. Finally, on August 7, Skinner announced his resignation in a conference room at Reading Municipal Stadium, where the Phillies were scheduled to play their Double A club that night. "The straw that broke the camel's back," according to the Phils' skipper, came earlier in the day when Allen refused to play because "his deal with Mr. Carpenter didn't include playing in exhibition games." When Skinner confronted Carpenter, the owner defended Allen's position. "That was it," Skinner told the press. "I have too much pride to stay in this job without support from the front office, especially in my handling of Richie Allen." He also intimated that Carpenter and the general manager John Quinn had been returning fines to Allen, which only served to undermine his authority even more.[70] Carpenter immediately rejected the notion and expressed regret over Skinner's decision to resign.[71]

Richie, on the other hand, expressed anger.

"If I was that much of a problem Skinner shouldn't have taken me back," said the Phillies' slugger when he learned of the manager's remark that he had made his job "unbearable:

> He was the manager. If he had the guts, he wouldn't have let me come back. I didn't want to in the first place. I was content in my heart to stay out the rest of the year. That's how bad I want to get out of Philadelphia, and he knew it, too.[72]

When Quinn made George Myatt the interim manager, the press asked him how he would handle Allen. "I believe God Almighty Himself would have trouble handling Richie Allen," remarked the Phillies' long-time coach.[73] Instead, Myatt took the path of least resistance, refusing to become embroiled in more controversy on a team of journeymen players and aging veterans. There simply wasn't much talent left. He suspended most of the club's rules for the remaining games and humored Allen's behavior, which by now included scratching messages to the disgruntled fans in the dirt around first base.[74]

On August 9, Richie wrote "Oct. 2"—the last day of the regular season and his date of liberation from the Phillies. Quinn phoned the National League president Warren Giles for a ruling on the action. Giles told him it was "inappropriate," and Quinn had the grounds crew erase the message. But Allen would not be deterred. The following night he scratched "COKE" with his cleats onto the first base cutout, later explaining that the fans were "getting on me and I wanted to hit a home run over the Coca Cola sign in left center field to shut them up." The next night he wrote "BOO"—and the fans happily obliged.

George Myatt with Allen before an August 8, 1969, game against the Reds at Cincinnati. Myatt was made the Phillies' manager after Bob Skinner abruptly resigned earlier that month. *Photo by Tony Bernato,* Philadelphia Evening Bulletin. *Courtesy of Temple University Libraries, Philadelphia, PA*

Richie continued scratching messages in the dirt with his cleats over the next six days, a span in which he hit five home runs. "I kept it up 'cause everyone made such a fuss over it," he admitted. Shortly after, Commissioner Bowie Kuhn attended a doubleheader, witnessed Allen's artwork, and ordered him to stop. Richie responded to Kuhn's edict during the second game by writing "NO" and "WHY?" Finally, the home plate umpire called time out, went

Allen responded to the negative treatment by Phillies fans by scrawling one-word messages in the dirt at first base. On August 11, 1969, the slugger returned their boos with one of his own. *Photo by Tony Bernato,* Philadelphia Evening Bulletin. *Courtesy of Temple University Libraries, Philadelphia, PA*

over to Allen, and told him that Quinn had called to complain. Allen begrudgingly erased the words. His final message came the next night when he scratched "MOM" into the dirt. It was a reference to his mother, Era, who Richie claimed was "the only one who can tell me what to do."[75]

The Phillies sputtered to a fifth place finish in 1969, thirty-seven games out. On October 8, six days after the season ended, Allen was traded to the St. Louis Cardinals in a seven-player deal that would go down in the annals of baseball history. The Phillies sent Allen, Cookie Rojas, and pitcher Jerry Johnson to St. Louis for Curt Flood, a Gold Glove center fielder; Byron Browne, a young outfield prospect; catcher Tim McCarver; and reliever Joe Hoerner. Flood, who was African American, refused to report to Philadelphia.[76] Calling himself a "well paid slave," Flood filed a $3.1 million damage suit against the Cardinals, challenging baseball's reserve clause, which prevented players from moving to another team unless they were traded.[77] The slave metaphor was not lost on Allen, either.

At his last game as a Phillie at Connie Mack Stadium on September 29, 1969, a homemade banner reminds Richie that his days with the team are numbered. *Courtesy of Temple University Urban Archives, Philadelphia, PA*

"You don't know how good it feels to get out of Philadelphia," Allen said when asked about the trade. "They treat you like cattle. It was like another form of slavery. Once you step out of bounds they do everything possible to destroy your soul."[78] Allen, who eventually agreed to a $90,000 contract with the Cardinals, also defended Flood's position. "My hat's off to Curt Flood," he told reporters from the *St. Louis-Post Dispatch*. "Would you have done it at that price? Would you walk away from $90,000? It takes a real man to do that. Maybe my kids will benefit from what he's doing, maybe yours will, too."[79]

Allen was not the only one who was happy about the trade. "When I told the children they jumped up and down," admitted his wife Barbara. "They wanted to know if we could leave for St. Louis tomorrow. No more boos. That's all they could say . . . no more boos."[80]

"Letters in the Dirt"

Chuck Brodsky, a singer-songwriter who idolized Richie Allen as a youngster, memorialized the slugger's early years with the Phillies in a song titled, "Letters in the Dirt." *Courtesy of Chuck Brodsky*

Chuck Brodsky saw Richie Allen play at Connie Mack Stadium for the first time in 1964. Seated with his father in a field box behind the visitor's dugout, the four-year-old was captivated by his surroundings: the plush green grass of the field, the huge scoreboard in right center field, and the curious, blended aroma of hot dogs, roasted peanuts, and beer. Most of all, the youngster was taken by his proximity to ballplayers he had only known from his baseball cards. He was so close to them it seemed as though he could reach out and shake hands with the on-deck batter. The vague memory of a rookie named Richie Allen playing third and hitting cleanup was nearly forgotten in the emotional overload.

Sometime during the next season, Chuck began to have more vivid memories of the Phillies' first African American superstar. Unforgettable memories, like his blinding speed on the base paths and the mammoth, tape measure home runs he launched well outside the confines of the ballpark. Those were wonderful memories, ones that would last a lifetime and result in the adoption of Richie as Chuck's boyhood hero.

There were other, more haunting memories, too. It seemed whenever Richie came to bat, the bleachers erupted with a hailstorm of boos. Occasionally, an ignorant fan would let loose the N-word with a bloodcurdling scream that sent a vicious chill across the stadium. If Richie was playing the outfield, it was not uncommon for him to be pelted with bolts, batteries, and coins from the stands.

"Home runs are surely something a little kid remembers," Brodsky recalled many years later. "So is racism. But at the time, I just couldn't understand it. Richie was the Phillies' best player, he hit lots of home runs, and my dad taught me to always root for the home team and its players. As a youngster I struggled with the contradiction."

Fortunately, Chuck's father, a man with a keen sense of social justice, used those ugly experiences to teach his son the lessons of "compassion" and "respect for human dignity." He understood blacks were not treated with the same respect afforded to whites. As a Jew in a predominantly Christian society, he could empathize with Richie Allen and the discrimination he suffered.

"Even as a youngster," said Brodsky, "I was keenly aware that some people didn't like Jews, which meant they didn't like me. I had no idea why, I just knew it was that way. So it was easy to identify with Richie Allen, and it was only natural to feel some of his pain."

Through the years Chuck often revisited the memories of his boyhood hero. They left an indelible mark on his heart and soul. Once he became a musician, he found a natural way to express those memories in a song titled, "Letters in the Dirt," a reference to Richie's habit of sending messages to the crowd by scrawling single words in the dirt around first base

Originally released in 1996 on a CD of the same name, "Letters in the Dirt" was later rereleased on a CD titled *The Baseball Ballads*. "Letters" is a profoundly moving ballad of a youngster's love for his father, who passed along his passion for baseball to his son, and for a boyhood hero whose painful experience taught the youngster compassion and respect for human dignity.

"Letters in the Dirt"

by Chuck Brodsky

Me & you, we never booed Richie Allen
I never understood why people did
He hit a homer every time he stepped up to the plate
That's what I remember as a kid

Richie in the field out there by first base
The target of some mighty foul words
With his shoes he'd scrawl between the pitches
"B-O-O" in great big letters in the dirt

Philly fans, they've been known to get nasty
When Joe must go, they'll run him out of town
I saw Santa get hit by a snowball
And then get hit again when he was down

Me & you, we never booed Richie Allen
Even if he did sometimes strike out
I was too young to read the papers
To know what all that booing was about

That big collapse of '64 was ugly
They blew a lead of 6 and one-half games
with 12 to play
Some might say their fans were justifiably angry
World Series tickets printed up in vain

Philly fans, they've been known to get nasty
When Joe must go, they'll run him out of town
I saw Santa get hit by a snowball
And then get hit again when he was down

Going back to old Connie Mack Stadium
You teaching me the rules of the game
We root-root-rooted for the home team
Those other people should've been ashamed

This was before the days of the million dollar contracts
Before the days of the artificial grass
He stood a bit outside the lines which made him fair
game for those times
Richie Allen never kissed a white man's ass

Me & you, we never booed Richie Allen
No, we'd pound our mitts & we'd yell, "We want a hit"
How could they call a guy a bum after he'd just hit a
home run?
That didn't make any sense to a kid

Now I've since found out all these days later
Now I know a lot more than I did
And if back then you knew, Daddy, why all those
other people booed . . .
Thanks for letting me have my heroes as a kid

Shortly after "Letters in the Dirt" was released, Chuck was invited to perform at the National Baseball Hall of Fame and Museum. As fate would have it, Dick Allen was attending a baseball function at Cooperstown the same day.

Tim Wiles, the director of research at the Hall of Fame and the individual who invited Chuck to perform, knew the songwriter was a huge Allen fan. He suggested Chuck drive over to the Otesaga Hotel where Dick was staying, leave a copy of his CD at the front desk, and request the clerk pass it on to the former ballplayer.

After his performance Chuck drove over to the hotel. Carefully rehearsing what he would say to the front desk clerk, he parked his car, placed a copy of "Letters in the Dirt" in his coat pocket, and proceeded to walk through the chilly wind and rain toward the grand entrance of the hotel.

Upon entering, the songwriter was astonished to see Dick himself. Chuck suddenly felt as if he was four years old again. Excited and nervous at the prospect of meeting his boyhood hero, he scrambled to find the right words to address him. Fortunately, Dick was in the middle of a conversation, so Chuck had some time to prepare as he waited patiently across the lobby.

When the conversation ended, Chuck mustered the courage to introduce himself to his boyhood hero. He told Allen he was raised in Philadelphia and that he was his all-time favorite player. Dick smiled and shook hands with the musician, which made it easy for Chuck to tell him about the song he had written for and about him.

Removing the CD from his coat pocket, the guitarist handed it to the Phillies slugger and waited eagerly to see his reaction. Dick held the disc in both hands, alternately studying the cover and then the songwriter. Chuck explained he used a photo of the word "Boo" written in the dirt for the back cover of the lyrics booklet and hoped Dick would appreciate it.

There was a pregnant pause. Dick, deeply moved, made no attempt to hide his feelings as a single teardrop slowly began to run down his cheek. This was a sensitive man, a caring person so few people had the privilege to know. Chuck, too, was touched by the moment, for he had just created another memory to treasure. Only this one would be shared with his boyhood hero.

March 23, 1970, *Sports Illustrated* cover. *Photo by Walter Iooss Jr.*, Sports Illustrated. *Courtesy of Getty Images*

CHAPTER 5: INTERLUDE

On Friday, March 13, 1970, Rich Allen arrived at Al Lang Field in St. Petersburg, Florida, the spring training camp of the St. Louis Cardinals. Looking resplendent in a light-brown, double-breasted Edwardian suit, orange shirt, and tan, high-button shoes, the former Phillie addressed the St. Louis sportswriters at a hastily arranged press conference. In his opening statement, Allen, with a smile as broad as his shoulders, assured the gaggle of reporters he was "very excited to be a Cardinal" and that he "hoped to play with peace of mind" for the first time in many years. When asked about his controversial tenure with the Phillies, Rich admitted he was "no angel" and that he had "taken a nip [of alcohol] here or there to calm down, but not to excess."

Another sportswriter asked why he thought St. Louis would be a better place to play. "In Philadelphia," Allen explained, "I was the center of attraction and that made it easy to be abused. But with the Cardinals I can be one of the team because there are other stars like Bob Gibson, Lou Brock, and Joe Torre. I expect to be booed by the fans, but not stoned." Allen discouraged any further questions about his tenure with the Phillies by saying, "Look, Philly isn't a bad town. It was just time for me to move on." Then he became more playful. When asked, for example, what he thought of the new artificial surface in St. Louis' Busch Stadium, Allen quipped: "If horses won't eat it, I don't want to play on it." The humorous quote was picked up by NBC's nightly news and went viral.[1] It was an auspicious beginning for a gifted ballplayer who desperately needed a change of scenery.

During the next few years Allen would play for two different teams: the Cardinals (1970) and the Los Angeles Dodgers (1971). Despite the fact he hit .287 and averaged twenty-eight home runs and ninety-five RBIs, neither team retained him. He seemed to become a "rental player," one who had the potential to help a contender clinch a pennant or a world championship, but whose controversial past did not warrant a long-term commitment. Major League Baseball, which clung to the belief that players were an integral part of all that was good about America, might have even encouraged the approach as the only way to treat a malcontented superstar. It would also serve as an example to other African American players who were beginning to speak their minds, such as Allen's former teammate Alex Johnson of the California Angels, Dock Ellis of the Pittsburgh Pirates, and Reggie Jackson and Vida Blue of the Oakland A's.[2]

Rich Allen, one of the most fashionable ballplayers, was the first major leaguer to grow an Afro. *Photo by Charles Bonnan,* Life Magazine. *Courtesy of Getty Images*

To be sure, Allen's experience in Philadelphia had made him a role model for the loners, nonconformists, and malcontents who emerged in baseball as the 1960s transitioned to the 1970s. While the sport exhibited little tolerance for self-expression, it did not know how to deal with it. Even stylistic self-expression challenged the status quo as ballplayers were expected to be clean cut. Neatly trimmed sideburns were acceptable, but facial hair was strictly off limits, and hair that grew below the collar was unimaginable. But Allen was the first to challenge that policy as he sported MLB's first real Afro, as well as mutton chop sideburns and a mustache that extended slightly beyond his lower lip. He even admitted the look "represented a threat to white people" because it emphasized blackness in a predominantly white sport. Within the next few years the Afro, which had already thoroughly permeated American popular culture, would be adopted by many other black baseball players who embraced the motto, "Rows, 'fros, anything goes!"[3] Hairstyles were not the only thing changing, either.

In St. Louis, Rich entered a conservative organization that was being directly challenged by the changing dynamics in player-management relations. The Cards' owner August "Gussie" Busch Jr. was facing a court battle initiated by the former Redbird outfielder Curt Flood, who refused to report to Philadelphia after being traded for Allen. Flood felt he had been exploited by the Cardinals. During the course of a twelve-year career in St. Louis, he had been a three-time All Star who batted over .300 six times and helped the Cards to two World Series titles in 1964 and 1967. When his batting average slipped during the 1969 season, general manager Bing Devine, with the blessing of Gussie Busch, traded the veteran outfielder to the Phillies.

Part of Flood's refusal to accept the trade was because of the heated racial climate in Philadelphia—something that Allen had brought to national attention. In addition, Flood and his family liked St. Louis, where they had a permanent residence. After consulting with a representative from the players' union, the disgruntled outfielder explained his decision in a letter to the MLB commissioner Bowie Kuhn. "After 12 years in the major leagues," Flood wrote, "I do not feel that I am a piece of property to be bought and sold irrespective of my wishes." While he expressed his desire to play in the 1970 season, the thirty-one-year-old insisted it would not be with Philadelphia, and he believed he had "a right to consider offers from other clubs before making any decision." When Kuhn denied his request, Flood filed a \$4.1 million suit against the commissioner and Major League Baseball, alleging the reserve clause violated antitrust laws and the 13th Amendment, which barred slavery and involuntary servitude.

Although Flood insisted the suit had less to do with the Black Power movement than with ridding baseball of an antiquated and unjust aspect of the game, the media painted him as a black militant, the baseball counterpart of a Black Panther.

Flood v. Kuhn would eventually go all the way to the US Supreme Court, where Flood's case was backed by the testimony of former players such as Jackie Robinson, though no active players agreed to testify. Although the Court ruled against Flood in a 5-3 decision in 1972, the action set in motion a chain of events that led to the

1975 arbitration ruling granting players the right to free agency. It was a legal explosion that would rock the game for years to come.[4]

As a result of Flood's challenge, Busch directed Devine to be tougher in salary negotiations with unsigned players like Steve Carlton, a supremely gifted twenty-six-year-old left-hander who won an average of thirteen games each season for the previous four years and set a major league record the previous season by striking out nineteen Mets in a game.[5] Carlton rejected the Cardinals' $31,000 offer for the upcoming 1971 season but refrained from taking the Cardinals to court. "I didn't use a lawyer," he said, "because this club has always wanted to deal on a personal level, and I believe in that, too." But Busch was adamant about holding his ground. "I'm fed up and I think the fans are, too," he complained. "The players have a great pension plan and we've been pretty fair with salaries. Now they talk strike. They must think [the owners] are a bunch of softies. I hope to God that Carlton's is not a majority view."[6]

Curt Flood refused to report to the Phillies when he was traded for Richie Allen in 1969. Instead, he challenged the reserve clause by suing Major League Baseball for $4.1 million. *Courtesy of the National Baseball Hall of Fame and Library, Cooperstown, NY*

While Allen shrugged off as "ridiculous" reports he originally sought a $150,000 contract from the Cards, he did test Busch's patience by trying to arrange the salary equivalent of the fringe benefits he enjoyed with the Phillies, who apparently placed his widowed mother on their payroll. Instead, Busch gave him a contract for $80,000 and a "take-it-or-leave-it" ultimatum and Allen signed.[7] Had it been manager Red Schoendienst's decision, the Cardinals would not have signed the controversial slugger at all.

Schoendienst had serious concerns about Allen's infamous reputation as a troublemaker. In fact, when asked whether he wanted the Cards to trade for the Phillies slugger, Schoendienst told Busch and Devine "no." But Devine went ahead with his plans anyway, pointing out that he had traded for "problem players" in the

When baseball commissioner Bowie Kuhn rejected Curt Flood's request to remain with the St. Louis Cardinals, he triggered a process that eventually resulted in free agency in Major League Baseball. *Courtesy of the National Baseball Hall of Fame and Library, Cooperstown, NY*

past and two of them—Orlando Cepeda and Roger Maris—helped the team win two straight pennants in 1967 and 1968. According to Devine, Allen's power and speed on the base paths could return the Cardinals to the postseason after last year's disappointing fourth-place finish in the newly created National League's Eastern Division.[8] Schoendienst would now have to reconfigure his infield, platooning at first, third, and catcher to make room for Allen, who still suffered bursitis in his right hand and shoulder as a result of previous injuries.[9]

The Cardinals opened the '70 campaign against the Expos at Montreal's Jarry Park on April 8. Allen hit a home run and two doubles, driving in three runs in the Cards' 7-2 win. After the game, he sat by his locker in the visitor's clubhouse reading an encouraging letter from his mother when a host of reporters penned him in. "Why don't you go over and interview Julian Javier?" he humbly suggested. "He drove in the winning run. Give him a little ink. He's been the best second baseman in either league over the last few years." It was a shaky but genuine way to act on his belief that in St. Louis he would be one of only several stars on a team.

But there was no way of avoiding the spotlight two days later when he debuted at Busch Stadium in the Cards' home opener against the New York Mets.

When Jack Buck announced Allen's name over the public address system, a record first-night crowd of 45,960 rose to their feet and began to applaud. The

1970 Rich Allen Topps baseball card. *Courtesy of The Topps Company, Inc.*

cheering was deafening, "almost as if [Cardinal Hall of Famer] Stan Musial was making a comeback," quipped the New York sportswriter Jack Lang. Standing at his first base position, Allen doffed his cap to the fans in the left field area, then turned to acknowledge the fans on the right side of the field.

"That's the greatest thing that ever happened to me," said Rich. "I never thought it could happen. I just wish Mom could have heard it.

"I usually have a heart of stone," he added. "But [the reception] almost brought a tear."

That night Rich went 0 for 3, with a strikeout, a walk, and a fly-out. "He was just trying too hard," explained the Cards' coach Dick Sisler. "He wanted so much to get a big hit that he could taste it. He kept swinging at bad pitches." The Cardinals still defeated the Mets 7-3.

In his first game as a St. Louis Cardinal on April 8, 1970, Rich Allen stroked a home run, two doubles, and knocked in three runs in the Cards' 7-2 victory over the Montreal Expos. *Courtesy of the National Baseball Hall of Fame and Library, Cooperstown, NY*

After the game, Allen told the St. Louis scribes, "No wonder they win here. I just hope I prove worthy of playing here. I know I'm going to like it now."

On April 12, in the series finale against the Mets, Allen hit a majestic 450-foot home run off Tom Seaver in the bottom of the eighth. After circling the bases, he tipped his hat to the Cardinal faithful and retreated to the dugout, but the applause continued. Rich finally acknowledged the reception by blowing kisses from the top of the dugout steps.[10]

By mid-May, Allen had slammed eleven home runs and was off to the best start of his career. "I was relaxed at the plate," he explained,

> maybe for the first time in my professional career. The result was that I could stay with breaking pitches longer, and that gave me more options. I could still go long ball, but I could also hit a flare down the line, and I could make the decision to do either in a microsecond with a downward flick of my wrist.

It was also in May that Rich returned to Philadelphia for the first time since being traded to St. Louis. Twelve thousand fans turned out at Connie Mack to boo him, and they were not disappointed when he struck out in his first at bat. When Allen came to the plate in the top of the ninth, with a runner on base and the Cards down 3-0, it was a different story. Jumping on a first-pitch fastball, he smashed a home run into an empty seat in left field. When he reached home plate Rich instinctively raised his first in the air, as if to say, "Take that." Naturally, he was booed. While the two-run homer cut the Phils' lead to one run, the Fightins held on to win the game 3-2.[11]

Allen would hit a total of thirty-four round-trippers and 101 RBIs that season, despite playing a good portion of it with an Achilles tendon injury that was aggravated by the Cardinals' new artificial turf. Among the most dramatic homers were a 450-foot shot off the Phillies' Lowell Palmer that ricocheted off the façade of the left field upper deck in Busch Stadium on May 12, and a 500-foot tape measure bomb off the Expos' Mike Wegener that sailed over the center field fence at Montreal's Jarry Park on July 3. At home games, Cardinal fans sitting in the seats above the club level in center field had to be especially watchful. Nine of Allen's blasts landed on those seats, providing the broadcaster Jack Buck with a frequent line: "Some of the folks in the stadium club might have choked on a chicken leg when they saw that one coming!"[12]

Redbird fans loved Allen for his sheer power. Until he was sidelined on August 14 by a torn hamstring, Rich was hitting homers at a pace of forty-six a season, threatening the club record of forty-three set by Johnny Mize at old Sportsman's Park in 1940.[13] There is no doubt that Allen's offensive prowess was a huge factor in the Cardinals' impressive home draw of over 1.6 million that season.[14] In addition, Rich earned another All-Star berth, and his personal problems seemed to abate. There were no controversies with teammates, nor with management. No reports of excessive drinking or a divided clubhouse. With the exception of one case, Allen arrived at the stadium on time, if not early. The Cardinals even acceded to his wishes regarding his name: the team broadcaster Jack Buck made a point of calling him "Dick" Allen, though the press, opposing players, and fans continued to call him "Rich" or "Richie."[15]

Richard Allen Jr., nicknamed "Dickie" as a child, remembers that his father was happier in St. Louis than he had been in years. "When he was first traded to the Cardinals I went out with him and spent the summer there," he said, smiling at the memory:

> I was five years old and had him all to myself. It was just the two of us. We'd go to the ballpark together every day, then back to the hotel, and do the same thing all over again the next day. I ate spare ribs for thirty days straight!
>
> On those rare days when he had off from the ballpark we'd sit and watch westerns on the TV and eat clams and shrimp cocktail, or he'd take me to the race track and we'd watch the horses. He'd teach me how to read a racing form.
>
> We were just hanging out, but those were some of the most special times I had with my father."[16]

In later years Barbara and the children joined Rich after school let out in June. It was a hectic schedule, but the couple wanted to keep their family together as much as possible throughout the year.

Rich also relocated his family to rural Perkasie, in Bucks County, Pennsylvania, where he purchased a farm to raise horses. Not only was the new home a welcome departure from Mount Airy, where he was more accessible to disgruntled fans, but a wonderful place to raise children. The large property offered privacy, the school system was among the best in the state, and Rich was able to unwind while riding his horses. But Barbara still had to accommodate her husband's demanding schedule. "Dick and I thought it was important for the family to eat dinner together," she explained. "That meant waiting for him to come home after a ball game and eating late at night, so we just kept the late dinner hour in the off season as well."[17]

"Family" was extremely important to the couple, who routinely invited extended family members to visit Perkasie. In that way, Terri, Dickie, and Heron were able to know and become close with their cousins, aunts, and uncles. One of the most frequent visitors was Hank's son, Rick, who was especially close to Dickie. Although Rick was older by a few years, the two cousins were inseparable when they were growing up, much like their fathers.

"Every summer Dickie—I called him 'Doobie'—[and I] visited each other either at our house in Bowie [MD] or his in Perkasie. We also spent a week in Wampum with our grandmother Era," recalled Rick Allen.

> During the school year when we were apart, Doobie and I would communicate by taping our thoughts on audio cassettes and mail them to each other. To this day we're like brothers.

Both cousins inherited their fathers' love of baseball and played the game at every available opportunity. "In Bowie, we had a garage and chalked a strike zone against the back wall," said Rick.

> One of us would bat and the other would pitch, throwing the ball as hard as he could to strike the other one out.
>
> We marked off certain distances for hits. For example, if you hit the ball on a line drive into the street it was a double. If it landed across the street in the air it was a home run. We pushed each other all the time so we could get better.

When they got older the Allen cousins played together in men's adult leagues. Dickie was a power-hitting left fielder and Rick a speedy center fielder. They were talented, too, being paid $75 for each contest. "The money didn't matter," Rick insisted. "We loved the game. What made us feel so good was that we were competing with and against former pro players, some had even been in the majors. It gave us a sense of belonging."[18]

Era Allen was also a popular guest at Perkasie; her visits were always special. Unlike many mother/daughter-in-law relationships, Era and Barbara were "very good friends." "I loved her and she loved me," said Barbara.

> Mrs. Allen was an extremely charming and personable individual, the very same traits that attracted me to Dick. Whenever she'd visit we'd go shopping together, and she always insisted on doing the cooking to give me a break. I learned a lot from her, and she made me feel as if I was her very own daughter.[19]

It was also important to Rich and Barbara that their children were raised to be well mannered and courteous to others; to ensure this, they shared the responsibility of disciplining them. "My

Terri Allen, age twelve. *Courtesy of the Allen Family*

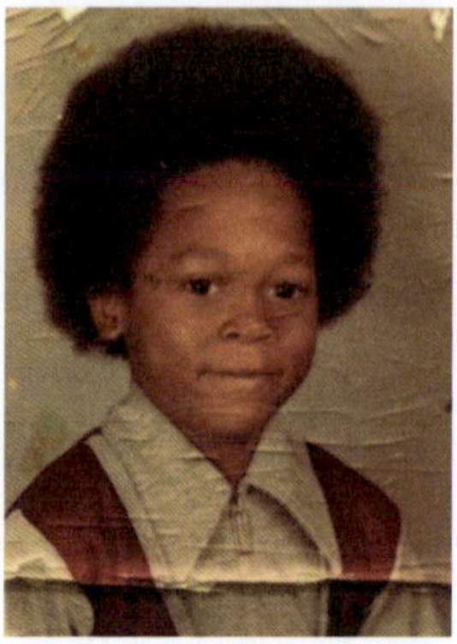

Dick Allen Jr., age six. *Courtesy of the Allen Family*

Heron Allen, age eight. *Courtesy of the Allen Family*

Growing up, cousins Rick Allen (left) and Dick Jr. were just as inseparable as their fathers Hank and Dick Sr. *Courtesy of the Allen Family*

father disciplined by the force of his personality," recalled Rich's son, Richard. "I only remember him hitting me once, and I deserved it:

> It happened one summer evening when I was playing outside and came indoors to get something to drink. Mr. Ogden, the scout who signed my dad, and his wife were visiting with my mother while waiting for dad to come home from the ballpark. Well, I came running into the house shouting, "What's there to drink?"
>
> My mother did not tolerate that kind of behavior. When I was rude like that she didn't answer me. So I shouted again, "Mom, what's there to drink?" But she still didn't answer me, so I took my plastic cup and started banging it on the counter.
>
> "You know what?" she said finally. "I don't have time for this. You go upstairs and wait for your father to come home."
>
> I did as I was told, and I must've fallen asleep because the next thing I remember dad was in the room. He grabbed me by the elbow and he taught me a *real* good lesson. That was the end of that. But that's the only time I can remember being smacked by him, and frankly, I deserved it.[20]

When reminded of the incident, Barbara chuckled, admitting that "it happened to be Dick's turn to discipline on that particular occasion." "We both handled that responsibility," she said. "When one of us disciplined the other would support the action. We made it very clear to our children that they were not going to play one parent against the other."[21] By all accounts the strategy worked: the Allen children grew up to become very courteous to each other, their parents, and others outside the family. "If you met someone who was older, we looked them straight in the eye and addressed them as 'Mr.' or 'Mrs.,'" Richard explained. "We were taught to ask others how they were doing and not to boast about ourselves or our accomplishments. And we were taught to share with others."[22] In fact, Dick set a fine example for his children in the way he interacted with teammates.

Like he did with the Phillies, Rich mentored the younger players on the Cards. "He was a very private person," said Jose Cardenal, who replaced Curt Flood as the Cards' center fielder. "Everyone on the team liked him. He treated me with respect and I considered him my best friend.

"Dick was also a very smart and knowledgeable baseball man, something that many people wouldn't know," Cardenal added. "Talking with him and watching him perform on the field definitely made me a better player and person. He may have taught me more in one year than I learned in the forty-eight years I was involved with professional baseball."[23]

Despite Allen's hot bat, the Cardinals got off to a terrible start in 1970, but they regrouped, and by August, St. Louis had gone from last place in the National League East to fourth, just 9½ games out. Instead of pressing forward, though, the Cards

Lithograph of Dick Allen by Charles Linnett.
Courtesy of Linnett Studios, Goffstown, NH

seemed content to be respectable. Then during the second week of the month, Allen tore a hamstring legging out a two-base hit. He would not return to the lineup until September 8, for one last game at Connie Mack, which was going to be abandoned by the Phillies in 1971 for a new stadium in South Philadelphia.

"I didn't belong on the field," he admitted. "My leg was throbbing. I had a few drinks to dull the pain. I had a lot of mixed emotions."[24]

Rich's last at bat came in the eighth against Rick Wise, and he nailed a second-pitch fastball into the left field bleachers. It was his ninetieth home run at Connie Mack, and his last.[25]

"As I rounded the bases I took one last look around," recalled Allen in his autobiography years later:

> I looked up at the press box, where so many negative stories had been written about me. I looked up at the Cadillac and Coke signs where I had hit so many home runs. I looked into the stands, where they had called me every name known to man. I touched home plate and kept running. When I got to the clubhouse I showered and left before the writers got there. I had nothing to say. I wanted to let that home run stand on its own.[26]

The Cards would go on to win the game 6-3 behind a solid performance by starting pitcher Steve Carlton. Allen, hampered by the torn hamstring, would play in only two more games that season.

When St. Louis finished the season a disappointing fourth in the National League's Eastern Division, Bing Devine traded Allen to the Los Angeles Dodgers for the infielder Ted Sizemore—1969 National League Rookie of the Year—and the catcher/outfielder Bob Stinson, the Dodgers' first-round pick in the 1966 draft. Ironically, the trade was made despite Schoendienst's protests.[27] The Redbird manager had grown to genuinely like Rich and appreciated his efforts on the playing field and in the clubhouse. Nor did it seem the Cardinals' front office had problems with him. The trade was simply a matter of numbers.

"Allen did everything we could hope for and more," admitted Devine:

> But we had to get someone for second base because Javier is 34 going on 35 and has a bad back. Joe Hague has established himself at first base, which is Allen's best position.
>
> Besides, middle infielders who can do a good job are scarce. Sizemore can do everything at second base and can move in at shortstop. Now we can have a set line-up and won't have too many men playing out of position anymore.[28]

To be sure, with Allen in the lineup, Schoendienst had to resort to platooning. If Dick played first, Joe Torre, the team's other potent bat, had to play third or catch. If Allen played third, Torre could play first, but it left Mike Shannon, previously the team's regular third baseman and a solid bat, on the bench. Complicating matters further was Joe Hague, who was only twenty-six and had just hit .271 and slugged .417 in 451 at bats as an outfielder/first baseman. The Cardinals were justifiably high on him, and his playing time at first would be limited if they kept Allen.[29] Trading Dick made sense if the Cards wanted to establish a set lineup.

What didn't make sense was trading him to Los Angeles. When the Phillies made Allen available the previous year, the Dodgers' vice president Al Campanis made clear the organization "didn't want his personality." "To acquire Rich Allen," said Campanis, "would have been making a travesty of everything that Dodger spirit represents."[30] So what changed his mind a year later?

The Dodgers finished second in the National League's western division in 1970, 14½ games behind the pennant-winning Cincinnati Reds. It was a huge improvement over 1969, when they finished the season eighth of the twelve teams in the National League. The Dodgers had improved their performance while going through a rebuilding process. Younger players like Steve Garvey, Bill Buckner, and Willie Crawford made successful adjustments to the majors more quickly than anticipated, but the Dodgers still needed a bona fide long-ball hitter to contend. Allen would fill that void, giving the Dodgers one of the top power hitters in the game. Without blinking, Campanis gave Rich the $105,000 he was asking, a salary higher than any other Dodger was making.[31]

Naturally, Rich was disappointed when he learned of the trade. "I hate to leave," he said, "but once you're traded the first time you're a marked man."[32] His younger brother Ron maintains that Rich realized early on "that baseball was not the same game he loved to play as a kid." "I think once he signed his first professional contract Dick understood that baseball was a business and that he had become a commodity," added Ron, who eventually made it to the majors with the St. Louis Cardinals in 1972.[33] What Allen really wanted after his horrific experience in Philadelphia was to "play in peace for one season," and the Cardinals gave him that opportunity. "The fans and the ball club were wonderful to me," he added. "I just wish I could have done a little more to repay them." At the same time, Rich was excited to be going to the Dodgers. "Putting on a Dodger uniform is something special for me," he said:

> The Dodgers broke the color line by signing Jackie Robinson and I idolized him growing up. My family lived just 30 miles away from Forbes Field, so every time the Dodgers came to Pittsburgh we would go there to watch them play. It's like coming home for me.[34]

As a youngster, Rich Allen idolized Jackie Robinson of the Brooklyn Dodgers. Allen would later carry on Robinson's legacy by challenging the racism that still existed in Major League Baseball in the 1960s. *Courtesy of the Library of Congress*

Interestingly, Rich Allen also challenged the racism that existed in Major League Baseball during the 1960s, though he did not do so as overtly as Robinson. Once the Dodgers' president Branch Rickey lifted the "no striking back" ban in 1949, Jackie became outspoken in his attack against racism, whether it was real or imagined. Often, he interpreted an opposing infielder's slap tag, a baserunner's take-out slide, or a brushback as "racially motivated" when they were really nothing more than tough, competitive play. And he responded with a verbal assault. Rich, on the other hand, sought retaliation in the batter's box. If a pitcher threw him a brushback or an infielder spiked him, it came at the expense of a hard line drive right back at him, or a game-winning home run. But never did Rich lower himself by making negative gestures to the fans or berating an umpire; he simply let his bat do the talking for him. In the process, Allen moved the moral conventions of the game past those that once condoned racism. For that he should have been admired like Jackie Robinson, instead of dismissed as a malcontent.

Rich reported to spring training at Vero Beach with renewed enthusiasm. He was the first one out on the field in the mornings and the last to leave in the afternoons.[35] "I'm working a lot harder than I have in a long time," admitted the twenty-nine-year-old veteran. "But it's fun again, like when I was a kid starting out."[36]

Allen's work ethic paid off immediately. "He was hitting at a .380 clip most of the exhibition season," recalled Tommy Hutton, one of the Dodgers' prospects. "Then he almost uprooted one of the palm trees chasing a fly ball."[37] Hospitalized overnight, Rich returned to the ballpark the next day ready for work. On his way out to the field, one of the sportswriters joked about him getting "carried away" the other day when it was "only spring training."

The remark stopped Rich dead in his tracks. Looking the offending reporter straight in the eye he said, "Spring training is a serious thing. This is my job and I take it seriously, and so should you if you care anything about what you're doing."[38]

During the first two months of the '71 campaign, Allen struggled at the plate, hitting .221, with just five home runs. His difficulty was in part because of the desire to prove himself again. Just as he did in St. Louis, Rich was pressing too hard. Opposing pitchers had also discovered a blind spot for fastballs that came up and in, roughly six inches under his chin, and began throwing to that location on a consistent basis. Throw him a slider or a breaking pitch, though, and he could easily it turn it into a tape measure home run.[39] Some of the Los Angeles scribes attributed his hitting woes to the race track, implying that he was a big better who was losing money on the horses. "Not true," said Allen when he learned of their stories. "Gambling is not my schtick."

"I love the horses," he admitted. "In fact, the pair of two-year-olds I own and the two mares for breeding got to my new home in Los Angeles before I got there. But I'm not a gambler. I enjoy working around horses and I plan to breed thoroughbreds."[40]

By June, Allen had straightened himself out at the plate and was back to hitting homers on a regular basis.[41] "Every time I watch him hit I see a World Series check," remarked his teammate Wes Parker. "He's been a large part of the success around here."[42]

Rich had also taken outfielder Willie Crawford and infielder Bobby Valentine under his wing. "Dick was the only guy who had a word of encouragement for me," said Valentine, a struggling twenty-one-year-old rookie. "I had only known him a few months and he talked to me daily about hitting, what I should do at the plate."[43] Allen took turns in the batting cage with Valentine and Crawford, giving them pointers on their hitting. Then he switched and commented on his own swing while driving pitch after pitch into the deepest parts of the stadium. Allen also showed his younger teammates a series of exercises to strengthen their wrists and forearms, as well as to get greater torque from their lower bodies. Crawford would later credit

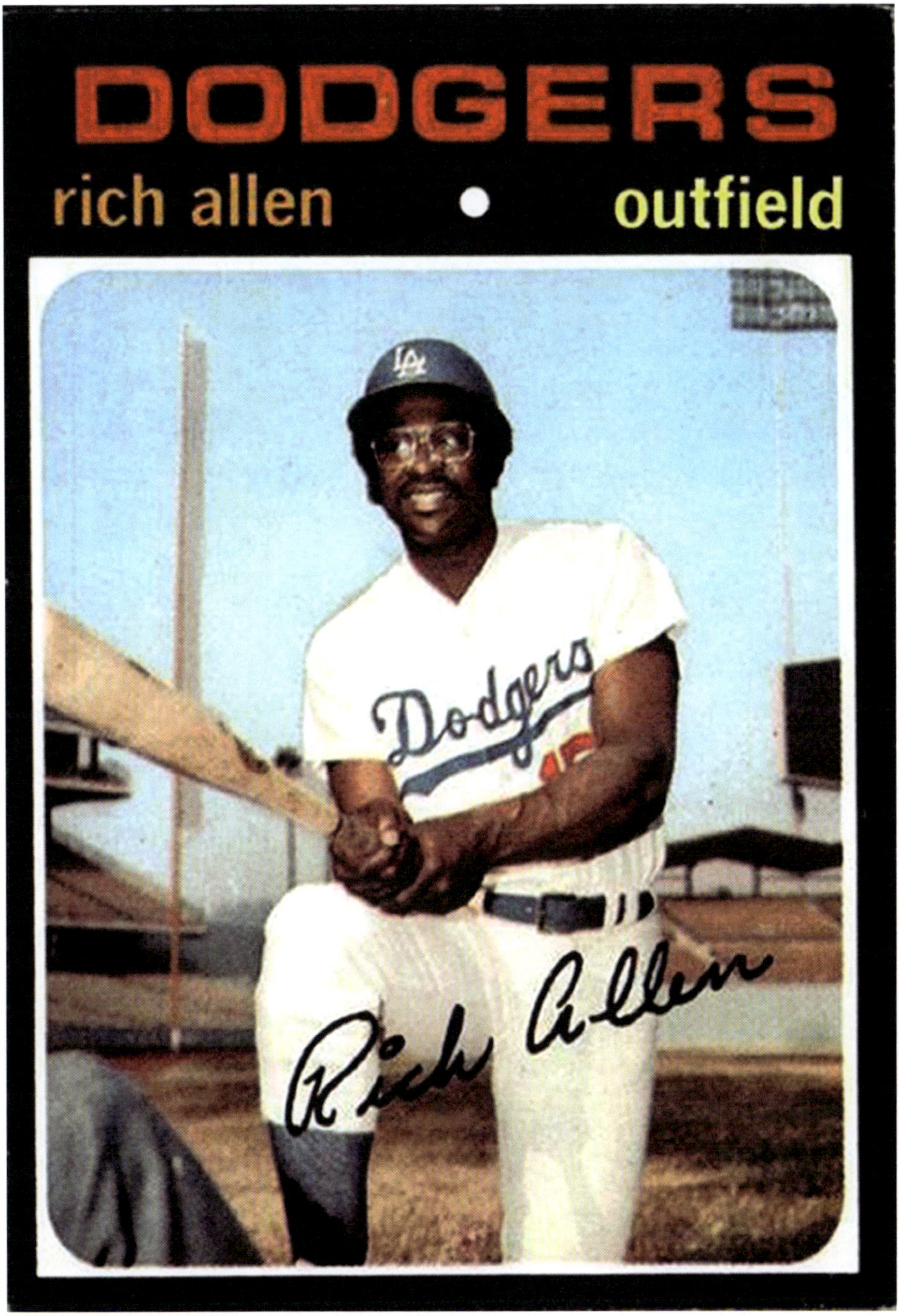

1971 Rich Allen Topps baseball card. *Courtesy of The Topps Company, Inc.*

him with raising his batting average nearly fifty percentage points that season, from .234 to .281.[44]

Down the stretch, Los Angeles and San Francisco battled each other for the National League West title. In the end the Dodgers finished second, a game behind the Giants. Allen had another fine year at the plate, hitting .295, with twenty-three home runs and ninety RBIs in 155 games.[45]

"Dick did a great job for us in LA," recalled Coach Danny Ozark. "He was a great base runner, the best I ever coached. I'd take the extra base with him and I don't think he was ever thrown out the entire year."[46]

Off the field Allen wanted no part of the public relations commitments that owner Walter O'Malley expected of the players, believing it distracted him from winning ball games. "The Dodger organization put a lot of pressure on players to sign autographs and have their picture taken," said Rich. "They want you to visit celebrities in the clubhouse before games. I kept telling the PR guys that I was there to play ball and that all that stuff distracted from the team's mission, which was to win ballgames."[47] Once O'Malley phoned manager Walt Alston and said he wanted Allen to show up for an appearance, Alston told him that he would ask the slugger, but that he already knew he would refuse. Alston would not forgive Allen for his refusal to court the fans, especially the celebrities. "You just didn't do that to O'Malley," said the Dodger's coach Carol Beringer:

> He was very big on image and expected the players to make public appearances. Truth is that O'Malley didn't ask a lot from the players, but when he did, he expected them to follow through. When Rich refused, Walt told me that it would hurt his chances to stay on with the club, and he was right.[48]

O'Malley never forgave Allen. On December 2, 1971, Rich was traded for the third time in as many years to the Chicago White Sox for the pitcher Tommy John and the infielder Steve Huntz.[49]

Worse, some sportswriters still continued to exploit Allen's "bad boy" reputation when it no longer applied. Shortly after he was traded to the White Sox, Larry Merchant, whose *Philadelphia Daily News* columns charged that Allen manipulated race to divide the Phillies, continued to disparage him as a writer for the *New York Post*. Merchant wrote that the Dodgers' decision to trade Allen was a "foregone conclusion." "While Allen produced for the Dodgers, he didn't produce their way," he wrote in a scathing March 1972 column. "His way is to go his own way: show up at the ballpark when the mood strikes him, take his cuts, get dirty if he has to, then disappear into the night until the next game."[50]

In fact, Allen had distanced himself from his infamous reputation during the previous two seasons. He worked hard, set a good example for teammates, willingly mentored young prospects, and continued to put up impressive power statistics. Despite all that, neither St. Louis nor Los Angeles retained him. "The Cardinals and the Dodgers only wanted me for a quick fix," said Rich. "I was in my eighth season in the majors and putting up good numbers, but baseball had become nothing but a fast shuffle to oblivion for me."[51]

Dick Allen, 1972 American League Most Valuable Player. *Photo by Leo Bauby. Courtesy of the Chicago Baseball Museum*

CHAPTER 6:
MOST VALUABLE PLAYER

Uncertain that he wanted to continue his playing career, Dick Allen failed to report to the White Sox spring training camp in Sarasota in early spring 1972. When he did arrive on March 15, he told the general manager Stu Holcomb to trade him because he did not want to be used for "public relations purposes," and that the club's salary offer of $120,000 would not change his mind. Then he turned around and walked out again.[1]

Allen was a proud man who believed in his heart the Cardinals and Dodgers had exploited him as a gate attraction, regardless of their apologetic explanations for trading him. Nor was he going to allow money to influence his decision. "I lived from age one to 18 without money," he explained. "So, if I'm going to make a living why not go and make $100 a week out in the country where I can live in peace?

"As my mother always said," he added, "if I don't use my baseball talent it's a sin. But I can't change my life to please anybody else. I have to live it my way."[2]

But the White Sox did have one thing in their favor if they hoped to sign Allen: their manager Chuck Tanner.

Tanner, a western Pennsylvania native, knew, liked, and respected Dick. They grew up ten miles apart from each other. Tanner, who went to Shenango High School in New Castle, competed in basketball and baseball against Dick's older brother Hank Allen when he was at Wampum High School.[3] Just as important for Dick, Tanner and his mother, Era, knew, liked, and respected each other.

White Sox Manager Chuck Tanner, a longtime friend of the Allen family, welcomed Dick to Chicago. *Photo by Doug McWilliams. Courtesy of the National Baseball Hall of Fame and Library, Cooperstown, NY*

"Sure, I knew Mrs. Allen," said the White Sox manager. "Back home everybody knew about Mrs. Allen and her boys. She was a wonderful woman, a tough woman raising all those boys."[4]

When Tanner learned the White Sox had traded for Allen, he traveled to Wampum to visit with Dick and his mother. Realizing Allen was considering retirement, the Chisox manager sat at the kitchen table and talked about the team's prospects as a pennant contender if he played for them. "I told him look Dick, Chicago will be your last stop," said Tanner. "You're going to make it with us. You're the guy who can make us a winner."[5] But it did not seem to sway Dick. Instead, he remained at his farm in Perkasie, Pennsylvania, when the White Sox opened spring training camp, pondering his future.

Finally, in mid-March, Allen phoned his mother and asked for her advice. "Listen, son, go help Chuck out. It might be a blessing in disguise."[6]

Chisox owner John Allyn and manager Chuck Tanner greet Dick at spring training in March 1972. *Photo by Leo Bauby. Courtesy of the Chicago Baseball Museum*

Allen did as he was told. Once again, he discovered his mother was right, and for that the entire White Sox organization was grateful. Just two years earlier, the White Sox had the worst record in the major leagues, losing 106 games. They also had the lowest attendance, drawing just 495,555 that year. The financially troubled franchise was struggling to stave off the image of a perennial loser. With the crosstown Cubs drawing much larger crowds on the North Side, rumors circulated that the Chisox would be relocating to St. Petersburg, Florida, or Seattle.[7]

The owner John Allyn, heir of the Francis I. DuPont brokerage firm, was intent on making his team relevant again. In 1969, Allyn purchased the White Sox from his brother, Arthur, and in the process staved off the sale of the team to Bud Selig, a car sales magnate who hoped to relocate the franchise to Milwaukee. Desperate to create some excitement at Comiskey Park, Allyn revamped the Sox's uniforms by abandoning the baggy blue, white, and gray woolen flannels and adopting a lightweight, double-knit polyester uniform with bright scarlet pinstripes. The new caps, undersleeves, stirrups, and shoes were also scarlet. Just as outstanding were the powder blue road uniforms with scarlet lettering. The vivid color scheme was similar to those of most other MLB teams who had adopted more dapper, form-fitting uniforms.[8] Changes were also made in the front office.

The general manager Stu Holcomb hired Chuck Tanner as his manager and Roland Hemond as assistant general manager and director of player personnel. The duo converted the White Sox from a singles-hitting, defensive team that relied on opponents' mistakes to more of a power-hitting team featuring Bill Melton, the American League's 1971 home run champion, and Carlos May, who ranked seventh among the league's leading batsmen that year.[9]

On April 1, 1972, Dick signed a $120,000 contract with the White Sox and later fielded questions from the Chicago sportswriters with owner John Allyn. *Photo by Leo Bauby. Courtesy of the Chicago Baseball Museum*

But convincing Allen to play in Chicago was the single most important factor in saving the franchise. Dick was a bona fide superstar who would solidify the heart of the batting order by protecting his younger teammates Melton and May. In addition, his powerful swing and tape measure home runs would immediately increase attendance and put the Sox back on the road to respectability, though White Sox fans would have to wait to catch their first glimpse of their new slugger.

Opening Day was delayed two weeks because the players walked out en masse after spring training ended. The antiauthoritarian spirit that had gripped college campuses in the late 1960s had finally surfaced in baseball. For the first time in the sport's history, players, led by the Players Association director Marvin Miller, conducted a strike. At issue was the players' pension fund, specifically the amount the team owners paid into it and how the fund's profits were to be invested. The strike lasted thirteen days. In the end, the owners compromised by agreeing to contribute $490,000 to the pension fund in 1972, with $500,000 of the fund's profits directed to additional benefits.[10]

Dick Allen would call Chicago's Comiskey Park "home" 1972–1974. *Courtesy of the National Baseball Hall of Fame and Library, Cooperstown, NY*

When the regular season began on Saturday, April 15, fans in other cities showed their displeasure by staying away from the ballpark in droves. The White Sox opened on the road against Kansas City, who swept the three-game series. When they returned to Chicago on Tuesday, April 18, for their home opener, they drew only 20,944 fans—considerably less than Comiskey Park's 46,550 capacity. But those who did show up saw the Sox demolish the Texas Rangers 14-0. Allen, hitting third, made an impressive debut, going 2-for-4, scoring three runs, and knocking in two on a pair of doubles.[11] It was the power with which he hit the ball that amazed teammates and opponents alike.

On Saturday, April 29, the White Sox were playing at Detroit's Tiger Stadium. Chicago was losing 5-0 in the top of the fourth when Allen stepped to the plate to face Tiger ace Mickey Lolich. Dick hit what appeared to be a nasty line drive that whistled by Lolich's ear, undressing him. The ball kept rising, sailing over center fielder Mickey Stanley's head, and skimmed off the fence for a home run.

As Allen was circling the bases he noticed Lolich was sitting on the mound with his arms around his knees, shaking, as if he were cold. Detroit manager Billy Martin jogged out of the dugout, concerned the vicious shot might have hit his star pitcher in the head as it whizzed by.

When Lolich insisted that was not the case, Martin asked, "Then why are you sitting on your ass?"

"Because I was afraid the fuckin' ball was going to ricochet off the center field fence and kill me!" he replied.[12]

At the end of April Dick was hitting .361, with four home runs and seven RBIs, and seemed to be comfortable with his new team.[13] In fact, manager Chuck Tanner's understanding for Dick's upbringing in a small, rural western Pennsylvania town, as well as his low-key style of handling ballplayers, would make it possible for Allen to thrive in Chicago.

Although the city's sportswriters insisted Tanner had one set of rules for the team and another set for Allen, it was not true. "I had twenty-five sets of rules," insisted the forty-one-year-old skipper. "I took every player case by case. My managing philosophy was a simple one:

Allen sporting the White Sox powder blue road uniform. *Photo by Doug McWilliams. Courtesy of the National Baseball Hall of Fame and Library, Cooperstown, NY*

Allen connects in an April 26, 1972, game against the Cleveland Indians. *Photo by Leo Bauby. Courtesy of the Chicago Baseball Museum*

Allen watches a home run leave Comiskey Park. *Photo by Leo Bauby. Courtesy of the Chicago Baseball Museum*

communication, not regimentation. But the media didn't get it."

"Most guys need to abide by rules," Tanner explained. "But Dick was one of several veterans on that '72 team, including Wilbur Wood, Bill Melton, and Carlos May. I gave all of them their freedom. Dick, in particular, was a creative person. I knew if I tried to box him in I wouldn't get results. He'd be unhappy and so would I."[14]

Accordingly, Tanner told Dick his measure of a player's worth was performance on the playing field, not appearance at practice sessions or adherence to curfew. The only demand that would be made on Allen was that he be "on the field when the game starts."[15]

To lessen the pressure on Dick defensively, Tanner gave him a regular position. For various reasons his previous managers had shuffled him around on defense, playing him at first base, third base, and the outfield in no particular order. The constant change in position almost cer-

Dick circles the bases after an April 26, 1972, homer. *Photo by Leo Bauby. Courtesy of the Chicago Baseball Museum*

tainly weakened Dick's defensive play and may have also contributed to his frequent injuries, as well as his perceived "bad attitude." Instead, Tanner played Allen exclusively at first base, allowing him to concentrate on hitting.[16] Free to do what he loved, Dick blossomed into the savior of the franchise. Whenever he came to the plate the public address system blared the music from the popular Broadway show, "Jesus Christ, Superstar."

White Sox teammates congratulate Dick after the homer. *Photo by Leo Bauby. Courtesy of the Chicago Baseball Museum*

Allen's offensive feats in 1972 are still spoken of reverently by Chicago's South Side fans. Although Comiskey was a cavernous old ballpark considered to be one of baseball's most pitcher-friendly stadiums, the Wampum Walloper blasted his home runs into some of its farthest reaches, including the roof and even the center field bleachers, 445 feet away from home plate. Among the most memorable homers was a June 4 blast against the New York Yankees in the second game of a doubleheader. The Sox had already won the first game 6-1, with Allen contributing two hits and a run scored. The victory enabled Chicago to stay in second place in the American League West at 24-17, just 3½ games behind the division-leading Oakland A's.

Some 52,000 fans packed Comiskey Park for the doubleheader, and all of them stayed around for the second game. Having played every inning of every game in the '72 campaign, Tanner decided to let Allen sit this one out for a well-deserved rest. With New York leading 4-2 in the bottom of the ninth inning, Bill Melton worked a one-out walk and Mike Andrews singled to left. The Yankee manager Ralph Houk went to his bullpen for left-handed reliever Sparky Lyle. Tanner countered by sending a batboy to the clubhouse to find Allen.

"I was eating a chili dog when I heard Chuck wanted me to hit," Dick remembered. "I had chili all over my shirt, so I put on a new one and a pair of pants with no underclothes."

Allen picked up his 40-oz. bat and strode to the plate as Tanner sent Jorge Orta in to pinch run for Andrews on first. When Allen was announced as a pinch hitter, Andrews, once Lyle's roommate on the Red Sox, shouted, "Hey, Sparky, you're in deep shit now!"

Allen evened the count at 1-1 and then crushed a slider 370 feet away in the left field grandstand, winning the game for the White Sox 5-4. Known in Chisox lore as the "Chili Dog Home Run," the blast was the ninth walk-off homer of Allen's career. The fans—giddy, almost delirious—refused to leave the ballpark. Instead, they spent the next thirty minutes on their feet cheering and hollering for Allen to take a curtain call.[17]

Dick called it "one of many memorable moments" during a summer in which he received more All-Star Game votes (1,093,658) than any other American Leaguer. "I feel good about that," said Allen:

> But I have to admit that I'm surprised, especially with all the things written about me as baseball's bad boy. I guess the fans really did judge me on what I did on the field, not what the writers said about my private life.[18]

Allen started at first base and batted cleanup for the American League in the annual midsummer classic. Unfortunately, he went 0-for-3 as the National League prevailed 4-3 in ten innings.[19]

On July 31, Dick made the history books with two inside-the-park home runs in the same game.

The White Sox were at Minnesota's Metropolitan Stadium for a two-game set with the Twins. The "Met" was a huge ballpark with wide power alleys, and Allen would take advantage of them that day. Facing the Twins' starter Bert Blyleven in the first, with Pat Kelly and Luis Alvarado on base, Dick hit a hard line drive to right center. When Twins center fielder Darwin took his angle to field the ball his feet slipped out from under him, and the ball took a strange hop over him and rolled to the fence. Allen, Pat Kelly, and Luis Alvarado scored for a quick 3-0 lead. Later, in the fifth inning, Allen, facing Blyleven again, followed Alvarado's RBI single with a sinking liner to left center. This time Darwin tried to make a shoestring catch but the ball got by him. Allen, who still had impressive speed for his age, raced around the bases for a major league record–tying second inside-the-park homer in a single game. Chicago romped the Twins 8-1 to split the series.[20]

Between July 22 and August 18, the White Sox won twenty-one of twenty-eight games to erase an Oakland lead that once stood at high as 8½ games.[21] Even with the slugging third baseman "Beltin' Bill" Melton sidelined by a back injury, Chicago led the division in late August.[22] "They're playing over their heads right now, and it's all because of Dick Allen," said the A's Reggie Jackson, a good friend of the Wampum Walloper:

Allen could still use his speed on the base paths if the situation called for it. Here he is sliding into home plate as the New York Yankees catcher Thurman Munson looks on. *Photo by Leo Bauby. Courtesy of the Chicago Baseball Museum*

Dick bowls over the Cleveland second baseman Luis Alvarez to eliminate a possible double play in a 1973 game. *Photo by Leo Bauby. Courtesy of the Chicago Baseball Museum*

> He's good for the players, he's good for the fans, and he's good for the owners because he brings people into the park. He's one of the most valuable players to come along to a team and to the league. People who rap Dick don't know anything about him.[23]

Allen genuinely believed the White Sox would prevail in the American League West that season. "The A's were talented but unhappy," he recalled years later:

> That's why I felt we could beat their ass, even though we were just a bunch of scrappers. When we'd play the A's and one of their guys would reach first base I'd get an earful about [Oakland's owner] [Charles] Finley. Especially from Reggie. He'd start talking about how cheap Finley was—the cattle car flights, no meal money, no food in the clubhouse. For a while that worked in our favor, but by

September the A's were united in their hatred of Finley. Once they were united they began playing for each other, not for their owner.[24]

Allen was not the only reason for the Sox's success, though. Wilbur Wood, a workhorse knuckleballer, was remarkably resilient during the '72 campaign. In one stretch he appeared in four games in ten days. Wood's reliever mentality and rubber arm allowed Tanner to do something unprecedented in modern times: work with a three-man starting staff of Wood, Stan Bahnsen, and Tom Bradley. The trio combined for 132 starts that season, with Wood leading the American League in starts (49) and innings pitched (376.2), and tied for the league lead in wins with twenty-four. Bahnsen won a career high twenty-one games in his first season with the Sox, and Bradley continued another fifteen victories. Rookie "Goose" Gossage and Terry Forster, both twenty years old, were a righty/lefty fireman tandem that combined

1972 Chicago White Sox. Front row (left to right): Batboys Jim Riley, Rory Clark, and Joe White. Second row (seated): Carlos May, Luis Alvarado, Bart Johnson, Coach Al Monchak, Coach Joe Lonnett, Manager Chuck Tanner, Coach John Sain, Coach Jim Mahoney, Jorge Orta, Walt Williams, and Jim Qualls. Third row (standing): Trainer Charlie Saad, Equipment Manager Larry Licklider, Batting Practice Pitcher Glen Rosenbaum, Wilbur Wood, Chuck Brinkman, Jim Geddes, Dave Lemonds, Rick Reichardt, Pat Kelly, Mike Andrews, Dick Allen, Traveling Secretary and Statistician Don Unferth, and Visiting Clubhouse Custodian Mike Morris. Back row (standing on bench): Ed Hermann, Bill Melton, Rich Gossage, Terry Forester, Tom Egan, Rich Morales, Jay Johnstone, Tom Bradley, Vincent Roma, Steve Kealey, and Stan Bahnsen. *Courtesy of the Chicago White Sox Baseball Club*

Heart of the White Sox batting order (left to right): Carlos May, Bill Melton, and Dick Allen. *Photo by Leo Bauby. Courtesy of the Chicago Baseball Museum*

for thirteen wins. Forster was also the closer, with twenty-nine saves.[25] The offense was just as impressive, and not only because of Allen.

The left fielder Carlos May, who hit .300 or better most of the season, also contributed clutch power with twelve home runs, sixty-eight RBIs, and a slugging percentage of .438. So did the previous year's American League Home Run champ, third baseman Bill Melton (.245, 7 home runs, and 30 RBIs in just fifty-seven games) and catcher Ed Hermann (.249, 10 HR, 40 RBI). While the Sox had great home run power, they also had a balance of line drive hitters like Pat Kelly (.723 OPS), who also boasted a team-best thirty-two steals.[26]

Despite all the talent, Chisox third baseman Bill Melton insists Allen's presence gave the rest of the team a "realty check." "We thought we were pretty good before Dick arrived," explained Melton in a recent interview:

> But when you add a player of his magnitude to your line up and pay him $150,000 when the rest of us are making $40,000 or less, then you realize what you need to become a contender.
>
> Dick did things on a baseball field that no one else had ever done before. He hit tape measure home runs in Comiskey, which was a pitcher friendly ballpark.

He could run like a deer, too. If he was on second base and there was a base hit up the middle he'd turn and watch as he was rounding third, put on the afterburners, and score. Rarely did he have to slide into home.

But most of all he led by example, and had a calming effect on the younger players. He just made us better as a team.[27]

Rich "Goose" Gossage, who was a rookie pitcher on the '72 Chisox, was one of those young players Allen took under his wing. One morning during spring training Dick walked out to the practice field and heard the distinctive pop of a 90-mph fastball hitting a catcher's mitt. Impressed with the young flamethrower on the mound, the slugger picked up his 40-oz. bat and stepped into the batter's box to get a better look.

"I'm throwing aspirins," recalled Rich Gossage, "and I say, 'Oh my God, that's Dick Allen standing up there.' The longer he stayed in the [batter's] box the more pumped up I became and the harder and faster I threw."

After watching him for twenty minutes Allen told Gossage, "You have one of the greatest arms I've ever seen. Just remember to keep those arms covered with sleeves. Keep the arm warm and you'll never have trouble with it."

"That's when he took me under his wing," said Gossage. "Dick taught me how to pitch."

Over the course of spring training, and then during the regular season, Allen would sidle up to Gossage and give him the benefit of his knowledge about pitching, as well as how to get inside the head of a power hitter. "We'd talk for hours on end about pitching and how to make pitches and what a hitter's looking for," recalled Goose.

Allen taught him the art of intimidation by teaching him how to fire his fastball at a right-handed hitter's front elbow, elevating it a bit for his out pitch when he was ahead in the count. "We as hitters see that pitch, but we can't get the barrel of the bat to the ball," explained Dick:

As a rookie pitcher with the White Sox, Rich "Goose" Gossage was mentored by Dick Allen, who taught the young hurler how to intimidate power hitters. Gossage would use that knowledge to forge a Hall of Fame career. *Photo by Doug McWilliams. Courtesy of the National Baseball Hall of Fame and Museum, Cooperstown, NY*

> We might even be able to get the bat on the ball to foul it off or hit it down the right field line. But we panic when we see that pitch coming inside on us because we know we have to get the barrel on it and we just can't do it. The pitch looks as big as a basketball, too. But believe me, God himself couldn't get the barrel on that ball if He tried. No one can. So what you want to do is get ahead of the batter 0-2 down in the strike zone, then come up and in on him with that pitch.

When Gossage expressed his concern that he might "drill the hitter," Allen's response was classic old school: "You probably will hit a few batters, but what's wrong with that? You can't worry about it. If you do, you can't be successful."

"Look at it this way," he added, "even if the ball gets away from you it's going to be a great purpose pitch. It'll keep the hitters honest."

"Besides, every guy in that dugout is watching. You'll have all the backup you need if the hitter charges the mound."

Under Allen's tutelage Gossage would perfect the art of intimidation on the mound. "Dick's the smartest baseball man I've ever been around in my life," said Gossage. "He taught me how to pitch from a hitter's perspective and taught me how to play the game, and how to play the game right. There's no telling the numbers this guy could have put up if all he worried about was stats."[28]

Despite his mentoring, Dick discouraged the title of "team leader," saying he was simply "part of a team" that over the course of the season "became tighter than pantyhose two sizes too small."[29]

Allen genuinely liked his teammates, especially Melton. The third baseman was the cleanup hitter and Dick batted third in the lineup. Pitchers didn't throw him many breaking balls in order to pitch around him because they still had to face Melton. As a result, Allen saw a lot of fastballs, many of which ended up as home runs. He appreciated that and made sure to credit his teammate just about every time he hit a homer. In fact, Allen seemed to like everyone in the White Sox organization except the newly hired broadcaster Harry Caray, whom he considered a nuisance, and his enthusiastic radio calls on WTAQ/WEAW irritating. Dick drove that point home during an August 23 game against the Yankees at Comiskey Park.

Caray was broadcasting the game from the center field bleachers directly under the scoreboard, as was his custom for Wednesday afternoon games. In the seventh inning of a tight game Allen came to bat against New York's Lindy McDaniel and rocketed a 2-0 offering deep into center field. Like many of Dick's home runs the ball started low, then suddenly took off. When Caray saw the ball heading his direction he hesitated momentarily because did not believe a pitch hit so low would be a threat more than 400 feet from home plate. Once Caray realized he was in harm's way, he dropped his famous fishing net—which he kept for just such an occasion—and scrambled out of range, spilling beer all over himself. Otherwise, Allen's line drive rocket might have killed him on the spot. Fans who were at Comiskey that day remember being sent into an initial state of shock, then amusement at the sight of Caray running for safety, and finally awe as Allen's blast cleared a wall 445 feet from home plate, highlighting a 5-2 win.[30]

Broadcaster Harry Caray called White Sox games from the bleachers on Wednesday afternoons. He would later become a Chicago institution with the Cubs. *Photo by Leo Bauby. Courtesy of the Chicago Baseball Museum*

"Dick didn't like Harry because Caray didn't like me," said Bill Melton, the reigning American League home run champion:

> Nineteen-seventy-two was Harry's first year with the White Sox, and he constantly criticized me on air because I wasn't hitting with the same power as I had the previous year. That was due to two herniated discs that became so aggravated that I was placed on the disabled list in July and stayed on it for the remainder of the season. While I didn't appreciate the criticism, I let it slide. But Dick, who has a fierce loyalty to his friends, didn't hide his animosity for Caray.[31]

In 1972, Dick Allen became one of the most beloved players in White Sox history for almost single-handedly carrying Chicago into contention. Even when he made an error, he immediately redeemed himself. One night in Cleveland Allen forgot how many outs there were in the bottom of the seventh. The Indians had runners on second and third with just one down. When the out was recorded at first base Dick, believing it was the final out of the inning, flipped the ball to the first base umpire and headed in to the dugout. Both Cleveland runners scored, giving the Indians a 4-2 lead.

Two outs later, when the inning finally did end, Allen, embarrassed, apologized to his teammates.

"Aw man, I'm really sorry guys," he said, humbled by the gaffe. "My fuck up. Tell ya' what, I'll get those runs back for us."

Dick, who had already struck out twice, came to bat again in the top of the eighth with two runners on base. Teammates sitting in the dugout and watching the slugger take his practice swings had seen his intensity before in similar situations.

"Hey, motherfucker!" they yelled out to Phil Heninger, the Indians' pitcher. "You better tie yourself down to the mound. He's goin' to kill your ass!"

Allen blasted a three-run shot over the center field fence, giving the White Sox a 5-4 lead. After circling the bases Dick entered the dugout, took himself out of the game, and said to his teammates, "Okay boys, I got you the lead. Now bring it on home."

"I never saw a guy set up pitchers like Dick Allen," insisted Gossage:

> He'd waste two at bats striking out and then come up in the eighth or ninth inning with runners on base and the game on the line and hit a dinger. It was a thing of beauty to watch.
>
> I can't tell you how many times Dick would get us a lead by the eighth inning and then take himself out of the game. He just put us on his shoulders and we rode his ass like he was a Clydesdale.[32]

Dick was a shoo-in to win the American League's Most Valuable Player award in 1972. He led the league in home runs (37) and RBIs (113), and came within ten points of winning the coveted Triple Crown with a .308 batting average. Here he is with the MVP award on Opening Day 1973. *Photo by Johnny Reyes. Courtesy of the Chicago Baseball Museum*

Although the A's eventually won the Western Division by 5½ games over the second-place Chisox, the '72 season was the high point of Allen's major league career. Not only did he win the American League's MVP Award despite the team's second-place finish, but he very well might have saved a White Sox franchise in terrible disrepair. Dick came within ten points of capturing the coveted Triple Crown, with a .308 batting average and a league-leading 37 home runs and 113 RBIs. He also led the American League in walks (99), on-base percentage (.422), slugging average (.603), and OPS (1.023), while winning a well-deserved MVP award.[33]

"It was one of the most impactful seasons a ballplayer ever had," according to Roland Hemond, the team's assistant

GM who is largely credited as the architect of the Allen trade. "Dick Allen is responsible for saving the White Sox franchise."[34]

To be sure, Allen's success not only drew thousands of fans to Comiskey Park, but expanded the team's appeal with radio listeners across northern and central Illinois. Before 1972, White Sox games were broadcast on WTAQ, a low-frequency AM radio station that had difficulty broadcasting clearly in the city of Chicago. Dick's monster season allowed the White Sox to regain a contract with WMAQ, a 50,000 watt AM radio station that could be heard throughout Chicago and its suburbs.[35]

On December 1—the day he was voted MVP by the Baseball Writers—Allen dropped by Comiskey Park for a press conference. He praised Chicago fans as being "among the most knowledgeable in baseball," his teammates as being "terrific," the front office as being "cooperative," and even expressed his unqualified gratitude for the way he was treated by the city's sportswriters.

"I really want to thank the fans of Chicago," said Dick. "They've done a lot for me. They made a human being out of me.

"Before I came here, I had to hide out. I'd never go out to eat at a restaurant. But it's different here in Chicago. I go out and enjoy meeting the fans."

Allen also said he was humbled by the MVP Award. "I believe that winning an honor like this takes more than just me," he added. "Baseball is a team game, and this award would mean a lot more to me if we had won the division title and the pennant.

"I still feel as if I haven't done enough," he concluded. "I believe I can do more, and I hope I can prove it next year. I came to Chicago to win and that's what I hope we can do."[36]

Allen spoke from the heart. Despite his team-oriented approach, Dick placed the blame on himself for the club's failure to make the postseason. Not only did he hate to lose, he internalized it. It was his way of driving himself to do better—to bring a pennant, if not a World Series, to the Windy City.

On February 27, 1973, the White Sox showed their appreciation by making Allen the highest-paid player in the history of Major League Baseball, signing him to a three-year $675,000 contract, topping Hank Aaron's three-year pact with the Atlanta Braves by $75,000.[37] Allen's record-setting contract, along with the acquisition of outfielder Ken Henderson from the San Francisco Giants, underscored the White Sox' intention to bring a pennant to Chicago.

Sox general manager Stu Holcomb pulled the trigger on that trade at the winter meetings in Honolulu, sending fifteen-game-winner Tom Bradley to the Giants for Henderson and the pitcher Steve Stone. Henderson was a rarity—a switch hitter with power. He was also an excellent fielder and fine base runner. "I did not expect the Giants to give up on me," Henderson said after he learned of the deal. "But I'm happy to be going to a contender. If I hit in front of Allen I can use my base running ability, and with Allen, Melton, Carlos May, and me in the lineup we have a good set of bats." With Henderson hitting third and Melton fifth, Allen would be even more dangerous in '73 because he would not be walked as often.[38]

Initially, many baseball insiders believed Dick's value would increase when the American League passed the designated hitter (DH) rule on a three-year trial basis. Allegedly there were many advantages to substituting a DH for a weak-hitting pitcher. The most obvious benefit was adding more power to the lineup, which in turn would attract more fans to the ballpark. The DH would also save pitchers a lot of wear and tear on their arms, according to the theory, and allow them to devote themselves fully to pitching. Similarly, aging power hitters could extend their careers by concentrating on hitting instead of having to play in the field, which taxed their bodies.[39] But the Wampum Walloper was not very happy when manager Chuck Tanner stated his intention to have him split time between DH and first base. Nevertheless, Allen reported early to spring training intent on fulfilling his promise to do more to bring a winner to Chicago.[40]

Dick made his debut as DH in a March 13 exhibition game against the Yankees in Fort Lauderdale. He grounded out, walked, and then singled to figure in the only

1972 Topps baseball card. *Courtesy of The Topps Company, Inc.*

1973 Topps baseball card. *Courtesy of The Topps Company, Inc.*

White Sox run in their 2-1 loss against New York. Allen admitted he "just isn't cut out for the role," though he realized that it "might lengthen my career." "When you're not in the field you get stiff. I'd rather be at first, talking to the opposing base runner, losing myself in the game." Still, Allen agreed to Tanner's arrangement to make him DH in day games and for the second game of doubleheaders.[41]

"Dick could've been a great designated hitter if his heart was in it," said Melton:

> He wasn't that big in stature, being just under six feet and 180 pounds, but he had huge hands and quick wrists, like Hank Aaron and Willie Mays. That's where he got his power from. But Dick still wanted to play first base every day. You just couldn't keep him out of the line up, and if he didn't want to do something there was no way anyone would get him to do it. That's just the way he was.[42]

Tanner eventually deferred to his star slugger and used Carlos May as the team's designated hitter.

1974 Topps baseball card. *Courtesy of The Topps Company, Inc.*

1975 Topps baseball card. *Courtesy of The Topps Company, Inc.*

If the White Sox skipper was annoyed with his star, he certainly did not show it. Instead, Tanner raved about Dick's hitting, his baseball genius, and how much he helped the younger players, especially pitchers. One of the reasons Allen was so effective with pitchers is because he was able to get them to understand his thinking as a power hitter. "I don't use the strike zone much," he explained to them:

> I'm looking for something to hammer. I don't have time to argue whether the pitch was two inches either way. Besides, that sumbuck in blue back there has more problems than I do.
>
> When I first see a pitcher I'm looking inside. Fight that hard stuff to right field, and the moment he comes in with that soft stuff, CLICK, pull it to left. If he can keep putting the ball on that outside corner, fine. I'll take five or six strikeouts until I understand the pitcher. Then, if I see that he's able to locate the pitch consistently outside, I'll start looking there, going to right. Then if he does come inside I can still come around on it.[43]

After hearing Allen's hitting philosophy, *Sports Illustrated*'s Roy Blount drew an insightful analogy to Dick's approach to life. "Allen wants everybody to be straight with him, to come in with their hard stuff," he wrote:

> He wants everybody to want him as eagerly as he and [Cardinal's pitcher] Bob Gibson want [to face] each other. He is set up to handle life that way—looking inside.
>
> When pitchers get shifty, trying to nip the outside corner, Allen disapproves but will adjust, grumbling all the while about pitchers who "want to fool everybody." But he cannot adjust to deviousness and compromise off the field.[44]

Allen *was* guarded, careful to protect himself from anybody knowing him completely. "Nobody can say they know me, or what I will do," he said. "If ever I am trying to keep up an image and something comes up that I want to do, I'll lose the image."[45] In other words, the only predictable thing about Dick was his unpredictability, and *that* quality prevented anyone from ever truly understanding him. Once he let down his guard, though, Allen could be exceptionally charming, personally insightful, and trusting, almost to a fault. As his tenure in Chicago unfolded, Dick let his guard down more often than not. Although he was still a shy, reserved individual, the first baseman admitted that the White Sox, their fans, and the city allowed him to be "truly at ease to be myself."[46] He even had a two-hour TV talk show, and was quite good at chatting up his sports guests on camera when he was in the mood.[47]

"Dick was a mercurial fellow," explained his teammate Bill Melton, now a broadcaster and analyst with the White Sox:

> I mean, there are not too many ballplayers who show up to the park dressed in a cape. He had a lot of confidence to wear something like that because most guys would get laughed out of the clubhouse. Dick wasn't looking for attention, though. Nor was he the kind of guy who looked for praise, either. He *always* put the team ahead of himself.
>
> Not many people realize that he was also a funny guy. Dick had great stories and one-liners, and kept us laughing on the bench and in the clubhouse. But he was also a sensitive guy. It meant a lot to him that his teammates befriended him pretty quickly after he was traded here. The young kids loved him, especially the pitchers, because he took the time to mentor them. And the fans cared about him, too. There's no doubt in my mind that Dick was one of the most beloved players in the history of the White Sox organization.[48]

Allen may have forced himself out of his comfort zone simply to avoid loneliness. His eleven-year marriage to Barbara was in distress. "Baseball wrecked my home," he admitted. "You don't get a chance to be at home during the season. That can be grinding on a guy." Still, Dick tried hard to save the marriage and remained extremely close to his three children, who continued to live with their mother at the family's horse farm in Perkasie.[49] His loneliness was tempered by the presence of his older brother, Hank, a steadying influence who the White Sox signed the previous year as a utility infielder.[50] The brothers shared a sparsely furnished two-bedroom apartment called "the flat" in the Windy City. "I don't need much," said Dick, "just a bed to lay my head on, something to feed my belly, a nice bathroom, and maybe a mirror to comb my hair. This place is close to the track and the stables and they are my beach. So what else do I need?"[51]

Allen began the '73 campaign like he hadn't taken any time off from the previous season. Despite an injured thumb, Dick played through the pain. By mid-June he was hitting at a .394 clip with sixteen homers, including a May 1 moon shot off Baltimore's Mike Cuellar that landed on the left field rooftop at Comiskey Park, an estimated 500 feet away from home plate.[52] Not only did he hit and hit with power, but he sacrificed himself to advance the runner, talked with the pitchers, taught younger teammates how to hit, and occasionally even persuaded manager Chuck Tanner to make an innovative move in the infield defense. Dick got along so well with his teammates that he bailed out a financially troubled rookie with a remarkably generous check and would occasionally pay their fines for infractions. "The day I can't get along with the guys I play with," he explained, "is the day I quit."[53]

With the world champion A's hovering around the .500 mark for most of the spring, the White Sox battled it out against the Royals for the lead in the American League West. Chicago's lineup was buttressed by the return of power-hitting third baseman Bill Melton and the indomitable pitching of Wilbur Wood, who was 13-3

Although manager Chuck Tanner experimented with Allen as a designated hitter, Dick preferred to play defense as well and was granted the request. *Photo by Leo Bauby. Courtesy of the Chicago Baseball Museum*

Dick was known to put the White Sox up by a few runs in the seventh or eighth inning and then take himself out of the game to watch the ninth from the bench. *Photo by Leo Bauby. Courtesy of the Chicago Baseball Museum*

Dick was reunited with his brother, Hank (left), on the White Sox in 1973. Here the two brothers pose with John Ogden (center), the scout who signed them to play pro ball, and Dick Jr. *Courtesy of the Allen Family*

by the end of May. In fact, things were going so well the Sox were favored to capture the western division. But those hopes were dashed on June 28 when Dick, in the sixth inning of a game against the California Angels, collided with Mike Epstein of the A's and fractured the fibula in his left knee. He tried to return five weeks later, but the pain was so severe it ended his season after just three games. At the time of his injury Chicago was just one game out of first with a 37-32 record. Wood tried to carry the load for the Sox, making forty-eight starts, including both ends of a July 20 doubleheader against the Yankees. Although he became the first pitcher in the majors to win twenty games that season with a July 29 victory over the Minnesota Twins, Wood faltered in the second half of the season, finishing with a 24-20 record.[54] Chicago, seven games out of first at the July All Star break, finished the season in fifth place, seventeen games behind the Oakland A's, who went on to capture their second straight world championship.[55]

Dick running the bases. *Artwork courtesy of Rob Larsen*

Dick completed his season with a .316 batting average, sixteen homers, and forty-one RBIs. After that, Allen sat in his flat and brooded for nearly a month until manager Chuck Tanner gave him permission to return home to Perkasie.[56] When the Chicago sportswriter Jerome Holtzman heard that Dick had left the club, he questioned whether Allen was really injured or simply shirking his responsibility. Roland Hemond came to Dick's defense. "If we were in the thick of the pennant race Dick Allen would have wanted to play," insisted Hemond:

> He gave us everything he had this season. He hurt his thumb earlier and it was a severe injury. He could've begged off and taken himself out of the line up, but he refused to do that. I think that's pretty courageous.
>
> Once we fell out of the [pennant] race we had to begin thinking about next year. We decided that rather than push him and risk further injury to his leg it would be better if Dick sat out and fully recuperated so he'd be ready to go for the next season. Why jeopardize his future for a few extra times at bat?

Hemond's explanation was sound, but it wasn't good enough for Holtzman, one of the most respected sportswriters in baseball, but one who could hold a grudge if he did not like you, as was the case with Allen. Holtzman continued to criticize Dick for "abandoning" the White Sox. He even enlisted the support of team physician Dr. Gerald Loftus, who claimed "Richie Allen was healed well enough to finish the season."[57] But that's not what Dick's physician told him.

"When I went to my own doctor for a second opinion he said the leg was broken," Allen insisted:

> I was told the fibula—the bone that was fractured—took away my lateral movement. Said I'd be out eight weeks, easy. But I returned after four, trying to make it back. Like another time, when I had a bad shoulder and they put me out in left field where I made an ass out of myself, lobbing the ball in underhand.

Referring to the Chicago team physician, Allen added: "I can't talk about aches and pains to someone who doesn't know what it's like to be hurt and still try to play major league baseball so I just walk away."[58]

The 1974 season did not begin well for Allen. "Things didn't feel right from the start," Dick recalled. "I felt confused, disoriented, but mostly depressed. My baseball career was slipping through my fingers."[59] Although he arrived early to spring training, Dick told the sportswriters he would not be joining the team until mid-March. His left leg was still bothering him, so he would return to his farm in Perkasie and prepare for the season on his own. When he did return to Sarasota, it was only long enough to make six plate appearances, which did not sit well with the Chicago scribes or the fans.[60]

On Opening Day (April 5), Allen was repeatedly booed by the fans whenever he came to the plate. Going 0-for-4 made matters worse. The Chisox lost the opener to the California Angels 8-2. But there was some comic relief. Despite the 37°F temperature, the game was repeatedly interrupted by nude fans streaking across the field, a custom that had recently exploded among college students. The most hilarious incident occurred in the third inning when a nude man sporting a plastic red souvenir Sox batting helmet lost his head wear as he was being chased by security. After he retrieved the helmet, the reveler did a handstand, flashing his bare buttocks to the crowd of more than 30,000 spectators. Somersaulting to his feet, he was finally apprehended. Appreciative of his efforts, several female fans in the upper deck cheered and flashed their breasts at him while a drunken fist fight broke out nearby.[61]

The White Sox would go on to lose six of their first seven games. Allen, who hit just .129 during that stretch, was excoriated by the Chicago press, with Jerome Holtzman leading the pack.[62]

Holtzman criticized Allen for not earning the $225,000 salary the Sox were paying him, and that he was "just going through the motions" instead.[63] Other writers

Despite rumors that manager Chuck Tanner and Dick had a falling out in 1974, the two remained close friends long after their years together in Chicago. *Photo by Leo Bauby. Courtesy of the Chicago Baseball Museum*

caught on and attacked Dick for "spending more time at the racetrack than at the ballpark," being a "cancer in the clubhouse," and "not delivering in the clutch."[64] Although Allen raised his batting average 180 points to .309 in May, and another twenty-one points to .330 in June, the sportswriters did not back off.[65]

Chuck Tanner had become as disgusted with the press as his premier slugger. "Just because you read it somewhere doesn't necessarily make it true," the Sox manager told the *Christian Science Monitor*'s Phil Elderkin in a June 1974 column. "I think Allen has taken a bad rap in the press, and that he doesn't deserve it. I think he's the best ballplayer I've ever seen, and when his playing career is over, I think he'll be a great manager if he decides to do that."

Disputing the charge that Allen was a divisive force in the clubhouse, Tanner insisted Dick was a "great teammate." "You'd be amazed at the number of kids on this ball club that he's helped," he added. "And he doesn't wait to be asked. He just goes to a kid who is struggling and helps him with his hitting."[66]

Third baseman Bill Melton maintained that the sportswriters' attack on Allen in spring 1973 was the only time it happened in Dick's three years in the Windy City. "Generally, the Chicago sportswriters were in awe of Dick because he did things that they'd never seen before," Melton insisted:

> He'd go hit these monster home runs, but he never took batting practice. He'd show up thirty minutes before game time, no batting practice, and you'd see him shadow boxing with Pat Kelly in the clubhouse. Then he'd go 3-for-4 in the game. The writers just couldn't wrap their heads around the notion that any ballplayer could do that. Nor could they understand why Dick was more thrilled with knocking the opposing shortstop over with a hard line drive than driving the ball 500 feet or more. Things were just different with him.[67]

In addition to the bad press, Allen found himself in an ongoing feud with a new teammate, Ron Santo. Santo, who played most of his illustrious career with the crosstown Cubs, was one of the first players to invoke the so-called five-and-ten rule, which held that any player with ten years in the majors and five with the same team had the right to determine where he was traded. When the Cubs tried to trade Santo to the California Angels, the veteran blocked the deal and ended up with the Chisox. Subsequently, the rule was nicknamed the "Santo Clause." Roland Hemond helped to engineer the trade so Santo could remain in Chicago and finish his long career by playing a final season for the White Sox.[68]

Dick had emerged as the team's leader in 1972, not by choice, but by example. But Santo tried to usurp that role when he arrived. The underhandedness did not bother Dick as much as the manner in which the former Cubs star tried to assert his authority. Instead of encouraging the younger players by mentoring them, like

Allen did, Santo tried to motivate by being openly critical. Dick sat by and said nothing until the middle of the season, when Santo began picking on second baseman Jorge Orta.

Orta was a young Mexican player whom Allen took under his wing. He was a sensitive individual who reminded Dick of himself as a young player. "I worked on that boy's confidence for two seasons," recalled the Chisox slugger in his autobiography. "I did it quietly, picking the right spots to build him up and the proper time to let him know when he screwed up."

One day Orta booted a grounder at second and Santo, who was playing third, tore into him. Between innings Dick approach the third baseman and asked, "Hey, how long you been in the big leagues?

"Fourteen years," replied Santo.

Era Allen joins her son on the set of "The Dick Allen Show." When Dick was asked to identify the best hitter he had ever seen, he responded, "my mother." Era quickly defended herself, insisting she "never gave a whipping that he didn't deserve." *Courtesy of the Allen Family*

Dick's official White Sox portrait. *Courtesy of the National Baseball Hall of Fame and Library, Cooperstown, NY*

"You ever screw up over those fourteen years?"

"Yeah," said the former Cub.

"Well, this is only Jorge's third season in the big leagues," Allen pointed out. "He's still learning. But he's going to be a good one. Instead of yelling at him, why don't you teach him a few things?"

Speechless, Santo just turned his back and walked away. Afterward the tension between the two veterans spread to the clubhouse. "We stopped being a team," Dick admitted. "I was still hitting the ball, but we weren't winning, and we weren't having fun."

Finally manager Chuck Tanner called Allen and Santo into his office and told them their feud was "ruining the team." "There's only room for one guy to run this team, and that's me," Tanner barked.[69]

Despite the turmoil, Dick put up MVP-like numbers in '74. He also continued to hit prodigious home runs. On July 6, at Detroit's Tiger Stadium, Allen lined a

Dick, a fan favorite, accommodates some autograph seekers. *Photo by Leo Bauby. Courtesy of the Chicago Baseball Museum*

Fans declare their loyalty to Dick with a homemade banner hung over the left field wall at Comiskey Park. *Photo by Leo Bauby. Courtesy of the Chicago Baseball Museum*

homer off the roof facade in deep left center field. The ball traveled 415 feet at an altitude of eighty-five feet. Anecdotal and mathematical evidence agreed the clout would have easily cleared some 530 feet on the fly.[70] Allen would hit five more homers before the All-Star break, two of them traveling 450 feet or more.[71]

Whatever problems White Sox fans had with Dick at the beginning of the season were forgotten by July, when Allen was voted to the All-Star Game as the American League's starting first baseman. Played at Pittsburgh's Three Rivers Stadium on July 23, the midsummer classic was dominated by the National League, but Allen did not disappoint his fans: he slapped an RBI single to left field to put the American League ahead 2-1. It was the last run they would get as the Nationals went on to win 7-2. The American League manager Dick Williams lifted Allen shortly after his RBI single, saying the Chisox slugger fouled a pitch off his foot during his first at bat and it was hurting him.[72]

Despite making the All-Star team for the third time in as many years, Allen grew so unhappy in Chicago that he considered retirement. His resentment for Santo had grown so strong that he purposely avoided him. In addition, Dick was playing in pain. Not only was he suffering from a serious shoulder injury, but he had severely strained his right Achilles tendon, and the left leg he had injured the previous year was acting up, as was his lower back.[73] With the Sox mired in fifth place and eleven games out, there was no reason for him to continue with the season.

On September 14, Allen called together his teammates and announced his decision to retire. "This is hard for me to say," he began, trying to choke back the tears. "I've never been happier anywhere than here. You're still going to be a good ball club without me." Now, with the tears welling in his eyes, he paused for a moment to collect himself. "It's tough to walk away from the game I've been playing since I was this high," he concluded, gesturing to the floor with his hand. Then he turned and walked away.[74]

"There were a few reasons for Dick's retirement," said Melton:

> He *did* have a problem with Ron Santo because he thought Santo was a "showboater." But their feud was on the field when Santo started yelling at the younger players. It didn't infect the clubhouse, though. Second, Dick was hurt, so he couldn't help the team. Finally, we were out of contention and he just didn't see the sense in hanging around. Dick had become bored with baseball, so he decided it was time to hang it up. That's just the way he was when he got bored with anything.[75]

In a recent interview, Hall of Fame pitcher Goose Gossage was less subtle in his explanation of why Allen left the team:

> Dick refused to play politics. What you see is what you get with him. He is the most honest person I know.
>
> Dick hated all the bullshit in the game, whether it was the sensationalist reporting of the sportswriters, his differences with Ron Santo, being told one thing by management and then seeing them do another; whatever it was Dick knew when people were lying to him. If you did that he lost all respect for you.[76]

Although Allen had not played since September 8, he managed to clout thirty-two home runs, enough to win the American League home run crown. He also led the American League in slugging (.563) and OPS (.938).[77]

Dick on deck on his final road trip with the White Sox in 1974. *Photo by Doug McWilliams. Courtesy of the National Baseball Hall of Fame and Museum, Cooperstown, NY*

Dick removes his batting gloves. *Artwork courtesy of Rob Larsen*

Said Kevin Hurley, a life-long White Sox fan:

> To compile those kinds of stats in an abbreviated season was amazing. It makes you wonder what he could've accomplished had he finished the season. Allen hit a ball harder than anyone I've seen. His home runs were line drive shots that kept rising even after it left the park. That kind of power is truly exceptional. It's just too bad he didn't play longer here.[78]

Dick's decision to leave the team with two weeks remaining in the season strained his relations with White Sox owner John Allyn and Roland Hemond, one of his strongest supporters in the front office. His ongoing feud with Santo had also created a rift between him and Chuck Tanner.[79] Those strained relationships would eventually heal in the future, but for now there were hard feelings on both sides, especially when Allen failed to file his official retirement papers with the league office.[80] The organization's parting shot came on December 3, when they sold Dick's contract to the Atlanta Braves for just $5,000.[81]

Dick Allen at bat, 1975. *Artwork courtesy of Rob Larsen*

CHAPTER 7:
RETURN TO PHILLY

Allen returned to his farm in Perkasie, Pennsylvania, in September 1974, intending to pursue another passion—raising thoroughbred horses. Although he had informed the White Sox he was "retiring," he never submitted a written statement to management, making his official status unclear. Having batted .302 with thirty-two homers the previous season, the thirty-two-year-old slugger certainly seemed to have a lot of baseball left in him. When the Atlanta Braves gave the White Sox $5,000 for the negotiating rights to Allen at the winter baseball meetings in New Orleans, there was at least one suitor for his services. That is, until the enigmatic slugger informed the Braves he "would never agree to play in the South again after the horrific experience [he] had in Little Rock as a Phillies' farmhand." At the same time Allen did suggest that he "might be interested in returning to Philadelphia."[1]

In 1975, Phillies general manager Paul Owens signed Allen to mentor young power hitters Mike Schmidt and Greg Luzinski. *Courtesy of the National Baseball Hall of Fame and Library, Cooperstown, NY*

While Allen's remark might have shocked the baseball world, it intrigued the Phillies' general manager Paul Owens, who was looking for a veteran power hitter to take some pressure off his two young, homegrown sluggers, Mike Schmidt and Greg Luzinski. Allen just might provide the veteran leadership the young club needed to become a perennial contender.

Between 1965 and 1972, Owens, as Phillies' farm director, rebuilt the organization's player development and scouting systems, making them among the very best in Major League Baseball. In the process he developed a homegrown nucleus of players who would make the Phillies competitive for years to come:

Larry Bowa, a temperamental shortstop from Sacramento, California; Greg Luzinski, a slugging outfielder/first baseman who turned down a football scholarship to Notre Dame to sign with Philadelphia; Bob Boone, a third baseman and Stanford graduate whose father once played for the Cleveland Indians; and Mike Schmidt, a power-hitting shortstop from Ohio University who would become the cornerstone of the team. The Phils made the Bobcat All-American their second-round pick in the June 1971 amateur draft.

Phillies team logo 1971–1992. *Courtesy of the Philadelphia Phillies Baseball Club*

In 1972, Owens assumed the dual responsibilities of the club's general manager and field manager to determine which players had a future with the organization. At the end of the season, he knew he had one of the game's most dominant pitchers in Steve Carlton, a twenty-seven-game winner who accounted for nearly 46% of the Phillies' fifty-nine victories that season; a fine defensive shortstop in Bowa; and an emerging cleanup hitter in Luzinski—but precious little else. Owens also realized that Schmidt, who had converted to third base, and Boone, who had converted to catcher, were ready for the big leagues. So he hired Danny Ozark, a longtime Dodgers coach known for his emphasis on the fundamentals, as his manager and went back upstairs to make the trades necessary to contend for a pennant.[2] In 1973, Schmidt joined the other homegrown prospects in the starting lineup. Although he demonstrated flashes of brilliance during his rookie year, the reserved third baseman struggled with the burden of high expectations. His breakout came the following year. Playing in all 162 games, Schmidt hit thirty-six homers and 116 RBIs to emerge as one of the top sluggers in the National League. But he still lacked the confidence and the experience to be a truly great player.[3]

Schmidt, Bowa, Luzinski, and Boone were all about the same age. They were also jealous of each other's talent, and too inexperienced to provide the kind of leadership the young club needed. In addition, none of them had any postseason experience. Nor did they know how to navigate the pressures of a pennant race. Only Carlton, the Phils' twenty-eight-year-old ace, had that kind of experience, having pitched in the postseason with the St. Louis Cardinals in 1967 and again in 1968. Owens would have to trade for veteran experience to complement his young but extremely talented core.

To solidify the bullpen, the Phils general manager acquired closer Tug McGraw from the New York Mets. McGraw, at twenty-nine, had also pitched in the postseason. He was a colorful character with a zany sense of humor. His antics kept the clubhouse loose and his example taught the young Phillies how to enjoy the game.[4]

While Carlton and McGraw contributed to the club's success on the mound, the Phillies really needed an everyday veteran player to provide day-to-day leadership. Owens filled the void by trading for Dave Cash, a scrappy veteran second baseman from the Pittsburgh Pirates, a team that captured three division titles, a pennant, and a World Series title between 1970 and 1972. Cash knew what it was like to win, and his enthusiasm, experience, and aggressive play gave the Phillies the confidence they needed to do so. He even coined the phrase "Yes We Can!," which became the team's mantra in 1974, when the Phils finally escaped the basement of the Eastern Division to finish third.[5] By 1975, the only missing piece was a veteran power hitter who could solidify the heart of the batting order and mentor the young sluggers Schmidt and Luzinski. Owens believed Dick Allen could fill that role.

In April 1975, Owens sent Cash, Schmidt, and Rich Ashburn, the star centerfielder of the 1950 pennant-winning Phillies and now a broadcaster for the team, on a mission to gauge Dick Allen's interest in returning to Philadelphia. Allen recalled:

Second baseman Dave Cash was acquired by the Phillies from the Pittsburgh Pirates. His enthusiasm and example inspired younger teammates to believe in themselves and in Cash's slogan, "Yes We Can!" *Photo by Doug McWilliams. Courtesy of the National Baseball Hall of Fame and Library, Cooperstown, NY*

Dick returned to the Phillies on May 7, 1975. After a press conference, he showed off his 40-oz. bat to the delight of the Phils' owner Ruly Carpenter (left), general manager Paul Owens (center), and manager Danny Ozark (partially obstructed). *Photo by Michael J. Maicher,* Philadelphia Evening Bulletin. *Courtesy of Temple University Libraries, Philadelphia, PA*

It was a conversation I wouldn't forget. Schmidt was talking about the Phils needing some additional clout, a big stick in the line up to go with his and Luzinski's. He said something about "Schmidt-Luzinski-Allen firepower." Cash [who was African American] was rapping about the brothers on the Phils' team and how they could use a veteran to inspire them. And ol' Richie Ashburn was telling tales about how much the city of Philadelphia had changed for the better.[6]

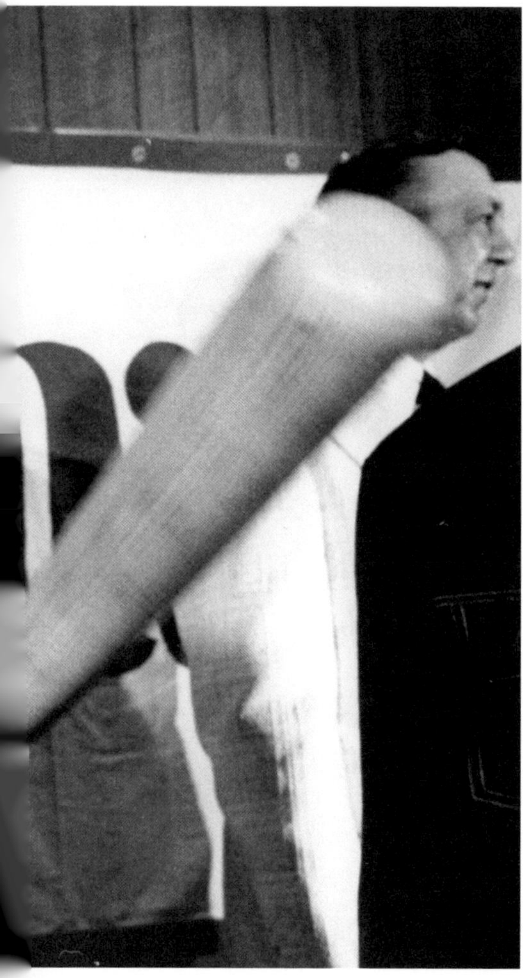

Ashburn was only partially correct. Philadelphia still struggled with race relations, but baseball was enjoying a renaissance in the city. There was no more Connie Mack Stadium. Instead, the Phillies played in the brand-new Veterans Stadium. The crowds were suburban and white. There was a new owner in Ruly Carpenter, who seemed more compassionate and approachable than his father was in the 1960s. Conditions seemed right for a reconciliation and, with a little luck, the pennant that Allen desired. In fact, leaks to the press that the Phillies were courting Allen were greeted with great enthusiasm by a new generation of fans who cared little about his controversial departure from the team in 1969.[7] Allen was a bona fide slugger without a team. That was all that mattered to them. Still, Allen admitted he was surprised by the overture:

> At first I figured it had to be a joke. It's not my style to return to the scene of the crime. But I had to admit the idea of coming home did fire me up a bit. I was touched to feel wanted by guys who played for the Phillies. When Cash, Schmidt, and Ashburn left that day I hugged them all.

That visit was followed by another in late April from Ashburn and Robin Roberts, the ace of the 1950 Phillies. Again, the team attempted to reconcile with their former Rookie of the Year. "No specific requests were made and no promises given," insists Allen.[8] A few days later, the *Philadelphia Inquirer* reported that Commissioner Bowie Kuhn was investigating the Phillies for tampering with the retired slugger.[9] Allen had no intention of playing for the Atlanta Braves, who purchased his contract from the White Sox. He would never return to the Deep South, not after the painful experience of Triple A ball in Little Rock, Arkansas. The Braves eventually accepted that fact. On May 7, after Kuhn dismissed the tampering charges, Atlanta dealt the veteran first baseman to the Phillies along with catcher Johnny Oates for young backstop Jim Essian and outfielder Barry Bonnell.[10]

Fans, sportswriters, and even the Phillies themselves began talking about winning the pennant. But Allen downplayed the popular expectation at a press conference the following day, insisting he was "no messiah" and that his primary goal was to "entertain the fans." Referring to his troubled early career with the Phillies, the veteran slugger said, "I'm not anticipating any trouble. I've learned a lot through my journeys. There's a lot of difference between the man I am now and the boy I was back then."[11]

Allen's decision to return to Philadelphia shocked the baseball world. To those who really knew him, though, it was consistent with his approach to the game. His career had always been distinguished by "predictable unpredictability." But two things were certain: Allen was blessed with the exceptional talent of a superstar, and at the age of thirty-three, he still had not realized his full potential. Instead, his career was troubled by an odd assortment of injuries and an inability to cope with people who had difficulty understanding him.[12] Perhaps a second chance in Philadelphia is what he needed. He admitted in a 2001 interview:

> Sure, I was excited about coming back to Philly. Back in the 1960s, I think I represented a threat to white people there. I wore my hair in an Afro. I said what was on my mind. I did my own thing. And I'll admit that I was something of a jerk. But in 1975, it was different.
>
> I saw players like Dave Cash, who represented a new generation of talented black ballplayers. They were proud of their playing abilities and sure weren't going to take a back seat to anybody. So the race thing wasn't an issue anymore.
>
> In terms of pure baseball, those Phillies had one of the best infields in the game with Schmidt at third, Cash at second, Bowa at short, and Boone behind the plate. I thought I could make a pretty solid contribution at first base. We also had the starting pitching to contend with, guys like Carlton and Jim Lonborg, and McGraw in the bullpen. Sure, I was excited about the possibilities.[13]

Not everyone was excited about Allen's return. Ozark, who coached Allen during his one-year stint with the Los Angeles Dodgers, had serious reservations about the kind of influence the new first baseman would bring to his young club. Shortly after the deal was made, the Phils' manager, usually known for his relaxed approach, instituted five team rules that he swore to enforce and distributed them in the clubhouse:

Players are to be in their rooms two hours after the team bus leaves the ballpark during road trips after a night game and midnight after a day game.

The manager controls alcoholic beverages on team flights and no beverage of any type will be taken out of the clubhouse.

All players must be on the bench five minutes before the game starts.

All players—except the starting pitcher—must be on the field for infield practice.

All players must report to the ballpark by the time the team bus arrives on the road and at posted times when the team is at home.[14]

It was no coincidence the rules targeted areas of personal behavior that Allen broke repeatedly throughout his career: drinking beer during games; arriving late to the ballpark, or not at all; and routinely breaking curfew. When sportswriter Bill Conlin of the *Philadelphia Daily News* pointed out the rules seemed to contradict his usually "laid back" style of managing, Ozark replied, "If my head's going to roll I want to be the one who rolls it."[15]

Tommy Hutton, who served as Allen's backup at first base, recalled that

> Danny did have some reservations about Dick coming to Philadelphia because of his "Bad Boy" reputation, but those concerns proved to be unfounded.
>
> In fact, Dick was a great teammate. I personally enjoyed talking about hitting with him. His knowledge fascinated me.[16]

Manager Danny Ozark knew Allen from 1971, when he was the Los Angeles Dodgers' third base coach. *Courtesy of the Allen Family*

Allen returned to the Phillies' lineup on May 14, in a home game against the Cincinnati Reds. It was a hero's homecoming. Before the game he was reunited with his close friend, Pete Cera, the assistant clubhouse manager, who presented him with a brand new uniform that bore his trademark No. 15. Allen had developed a close friendship with Cera in the minor leagues when he was experiencing the turmoil of racial discrimination. The slugger nicknamed him "Mother Cera" because Cera was always checking up on him, taking care of his needs, and lending a sympathetic ear whenever he needed it. As the two men embraced, the Phillies' prodigal son promised the clubhouse attendant it was "My turn to take care of you."[17] On the playing field, Allen was greeted just as warmly.

As the Phillies were taking the field, a few members of the grounds crew, finishing up their work on the base paths, yelled out, "Hey 15! Welcome back!" "We didn't expect any response," said Mark Carfagno, a member of the crew, "but he turned our way and said, 'Thanks.' After that, he referred to us as his 'Gang.'"[18] Allen's new teammates also embraced him. The energy level in the club seemed to soar. The fans were even more receptive, almost patronizing. After singling to center in his first at bat, Allen received a tremendous ovation. Although he failed to reach base again, going 1-for-3, the Phils defeated the Reds 4-0.[19] The lovefest continued for the next three weeks. If Allen made a miscue —as he did several times, having missed spring training —it was excused. He was cheered constantly for regular defensive plays and routine fly ball outs, even though he was in the middle of a .233 slump—a career low. Perhaps the most exaggerated expression of fan appreciation came in a May 26 game against San Francisco. After struggling all evening against Giant pitching, Allen, in the tenth inning, hit a sharp liner that was misplayed by third baseman Ed Goodson. When the winning run scored on the error, the Phillies' faithful erupted in applause and demanded a curtain call from their new hero.[20]

Even the press was friendly. Allen found himself glibly answering the questions of sportswriters he had once refused to speak with. Now they were a band of admirers toting pads and pencils, hanging on his every word. Six years earlier the press had run Allen out of town, steadfastly calling him "Richie," knowing fully that he found the name denigrating because it sounded childlike. Instead, he had repeatedly requested he be referred to as "Dick Allen." Now they graciously complied with the request.[21]

While all the media hype unfolded, owner Ruly Carpenter, who understood the fickle nature of the local media, stood watching, praying the sportswriters would not run the slugger out of town again. "I hope to hell they leave him alone," he said quietly as he listened to an early press interview. "I could never understand why they got on him so when he was here before."[22]

Mark "Froggy" Carfagno, a member of the Phillies grounds crew, became one of Dick Allen's closest friends after he returned to Philadelphia. *Courtesy of Mark Carfagno*

The scoreboard at Veterans Stadium welcomed Dick back to Philadelphia on May 14, 1975, when he played his first game as a Phillie since 1969. *Photo by Salvatore C. DiMarco Jr.*, Philadelphia Evening Bulletin. *Courtesy of Temple University Libraries, Philadelphia, PA*

Carpenter stated in a recent interview:

> Dick was a serious, dedicated athlete, he was a great team player, and he really never did anything you could consider "bad" for the game of baseball when you consider some of today's players. Hell, he behaved better than some of the greatest players of all time. Babe Ruth was drunk virtually every night. He whored around like mad, set a lousy example for kids, and there was never a bad word written about him. Dick would show up late for a practice once and the sportswriters would crucify him. It just wasn't fair.[23]

Philadelphia's Veterans Stadium seemed like an ideal park for Allen. It was one of the concrete, multipurpose stadiums that had become popular in many cities in the 1970s. While it lacked the physical intimacy and quirky dimensions of the older concrete and steel ballparks, the "Vet" was a hitter's park, much more conducive to hitting home runs than Chicago's cavernous Comiskey Park. The distance from home plate to center field was only 408 feet, whereas it was 330 feet down both foul lines—

easily short of Allen's average home run distances. The Vet also sported artificial turf that allowed Dick, who was never known for his defense, to play deeper, and the density of the fabric meant there was little chance of the ball taking a bad hop. The artificial surface also provided much better traction than natural grass, something that allowed him to double his stolen base totals from the previous two seasons. The only drawback of artificial turf for an aging player like Allen was that it retained and reflected heat, and in the dead of a Philadelphia summer on the field, day game temperatures at the Vet could rise as high as 140°F, sapping his energy.[24]

But Allen's struggles at the plate continued into the month of June. His offensive woes were due to a weak Achilles tendon in his right leg. He was spiked there during his final season in Chicago and, though he had the tendon surgically repaired, it was still painful for him to play. A torn Achilles is the death knell for a power hitter, who relies on his legs to generate the force he needs to drive the ball long distances. Allen was a right-handed hitter, and his ability to hit home runs was due in part to planting his back (right) foot in the batter's box and driving it into the ground. After tearing his Achilles, Dick could no longer do that, though he never used it as an excuse. Nor did he ever inform the Phillies of the ongoing problem.[25] The injury would plague him for the remainder of his career, severely diminishing his ability to hit with power.

Hampered by the weak Achilles, Allen hit just .233 with four home runs in his first fifty games. In July, his batting average dipped to .220 and he hit just one home run. There were flashes of his former self, though. On June 8, Dick crushed a pair of home runs to help Steve Carlton defeat the Dodgers 4-0 at the Vet.[26] In an August 22 game against the San Diego Padres, Allen went 3-for-4 with a single, double, and a tape measure home run into the seldom-reached upper deck at San Diego's Jack Murphy Stadium, pacing the Phils to a 6-5 win.[27] Occasions like that gave the Phillies and their fans hope that Dick could once again become a feared slugger, though he had become a liability in the field. Allen lacked the defensive range he once enjoyed and had trouble digging balls out of the dirt; an imperative for a first baseman.[28] The team was also underachieving.

Despite a hugely talented roster that featured both 1974 home run champions (Schmidt and Allen), two former Cy Young Award winners (Carlton and Lonborg), and the best second base/shortstop combination in the game (Cash and Bowa), the Phillies just could not put it all together, slumping down the stretch. At season's end, Allen was hitting .233 with a total of twelve home runs and sixty-two RBIs. Worse, he struck out 109 times in 416 at bats.[29] Owens blamed the mediocre performance

The 40-oz. bat used by Dick 1973–1975. *Courtesy of the Allen Family*

Philadelphia's Veterans Stadium ca. 1975. *Courtesy of the National Baseball Hall of Fame and Library, Cooperstown, NY*

on the fact that Allen had a long layoff, missing all of spring training, and re-signed him for the 1976 campaign.[30]

At the same time, Allen's presence in the batting order behind Schmidt, who hit third, and Luzinski, who hit cleanup, enabled the two power hitters to see more fastballs. Opposing pitchers knew they could not pitch around Schmidt because Luzinski followed him, and they couldn't pitch around the Bull because Allen came next. As a result, Schmidt captured his second straight National League home run crown with thirty-eight round-trippers, and Luzinski clinched the league's RBI title with 120. Still, the Phillies finished second, 6½ games behind the Pittsburgh Pirates, in the National League's Eastern Division. It was the team's first winning season in eight years, and expectations were high entering the next season.[31]

"I owe the Phillies something," said Allen. "I'm thirty-three years old and maybe I can't do the same things guys like Greg Luzinski, Mike Schmidt, and some of the others can do. But I swear I feel as young as those guys. That's what makes me want to play."[32]

Determined to make good on his promise, Allen arrived early to spring training in 1976. No longer plagued by the strained Achilles in his right leg, the thirty-four-year-old veteran worked hard and for long hours, and it paid off. He batted .294 and

struck out just once in seventeen plate appearances during the exhibition season. "I don't know how Dick feels about it," said manager Danny Ozark, "but he impressed the hell out of me." Allen admitted it was "a lot easier to hit on two good legs," and that spring training was "fun," except for one thing: the sudden and unexpected death of his close friend and agent, Clem Cappozzoli. "Dick was so happy and outgoing before Clem's death," observed Ozark. "Now he's quiet and withdrawn. No doubt it was a terrible shock. Clem was like a father to Dick, and it may take him a while to get over it."[33] Cappozolli's death had a profound impact on Allen.

While the Phillies did not seem to lose during the first few months of the 1976 campaign, Allen's performance was worse than the previous year's. Ten games into April Ozark replaced him with Tommy Hutton, a better defensive first baseman. "Don't get me wrong," said Hutton in a recent interview:

> I liked Dick a lot, but I can't say that I was disappointed when Danny benched him, especially after the limited playing time I had the previous season. Actually, it was kind of funny.
>
> Danny came up to me in early June '75 and said, "I'm giving Dick a rest tomorrow, so you're playing first." The next day before I left for the Vet I told my wife to get there early because I was playing.
>
> Well, I walked into the clubhouse, checked out the line up, and there's Dick's name hitting fifth and playing first. I found Danny and asked what was going on. He told me that Dick came in that afternoon and said he wanted to play.
>
> I understood it the first time, but after it happened again I told Danny, "Forget it, I don't want to know when I'm playing. Just let it be a surprise."[34]

To Hutton's benefit, Allen's playing time waned over the remainder of the month. When Dick returned to the lineup on a regular basis in May, Allen was dropped from fifth to seventh in the batting order.[35] Dejected, he found other ways to be useful to the club. He spent time mentoring his younger teammates, especially Mike Schmidt, who was at a critical juncture in his career. Like Allen in the mid-1960s, Schmidt in 1975 had superstar potential but an extremely sensitive ego. Both men were natural athletes in the truest sense of the term. Both were blessed with muscular, athletic builds. Both were power hitters with high strikeout ratios. And both were forced to labor under the unrealistic expectations of the Philadelphia fans and the local media.

The two teammates quickly realized the similarities and often expressed their respect for the other. Recalled Schmidt:

> Growing up I admired Dick Allen. I pretended I was like him when I was up at bat playing Legion ball in Dayton, Ohio. I was fortunate we became good friends on the Phillies and that I learned a lot from him.[36]

Allen would help the young slugger learn to cope with the intrusive press, the fickle fans, and the impossible expectations they had for their star players. He was really the only person who could do that, having experienced it himself six years earlier. "Schmidt had as much talent as anybody I've ever seen play the game," said Allen of his younger teammate. "Quick wrists, strong, perfect baseball body. But he battled the strikeout because he was trying to hit every pitch out of the park, and when he didn't he'd sulk about it."[37]

Like all prodigious power hitters, Schmidt battled the strikeout. As much as he was revered for his ability to produce home runs, he struggled to become a better hitter. His statistics over the previous three years reflected the severity of the problem. In 1973, his rookie year, Schmidt hit eighteen home runs, batted a career low .196, and struck out 136 times in 367 plate appearances. The following year, he led the National League with thirty-six homers and improved his average by nearly 100

Mike Schmidt credited Allen with mentoring him during the early years of his career. *Courtesy of the National Baseball Hall of Fame and Library, Cooperstown, NY*

points (batting .282), but also continued to lead the league in strikeouts with 138. In 1975, Schmidt's home run production increased to thirty-eight, but his strikeout total jumped to 180 and his average dropped to .249. The frustration began to mount.[38]

Allen noted:

> When I went to Philly in '75, Mike didn't seem to be hitting for average. I talked to him about swinging down on the ball. That's the ticket for a good hitter, and Schmitty picked up on it pretty quickly.
>
> The other thing about him was his attitude. Mike was moody, and if he had a bad game, he'd take it home with him. I used to take him out after a game for a couple beers and we'd talk about things, have a few laughs, put the ballyard behind us. I used to tell Schmitty to pretend he was back on the sandlots of Dayton, where

Dick often stood outside the batting cage, offering hitting tips to his younger teammates. *Courtesy of the Allen Family*

> he grew up. Get out there and bang that ball like you did in high school. He began to get the message.[39]

Schmidt was mired in a slump at the beginning of the 1976 season. The harder he pressed, the less success he had. Ozark tried to break the slump by hitting the struggling third baseman in the lead-off spot, believing he would be forced to take more pitches there. It didn't work. Then, at the suggestion of Rich Ashburn, a former Phillies' star and one-time batting leader, Ozark dropped Schmidt to the sixth slot, where he could take pitches just as easily and also drive in some runs.[40] The change was made on April 17, before the first contest of a three-game series against the Cubs at Chicago's Wrigley Field. It was a beautiful but windy spring day, a hitter's day. Before the game Allen pulled Schmidt aside. "Mike, you've got to relax," he said. "You've got to have some fun. Remember when you were a kid and you'd skip supper to play ball? You were having fun. And with all the talent you've got baseball ought to be fun. Enjoy it. Be a kid again."[41]

Schmidt took the advice to heart. He put on an impressive display of firepower. After a fourth inning single, he homered in each of his next four at bats. Two of the home runs—a two-run shot in the fifth inning and a solo homer in the seventh—came off Cub starter Rick Reuschel. The third home run came in the eighth inning, a three-run shot off the right-handed reliever Mike Garman. With the game tied 16-16 in the tenth, Schmidt stepped to the plate again and drilled a Paul Reuschel fastball into the left field bleachers for his fourth home run of the game. The Phillies went on to win the contest 18-16, as Schmidt became the tenth player in major league history to collect four homers in a single game.[42] After that the Phillies could not seem to lose for the next three months, and Schmidt's bat was at the heart of their success. "Dick was like the wise soothsayer of the team," recalled Schmidt:

> He just had this way of inspiring the younger guys with his knowledge of the game as well as his counsel. The day I hit those four homers at Wrigley [Field] was a perfect example of his wisdom. He knew I was pressing and that I needed to relax, to have fun again. And he was right.[43]

The Phillies pitcher Larry Christenson, a twenty-one-year-old starter, was also the beneficiary of Allen's counsel:

> After a rough inning I'd be in the dugout and Dick would come up to me. He would put his hand on my shoulder and say, "Kid, you've got good stuff tonight. Stay with it and they won't touch you!"

Allen hits a home run against the Cincinnati Reds in a June 24, 1976, game at Cincinnati's Riverfront Stadium. The Phillies won the game 5-4. *Photo by Bob Bartosz. Courtesy of the National Baseball Hall of Fame and Library, Cooperstown, NY*

> Not often, but once in a while when he could tell I was pressing, Dick would come out to the mound and remind me to "stay strong" and to "pound the hitters inside." It was always short and to the point, but he just made me feel so confident about my ability that I didn't want to let him down.[44]

Perhaps the highlight of Allen's season came on June 25, in a home game against the St. Louis Cardinals. By that time, Ozark was platooning him at first base with Bobby Tolan, but the rest allowed the veteran slugger to raise his average near the .300 mark. Returning to his old form, Allen went 2-for-3 with two homers and four RBIs, bringing the hometown fans to their feet with a standing ovation.[45] It was his last brush with glory, though. In July Allen slumped, struggling to maintain a .250 average. Ozark tried to take the pressure off by dropping him from the fifth to the seventh slot in the batting order, but it didn't help.[46] Age had caught up with the Wampum Walloper. No longer was he the feared slugger of just a few years earlier. Then he began to have problems off the field.

On July 25, Allen was injured in a collision at first base with Pirate pitcher John Candelaria. Complaining of dizziness, he phoned Ozark the following afternoon and told him he could not play. Over the next three days, Allen appeared in uniform once and played just three innings before leaving the stadium. The other two nights he didn't bother to show up, nor did he phone to tell anyone he wasn't playing. Ozark called a team meeting and informed his players that Allen went AWOL. In a subsequent press conference, the Phils' skipper announced that Allen would be fined for his unexcused absences, but days later Ozark changed his position. Rescinding the fine, he told the press that the first baseman was injured and would be placed on the disabled list.[47]

On August 10, the day his disabled stint was scheduled to end, Allen phoned Ozark and told him he was still hurting. He remained sidelined for the next three weeks. When he finally returned to the lineup on September 3 he struggled, unable to help the Phillies, who were trying to fend off the hot second-place Pirates in the National League East. Predictably, the sportswriters and fans began to evoke the ghosts of 1964 when the Phillies, with a 6½-game lead and twelve left to play, lost ten straight to blow the pennant.[48] As the pressure to win mounted, players' tempers became short. Tension filled the clubhouse as teammates started to blame each other for the losses. When Larry Bowa openly criticized Allen's inability to dig low throws out of the dirt, Dick, who was mired in a 3-for-40 slump, refused to say anything about the criticism to the press. Instead, he confronted Bowa, suggesting he make more accurate throws to first base.[49]

Schmidt recalled in a recent interview:

> To tell you the truth, Dick was extremely valuable in the clubhouse down the stretch. He kept us loose in the infield, clowning around and throwing "down-and-out patterns" to us [during warm-ups] between innings. Dick was always telling guys how good they were, too. That was important because we weren't hitting. Those are the times you need to hear that kind of encouragement because you might be losing confidence in yourself.
>
> I knew he was struggling at the plate, but I didn't care if he never got another hit. Just having Dick with us meant a lot because you knew his mere presence intimidated the other team. They saw him in the lineup. They knew he could hit the ball out of the yard, steal bases, and that put some fear into their pitchers.[50]

Allen was no longer a threat in the Phillies batting order. Shortly after the regular season began, he strained the previously injured Achilles tendon in his right leg. He

1976 Topps baseball card. *Courtesy of The Topps Company Inc.*

kept it a secret. The more he played on the injured leg, the less he was able to hit with power. Owner Ruly Carpenter noted:

> Dick still had tremendous bat speed but the brute strength was gone. He was just thirty-four years old. That's the prime of a player's career, so we thought Dick would make *the* difference in our lineup hitting behind Schmidt and Bull [Luzinski]. But we were not aware that he reinjured his Achilles. And if you have that problem, it's hard to hit with power. So it was clear to us midway through the [1976] season that Dick was no longer the same [offensive] threat he had been in the past.

Having said that, Carpenter still insisted Allen's "mentoring of his younger teammates, especially Schmidt and Luzinski, was instrumental in helping the Phillies reach the playoffs in 1976."[51]

Allen's impact on Larry Christenson's pitching was also unmistakable. The best years of Christenson's career came between 1975 and 1978, and Dick was his teammate for the first two of those seasons. During that four-year span, the young hurler won fifty-six games, struck out 391 batters, and recorded a 3.66 earned run average. Allen was such an inspiration that Christenson, in a September 5, 1976, game against the New York Mets at Shea Stadium, mustered the courage to use the Wampum Walloper's 40-oz. bat. "Kid, if you can swing it, you can use it," Dick replied, handing him the war club.

Larry Christenson was another young pitcher Dick took under his wing. *Courtesy of Larry Christenson*

Christenson won his own game that afternoon 3-1, belting two home runs against the Mets' Mickey Lolich. Afterward, Allen handed him the bat with the inscription, "To L.C. – Two homers with my bat. How about that! Dick Allen."

Said Christenson:

> When Dick came to Philadelphia he was already a legend and one of the top power hitters in the game. I think all of us were in awe of him. He wasn't a rah-rah guy, didn't say a lot. But when

> he spoke we all listened. He was a very kind and generous teammate and always very positive, very supportive. Just his sheer presence on the team made us better. In that sense, Dick made the difference in getting to the playoffs in 1976, just like Pete Rose got us to the World Series four years later.[52]

Nevertheless, Allen continued to be dogged by controversy. After the Phillies clinched their division on September 26 with a 4-1 victory over the Expos in the first game of a doubleheader at Montreal's Jarry Park, the Philadelphia press went on the attack again.[53] As the team celebrated the division-clinching victory in the visitors' clubhouse, Allen, Cash, Maddox, and Schmidt gathered in a nearby equipment room, where Dick offered a prayer of thanks. Tug McGraw, who was frolicking around the clubhouse dousing his teammates with champagne, noticed the four players were missing from the celebration and made a flippant remark about the "brothers meeting" elsewhere. Some of the other players noticed the absence as well and complained about the "attitude" of their four missing teammates.[54] Afterward, the Phillies headed to St. Louis for their final regular season series and Allen returned to Philadelphia alone. He was mired in a slump and Ozark agreed to let him have the time off, but that is not how the sportswriters reported it.

Bill Conlin of the *Philadelphia Daily News* labeled the small gathering of Allen, Cash, Maddox, and Schmidt the "Broom Closet Incident" and suggested that Allen, who "chose" to fly back to Philadelphia alone, had divided the team along racial lines, just as he had done a decade earlier.[55] Conlin continued to raise the specter of racism over the next two days in his column by selectively quoting Tug McGraw.[56] In fact, Dave Cash insists that "there was nothing racial about the [separate] meeting" and that it "should never have been reported that way by the *Daily News*":

> To set the record straight, yes, we did have a meeting in the back of the clubhouse after the first game of the doubleheader. It was 9:30 at night and it was about 35° outside, too cold to hang out in the dugout. Dick, Garry, Mike, and myself just wanted to get together to thank the good Lord that he had taken us that far. But Conlin purposely misinterpreted the remarks of one teammate [Tug McGraw], which was meant to be taken humorously, and made a racial thing out of it.[57]

Maddox echoed Cash's belief, stating "race never entered [his] mind" when the four players isolated themselves for a prayer meeting. "Somebody's been fooling me this season," added the black center fielder. "I never saw a single race problem all year."[58]

To be sure, Allen, Cash, Maddox, and Schmidt were the core of a small but growing group of Christian athletes on the team.[59] Because of the negative stereotype associated with fundamentalist Christianity among most ballplayers, it would have been logical for them to separate themselves to worship God.[60] While McGraw, who gave new meaning to the term "free spirit," would never be mistaken for a "born again Christian," he certainly was not racist, either. The relief pitcher respected and was genuinely interested in the religious, ethnic, and racial backgrounds of others. "Tug would've never made a racial thing out of that incident," insisted Mike Schmidt in a recent interview. "He wasn't that type of person. He just saw that we were missing [from the clubhouse] and wanted us to be part of the celebration."[61]

What *did* disturb McGraw, a consummate "team player," was the double standard he felt was being created for Allen, specifically allowing the veteran slugger to be excused from traveling with the rest of the club after the Montreal series concluded. When the Phillies arrived in St. Louis on September 27 for a three-game series against the Cardinals, Ozark called a clubhouse meeting to clear the air. Now that the Phillies had clinched their division, he believed it was time to stop all the finger pointing and feuding so the team could focus on the playoffs. During the meeting, McGraw criticized Allen for flying back to Philadelphia. "He makes $250,000 a year," said the reliever. "Doesn't that mean he has a responsibility to be with the team on the road?"[62]

Center fielder Garry Maddox was a member of the small group of Christian athletes on the Phillies who gathered together for a prayer after the team clinched the National League's Eastern Division title in Montreal on September 26, 1976. *Courtesy of the National Baseball Hall of Fame and Library, Cooperstown, NY*

Maddox took exception to the remark. "Why should anybody be upset at Dick's going home?" asked the center fielder. "He got permission from Danny and he told him he could [go home.]"[63]

Years later McGraw was asked about the clubhouse meeting and whether there was a racial divide on the team because of Allen:

> I never saw it as a strictly racial thing. Remember, there were black and white guys on the team who really admired Dick. Schmitty [Mike Schmidt] and Bull were two of his biggest admirers and they're white. Others, like Dave Cash and Garry Maddox, are black. What bothered me was that I felt Dick's independent ways were influencing them, and that wasn't good for the club.[64]

It would be difficult to argue with McGraw. If nothing else, Allen was an independent thinker and doer, and that was a mixed blessing. On one hand, the quality made him fiercely loyal to friends, but on the other, it caused friction with managers and teammates who really did not know him. Perhaps the best illustration of the dichotomy in Allen's personality was his defense of Tony Taylor at the end of the season.

After the Phillies clinched their division, management announced the postseason roster would have to be cut to twenty-five players and Taylor, a forty-two-year-old veteran second baseman, would probably not be eligible for the postseason. The Cuban-born infielder was a fan favorite, having played for the Phillies for fifteen seasons, and had never made it to the playoffs. Allen was furious. He was a close friend of Taylor's, having known him since the mid-1960s, when they were young teammates. Allen fumed:

> To my way of thinking, nothing could be more unfair than to take Tony Taylor's uniform. He played nineteen seasons in the big leagues, but never in a World Series. He was a model player for the Phillies organization, mostly through the club's worst times. He was the one guy who would walk to the box seats and sign autographs before every game. He was the one guy who would volunteer to do a post-game interview when the rest of us were turning our backs on the press. In all his years he never complained. Tony Taylor was Philadelphia Phillies baseball.[65]

Dick took the snub personally. Before he boarded his flight home from Montreal, Allen gave Ozark an ultimatum: he would refuse to play in the postseason unless Taylor was made eligible. When he got back to Philadelphia he went to see owner Ruly Carpenter and told him the same thing.[66] "With God as my witness," Allen vowed, "if you take Tony Taylor's uniform off his back you'll have to take mine, too."[67] It wasn't an idle threat, either. Allen desperately wanted a World Series ring, but it was not going to come at the expense of loyalty to a close friend. Initially, Ozark rejected the demand. "Much as I love Tony Taylor and as much as I'd like to see him play in a World Series," he told the press, "I'm not going to go to one of my pitchers and ask him to sit out."[68] But Carpenter, who wanted Allen's bat in the lineup, hoping he would get hot in the postseason, ordered his manager to keep Taylor on the roster as a coach.[69]

Allen was not happy with the decision, wanting his friend to have an opportunity to play, but Taylor asked him not to challenge management anymore.

Said Taylor years after his playing career ended:

> It really was a dirty deal. I was forty-two years old at the time, but the club could have made room for me. I was happy that they included me as a coach, but it's not the same thing as being a player.

When Tony Taylor (left) was cut from the postseason roster, Allen took the snub personally. The two ballplayers had been close friends since the mid-1960s, when they were teammates with the Phillies. Allen threatened to boycott the playoffs if Taylor was not allowed on the roster. *Photo by George D. McDowell,* Philadelphia Evening Bulletin. *Courtesy of Temple University Libraries, Philadelphia, PA*

> I told Dick, "Look, there's nothing we can do about it. Just go play ball. The team needs you." Then the press made the whole thing into a race issue. I don't think it was. I just think the Phillies wanted to go with younger players.[70]

Ultimately, the decision had little effect on the Phillies' postseason fortunes. They were swept three games to none by the powerful defending World Series champion Cincinnati Reds, who would go on to sweep the New York Yankees in four games for their second straight world championship. Allen hit .222 in the playoffs, collecting just two singles in nine at bats.[71]

Allen was released shortly after the playoffs. In the two seasons since his return to Philadelphia, the veteran first baseman hit just .250, averaging thirteen home runs and fifty-five RBIs each season.[72] Now a free agent, Dick was compelled to negotiate with any club that drafted him according to the rules governing free agency at the time. The

Phillies would have received compensation if two or more teams drafted Allen, but only one team expressed an interest—the Athletics. Dick tried to negotiate with other clubs, hoping to use other offers as leverage with the A's owner Charlie Finley, but no one else wanted him. With no other options, Allen signed a one-year, $150,000 contract to play with Oakland for the 1977 season.[73]

Mike Schmidt (left), Dick Allen, and Greg Luzinski were the heart of the Phillies' batting order in 1975–76. *Artwork courtesy of Dick Perez*

It seemed to be a fitting marriage. Charlie Finley, like Allen, was not only a nonconformist but also the game's greatest showman in the 1970s. Finley distanced himself from baseball's conservative establishment with such zany experiments as orange baseballs and the three-ball walk. He dressed his players in bright colored, mix-and-match Kelly Green and yellow uniforms and white spikes and encouraged them to grow facial and longer hair.[74] The high fashion and permissiveness were appealing to Dick, but even more attractive to him was the fact that the A's had a history of winning, and winning big.

Portrait of Dick Allen, 1976. *Artwork courtesy of Dick Perez*

Between 1972 and 1974, Oakland captured three straight World Series titles, the most dramatic coming in 1972, when they played Cincinnati's more traditional looking "Big Red Machine." The Series was appropriately dubbed the "Hairs vs. Squares."[75] Although Dick's good friend Reggie Jackson had been traded to Baltimore, the A's still had Vida Blue, Billy North, and Rich McKinney from those championship teams, as well as veteran stars like Manny Sanguillen, Willie Crawford, Dave Guisti, and Doc Ellis, who had played on world championship teams in other cities. Oakland also had some young talent, including Tony Armas, Jeff Newman, and Rick Langford. As a result, the Wampum Walloper probably believed he could finally secure the ring that had eluded him for so long.

Encouraged by Finley, Allen donned the letters "W-A-M-P-U-M" on the back of his uniform in place of the traditional surname and selected the uniform No. 60. While the former acknowledged his western Pennsylvania hometown, the latter was a reference to the year he entered professional baseball. When the A's tried to make Allen a full-time designated hitter, though, he bristled at the idea of becoming a one-dimensional player. Dick's relationship with Finley deteriorated quickly after that, and he left the team abruptly in June after playing in just fifty-four games. Soon after, the A's released Allen, and he retired for good the spring of the following year.[76]

Topps 1967 bonus card

Topps 1968

Topps 1969

Topps 1970

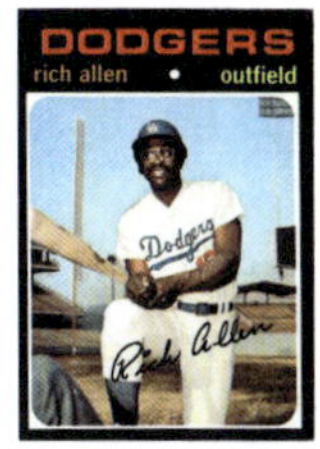

Topps 1971

Topps 1967

Richie Allen, 1964. *Artwork by Rob Larsen*

Topps 1972

Topps 1966

Topps 1973

Topps 1965

Topps 1974

Topps 1964

DICK ALLEN

Philadelphia Phillies
1964–69, 1975–76

St. Louis Cardinals
1970

Los Angeles Dodgers
1971

Chicago White Sox
1972–74

Oakland A's
1977

Topps 1975

Topps 1976

Dick with "Trick Fire," a two-year-old filly, at the Bowie, Maryland, racetrack. *Photo by Walter Iooss Jr. Courtesy of Sports Illustrated/Getty Images*

CHAPTER 8: RECONCILIATION

Dick Allen had imagined himself as a horseracing entrepreneur after his playing career ended. For a while he raised thoroughbreds at his farm in Perkasie, Bucks County, Pennsylvania. He owned eleven horses, including "Designated Runner," "Briar Bend," "Getting Ready," and "Pisces' Dream."[1] When an electrical fire destroyed their house in 1979, Allen was forced to abandon the enterprise. Instead, he kept several thoroughbreds at a Maryland stable owned by his brothers Hank and Ron.[2] Hank recalled:

> While Dick was still playing I took care of "Getting Ready," "Pisces' Dream," and "Briar Bend." Then Dick talked me into learning how to train horses. He set me up with a ninety-seven-year-old trainer from Chicago, Nate Cantrell, the first black trainer I'd ever met.
>
> Nate taught me well. Soon after I bought my first horse, "Sweet & Fast," and started my own training. Seven years later Hank won his first stake race at Keystone Park with a horse named "Destry." After that the Allens started winning stake races on a routine basis.[3]

Hank and his brothers established a base at the Bowie and Pimlico race tracks in Maryland. The business became so successful that the Allen brothers expanded to thirty-eight thoroughbreds by the mid-1980s.[4] In 1989, Hank made history when he became the first African American trainer in seventy-eight years to saddle a horse in the Kentucky Derby when "Northern Wolf" ran sixth to winner "Sunday Silence." The following year he conditioned "Northern Wolf" when the horse set a new Laurel Park track record of 1:08⅘ for six furlongs while winning the "Duck Dance Handicap." Two months later, "Northern Wolf" set a new Pimlico track record of 1:09 flat for the same six-furlong distance, winning the Frank J. De Francis Memorial Dash Stakes.[5]

Dick, a licensed trainer since 1974, was also well respected at the racetrack. "There are many trainers who are excellent horsemen," said Eddie Smith, a steward at Keystone Racetrack outside of Philadelphia,

> but they don't have the affection Dick feels for the animal. I always say horses are like people. Each one's got a different personality and you have to handle each one a little different. Dick does that, and he does it extremely well.[6]

Once Allen even admitted that his special abilities as a "horse whisperer" were because he could relate better to thoroughbreds than to people. "I can communicate with horses," he said. "I have a mare who's very sensitive. You can tell by the way she lowers her ears, the light in her eyes. I can talk to her."

"Some of 'em need that soft talk, easy handling. Others need to be roughhouses, hollered at. Like me, I guess."[7]

Dick with son, Dick Jr., at Veterans Stadium, 1989.
Courtesy of the Allen Family

Richard Jr. sometimes feels it might have been nice if he and his brother, Heron, had joined their father as trainers. But Heron was more interested in reading and writing than sports, and Richard was still trying to fulfill his own ambitions to play professional baseball. An outfielder/first baseman at Bowie State University in Maryland, Dick's namesake admitted he has "always loved baseball." During his summers in college in the mid-1980s, he worked on the Phillies' grounds crew at Veterans Stadium. Since he could not do that and play on a summer league team, Richard made frequent use of the batting cages and spent time shagging flies in the outfield whenever he wasn't working.[8]

"I gave it a shot," said Richard in a recent interview:

> I played at Bowie State. I had a brief tryout with the Atlanta Braves at Bradenton, Florida. I was invited to spring training with the St. Louis Cardinals, and I also played in the Instructional League in Mesa, Arizona, with the Dodgers. But I was my own worst critic. I used to get down on myself when I didn't get a hit. I needed to have more confidence in my playing ability."

The pressure was self-inflicted; it did not come from his father. If anything, Dick supported his son's effort. They would talk baseball for hours when he came east to visit, or by phone when he was in Los Angeles.

> If I put pressure on myself to succeed in baseball it was not so much because of my father as it was his brothers. They were all very good athletes. Growing up, I felt I had a certain family standard to uphold, so I had pretty high expectations for myself as an athlete. If I had just relaxed, I think I could've been more successful than I was.

In fact, Richard did experience considerable success playing in men's semipro leagues during his late twenties and thirties. Although he had been a line drive hitter in college, he began hitting for power and distance, much like his father. His success was due to a more relaxed approach. He finally allowed himself to enjoy the game.[9]

On the other hand, his father continued to lead a semireclusive life, at times seeming as though his preoccupation with horses was therapy for the pain that came his way after his playing career ended. Dick and Barbara divorced in 1981.[10] Ten years later, on May 30, 1991, Dick's twenty-seven-year-old daughter, Terri, died suddenly.[11] The eldest of Dick and Barbara's three children, Terri Allen was a sweet, caring person with her mother's gregarious personality. Introduced to baseball through her father, Terri worked as an usherette at Veterans Stadium during her summers in college at Howard University. She graduated from Howard in 1987 with a degree in broadcast journalism and secured internships at ABC News and WUSA-Channel 9, both in Washington, DC. She had a very bright future ahead of her.[12] "Everybody who knew Terri was special to her," said Barbara, "and she was special to them. She was so full of hugs and kisses. Everyone loved her."[13]

Richard noted:

> I am the quiet one in the family, probably like my father when he was growing up. My younger brother Heron is more outgoing, but Terri had all the personality. She was like my mother in that way. All you had to ask was, "How was your day?" and that was a good hour and a half gone!

"But my sister was also 'Daddy's Little Girl,'" he added, tears welling up in his eyes at the memory of her death. "When we were kids, we'd be sitting in the back seat of the car as Dad was driving and there was Terri with her arms wrapped around him. Dad was crazy about her, just loved her to pieces.[14]

Terri Allen, Dick's only daughter, died suddenly on May 30, 1991. Her death motivated him to return to baseball to give something back. *Courtesy of the Allen Family*

Dick was living on the West Coast at the time of his daughter's death and flew to Maryland immediately after hearing the tragic news. "He was devastated," recalled Richard. "When my father arrived he checked into a hotel and my mother asked me to go and see if he was all right. He was just torn to pieces, as any father who lost a child would be. What could I say? All I could do was just be there for him."[15]

For years Dick claimed he had no interest in returning to baseball as a coach, though his fertile baseball mind was that of a manager's. In the early 1980s, however, he began to reconsider. Dick finally agreed to serve as a hitting instructor for the Texas Rangers during spring training 1982. He also began to appear at baseball card shows in the Philadelphia area and playing in several Old Timer's games throughout the major leagues.[16] In 1989, his autobiography, *Crash*, cowritten with Tim Whitaker, was published and received a number of favorable reviews. It also softened his one-time image as "Baseball's Bad Boy." "I was mild-mannered compared to players today," said Dick, after the release of the book. "Maybe I was ahead of my time."[17] All of these activities allowed the former Phillie to feel good about himself, but it was Terri's death in 1991 that prompted him to rebuild his life by returning to the game he still loved.

"Terri was born while I was playing ball, and that's what fed her," said Dick in a July 1993 interview with *Sports Illustrated*. "I thought maybe I should get back into the game, if only to get my mind into something solid. I still love baseball, I really do."[18]

Soon after, Allen began working with the White Sox as a part-time hitting instructor. Then, in 1994, he agreed to return to the Phillies. Hired as a spring training batting instructor, Dick worked primarily with minor leaguers. His patience, understanding, and excellent communication skills made him an instant hit with the young prospects. When camp broke, the Phillies, eager to retain his services in any capacity, persuaded Dick to work with the newly established "Reviving Baseball in Inner Cities" program.[19]

The program was initiated by the Phillies in 1989 to address the dwindling number of children from the inner cities involved with baseball. Initially, "RBI" was geared toward children ages twelve and younger in areas that had not housed an organized baseball league in almost twenty years. The coaches taught the fundamentals of the game in a noncompetitive atmosphere with the goal of inspiring an interest in the sport. In 1993, the Phillies expanded the program as part of MLB's international RBI campaign, which introduced competitive baseball to preteens and adolescents. Since that time the program has grown to encompass over 8,000 children playing baseball and softball in more than fifty locations throughout Philadelphia, southern New Jersey, and Delaware.[20] Dick's involvement as a part-time coach and popular speaker at clinics allowed him to fulfill a desire

Dick was inducted into the Phillies Hall of Fame in 1994. *Author photo*

Dick is a regular at Phillies alumni events. *Photo by Steve Mucha*

he expressed years earlier to "stay in baseball by helping the young black kids coming up, so they could avoid the mistakes I made."[21]

In 1997, Dick assumed an even more active role in the Phillies organization as "elder statesman," a role he continues to serve with grace and humility. That year, third baseman Scott Rolen became the first Phillie since Dick to be named Rookie of the Year. When asked to compare himself with Rolen, Allen said they were both "team first players," but Rolen was much better defensively. "In my early days as the Phillies third baseman I was nicknamed 'E-5,'" he joked.

In 2005, when Ryan Howard became the fourth Phillie to win Rookie of the Year, Dick was among those on hand to congratulate him. He had first worked with the young slugger as a coach during spring training four years earlier. Dick, now older and mellower, said that Howard reminded him of "what it felt like to be a young star with his entire future ahead of him."[22]

Dick receives a hug from a fan. *Photo by Steve Mucha*

A regular at Phillies alumni events, including the Wall of Fame induction each August, Allen, now beloved, is always warmly received by former teammates and fans. "You see how things turn around?" he told Frank Fitzpatrick of the *Philadelphia Inquirer* at a 2010 alumni event. "You see how rewarding it is? I'm proud of this city. It's in my heart."[23]

Waving to the crowd at Citizens Bank Park in April 2015, Dick takes a ride in a 1970s Corvette. *Photo by Steve Mucha*

Nor has Dick forgotten his friends back home in western Pennsylvania.

While most professional athletes who have experienced Allen's tremendous success ignore their past, Dick has maintained his boyhood friendships and strong ties to Wampum. In fact, those relationships continue to define him as a person. "Sleeper is extremely loyal to his family and friends," said Guy Demaio, his American Legion coach. "When I moved to New Castle, he was still playing in the majors. But when he came home during the offseason he looked me up and came to visit. I was very touched by that. He's not an outgoing person, but if he likes you he opens up.

"Sleeper's always been very careful in choosing his friends," added Demaio. "But if you're his friend, you're a friend for life."[24]

In 2010, when Allen's senior high school class was celebrating their fiftieth reunion, he paid for the entire event but was too shy to attend it. Unlike many of his

The author (center) with Johnny Callison and Dick at an appearance at Chester County Historical Society, West Chester, Pennsylvania, in April 1999.

Tony Taylor and Dick at Phillies alumni weekend in August 2013. *Photo by Steve Mucha*

Dick joined former Chicago teammates Bill Melton (center) and Rich "Goose" Gossage (left) during a ceremony to honor the 1972 White Sox in 2012. *Photo by David Fletcher. Courtesy of the Chicago Baseball Museum*

teenage friends, he can still recall school plays, basketball games, and pranks, and is happiest when he is in the company of his friends from Wampum High School's 1960 state championship basketball team.

Jim Santelli, one of those teammates, noted:

> Sleeper's really a hometown guy at heart. He loves Wampum and our basketball team so much that he'll do anything for us. It's not unusual for him to pick up the phone and call just

White Sox golf outing, 2012 (left to right): former general manager Roland Hemond, former manager Chuck Tanner, Dick, and Rich "Goose" Gossage. *Photo by David Fletcher. Courtesy of the Chicago Baseball Museum*

Dick holds his 1972 MVP Award, 2012. *Photo by David Fletcher. Courtesy of the Chicago Baseball Museum*

to see how we're doing. If he's in town he'll take us out to a nice restaurant and pick up the check. He's just a really genuine and generous guy.

For someone as successful as Sleeper was in baseball you'd think he'd go around bragging about it, or carry himself like he was better than other folks. He never does any of that. When he comes back home he *never* talks about himself, or his achievements. He was always very humble, never too good to talk to us.[25]

Outside of Wampum it took others to catch up, to understand that Dick Allen has always been and remains the product of a rural, small town where people are judged by their candor, humility, and fierce loyalties to family and friends. Perhaps that is why Allen has been the recipient of many belated honors over the past two decades, including a June 25, 2012, tribute cosponsored by the Chicago White Sox and Chicago Baseball Museum; the Philadelphia Sportswriters' Living Legend Award (2005); and inductions into the Phillies Wall of Fame (1994), Philadelphia Sports Hall of Fame (2010), and the New York-Penn League Hall of Fame (2016).[26] In fact, the only conspicuous absence among those honors is a bronze plaque in the National Baseball Hall of Fame at Cooperstown, New York. But Dick is a humble man who does not like to talk about his major league career, let alone campaign for his own Hall of Fame induction. Consequently, family members, former teammates, friends, and fans have taken up his cause. Their loyalty to and love for Dick are unconditional.

Mark "Frog" Carfagno, a former member of the Phillies grounds crew at Veterans Stadium and one of Dick's closest friends, has managed the Hall of Fame campaign. He explains Allen's refusal to become involved in the campaign is because of his pride and introverted nature—something he attributes to the racial tensions that prevailed in Philadelphia during the civil rights era of the 1960s. "Those were tough times," said Carfagno:

Mark Carfagno (right) led the campaign to get Dick elected to the National Baseball Hall of Fame for six years. He is shown with Dick Allen Jr. and the late Pete Cera, the former Phillies' clubhouse attendant and a close friend of the Allen family. *Photo by Steve Mucha*

The Phillies were the last National League team to integrate, and Dick was their first black superstar. Really, he was just ahead of his time.

I saw the way he was abused. They called him every name in the book; every racial epithet. It's hard to believe that he could play with all that pressure on him. After games he would blow off steam by hanging out with the grounds crew. We understood him. Nobody else did.

Carfagno considers it a "slap in the face" that Allen is not in the Hall of Fame. During the past decade he has lobbied for his friend's induction with former Phillies and White Sox teammates and baseball writers, reaching out to the Golden Era voters and keeping Allen's name in the news.[27]

The film producer Mike Tollin is another close friend. Growing up in Havertown, a suburb of Philadelphia, Tollin was one of Allen's biggest fans.

"I guess it was the regal way he carried himself, the way he strode to the plate with that 40-oz. bat," said Tollin of his boyhood fascination with Allen. "I connected with him on a visceral level." In 1977, when Dick was playing in Oakland, Tollin, a college student at Stanford, met his hero for the first time, and a friendship was born.[28] Tollin went on to become a successful Hollywood producer with such feature films to his credit as *Radio* and *Varsity Blues*. In 2001, he invited Dick to make a cameo appearance in *Summer Catch*. Allen agreed, and had so much fun that he returned for another cameo as a racetrack bookie in Tollin's 2005 film *Dreamer*.[29]

"He's not really reclusive by design," said Tollin, who is currently making a documentary on Allen's life. "But outside the race track he's a little bit out of his comfort zone. He's a good soul, but it's hard for him to let people embrace him and thank him."[30]

For those who befriended Allen during his playing days—and who witnessed the horrific treatment he suffered—there is a fierce loyalty that borders on protectiveness. "I've always considered Dick to be like a brother to me," said Howie Bedell, who played for the Phillies in 1968. "Not only were we teammates, but both of us are

Film producer Mike Tollin idolized Dick while growing up in Havertown, Pennsylvania, and later invited him to make a cameo appearance in his 2001 feature film *Summer Catch*. *Courtesy of Mike Tollin*

Dick had another cameo appearance in Tollin's 2005 film *Dreamer*. Here he poses with the actor Kurt Russell (left), who starred in the film, and producer Tollin. *Courtesy of Mike Tollin*

Pennsylvania boys who were courted and signed by John Ogden, so we share that special bond." Bedell, who went on to a very successful career as a player development director with the Phillies, Kansas City Royals, and Cincinnati Reds after his playing career ended, agreed to serve as Allen's agent without any remuneration. He negotiated a film documentary and public appearances in Chicago and Philadelphia to give Dick greater visibility before the Golden Era balloting in 2014. It was a labor of love.

The public demand for Dick became too much for Bedell, though. When he suggested his former teammate find another agent, Dick worried that he had done something to hurt his longtime friend. Howie assured him that was not the case, but that the responsibility had become too demanding and that he was better off with another more experienced agent. Admitted Bedell:

> One of the reasons I love Dick so much is because of his sensitivity. If he feels he's done something to upset a friend, he goes out of his way to apologize. He *always* remembers his friends, most of whom are just common everyday people, not celebrities or superstar athletes. Whether it's a birthday, a personal loss, or offering congratulations for an achievement, Dick always seems to find out about it and either calls or visits. People who don't know him never see that side of him.[31]

Today, Dick Allen, age seventy-five, spends most of the off-season with his second wife, Willa, at their home in Wampum, and with his two grown sons Richard and Heron and his grandson Dick III in Williamsport. But once spring training rolls around, the Wampum Walloper is back in Clearwater with the Phillies as a hitting instructor. More important, Allen is at peace with himself, the Phillies, and Major League Baseball.

"I wouldn't change a thing in my life," he said in a recent phone conversation. "What I've done, I'm pretty happy with it. So whatever happens with the Hall of Fame, I'm fine with."

"Besides, I'm just a name," he added. "God gave me the talent to hit a baseball, and I used it the best I could. I just thank Him for blessing me with that ability and allowing me to play the game when I did."[32]

Era Allen (1960) was the matriarch of the Allen family. A compassionate woman and strict disciplinarian, Era nurtured a strong sense of self-esteem and loyalty to family in all of her children. *Courtesy of the Allen Family*

We Are Family

"Family" is the most important blessing in Dick Allen's life. Growing up in Wampum, Dick's parents created a loving, supportive home life for him and his siblings. Although the children were from two marriages, no one ever used the terms "stepbrother," "stepsister," or "stepchild." All of Era Allen's children were treated and loved equally.

Dick and his siblings cultivated that same love of family in their own children. As a result, many of the cousins are as close as brothers and sisters. Although some extended family members live in California, others in Maryland, and still others in Pennsylvania and Ohio, they stay in contact on a regular basis and hold a family reunion every two years in the summer.

In November 1972, Era Allen was honored as "Mother of the Year" and Dick as the American League's Most Valuable Player at a banquet in New Castle, Pennsylvania. During that event, the Allen family posed for this photograph (left to right): Dick, Coy Jr., Era, Barbara, Caesar, Marthela, Hank, a family friend, and Ron. *Courtesy of the Allen Family*

Dick with his grandson Dick III. *Courtesy of the Allen Family*

Dick's three children (left to right): Dick Jr., Terri, and Heron. *Courtesy of the Allen Family*

Three generations of the Allen family (left to right): Hank; Caesar; Dick Jr.; Heron (standing in rear); Rick holding his infant son, Ricky; and Ron Jr. *Courtesy of the Allen Family*

Barbara Allen, Dicks' first wife, with Dick Jr. (left), Dick III (center), and Heron. *Courtesy of the Allen Family*

Celebrating the fortieth anniversary of Dick's 1972 MVP season with the Chicago White Sox are (left to right) Dick III, Hank, Dick, Dick Jr., and Ron. *Courtesy of the Allen Family*

Dick Jr. with his son, Dick III, a shortstop at Cecil College (Maryland), 2015. *Courtesy of the Allen Family*

Dick and Willa Allen at spring training in Clearwater, Florida, 2016. *Courtesy of the Allen Family*

Dick Allen today. *Photo by Charles Fox. Courtesy of* The Philadelphia Inquirer. *Copyright 2016. All Rights Reserved*

CHAPTER 9:
HALL OF FAMER IN WAITING

Dick Allen became eligible for induction into the National Baseball Hall of Fame in 1982, yet never did he receive more than 18.9% of the vote during his fifteen years on the ballot. Eliminated from annual consideration in 1997, Allen's candidacy resurfaced in 2014, when his name appeared on the Hall of Fame's "Golden Era" Committee poll of ten candidates who played between 1947 and 1972.

Along with Allen, Gil Hodges, Ken Boyer, Jim Kaat, Minnie Monoso, Tony Oliva, Billy Pierce, Luis Tiant, Maury Wills, and former Reds general manager Bob Howsam were considered. To be elected, each candidate had to appear on 75% of the ballots, or secure twelve of the sixteen votes cast by the committee. No one was elected. Allen and Oliva received eleven votes, one vote shy of election.

The Golden Era Committee of Baseball Writers was divided into two separate committees in 2016. The "Golden Days" Committee will consider those candidates who played between 1950 and 1969, and will vote in December 2020. The "Modern Baseball" committee will consider those candidates who played between 1970 and 1987, and will vote in December 2017. Since Dick Allen's career spanned both eras, he should be eligible for consideration this year.[1] Allen's family, friends, and fans are hoping that in the summer of 2018 he will finally achieve the baseball immortality that has eluded him for forty years.

Does Dick Allen deserve a place in Cooperstown?

His career statistics and rarefied achievements indicate he does. Allen was an All Star for seven seasons. He won the 1964 National League Rookie of the Year Award when he played for the Philadelphia Phillies, hitting .318 with twenty-nine home runs and ninety-one RBIs, and led the league in games played (162), runs scored (125), and triples (13). Allen was voted the American League MVP in 1972 while with the Chicago White Sox, when he led the league in home runs (37), RBIs (113), walks (99), and slugging percentage (.603). During his fifteen-year major league career, the Wampum Walloper batted .292, including seven seasons (1964–67, 1972–74) at the .300 mark or higher.

Allen was also one of the most dominant sluggers in the most difficult era for hitters in baseball history. He hit 351 homers, leading the American League twice (1972, 1974) in that category. He combined massive strength and body torque to

Dick Allen is among the all-time offensive leaders of the era in which he played (1963–77). *Artwork by Drew Davis. Statistics courtesy of Baseballreference.com*

produce remarkable bat speed, assets that enabled him to drive the ball long distances. In fact, Allen's home runs were more prodigious than those of any power hitter in the history of the Phillies organization, including Hall of Famers Ed Delahanty, Chuck Klein, and Mike Schmidt.[2]

Swinging a 40-oz. bat—one of the heaviest in major league history—the Wampum Walloper crushed the ball, sometimes 500 feet or more. Eighteen of his drives cleared Connie Mack Stadium's sixty-five-foot-high left field grandstand. Twice Allen cleared that park's sixty-five-foot-high right center field scoreboard, a feat considered virtually impossible for a right-handed hitter. Bill Jenkinson, a historian who has chronicled the feats of baseball's greatest power hitters, ranks Allen with Jimmie Foxx and Mickey Mantle and just a notch below Babe Ruth as the four top long-distance sluggers ever to wield a baseball bat.[3] Willie Mays still says that he has never seen anyone hit the ball harder. Not surprisingly, Allen compiled 1,119 RBIs and a lifetime slugging percentage of .534, leading the National League in that category in 1966 and the American League twice (1972,1974).[4]

Compared with other Hall of Fame first basemen of his era, Allen, who played most of his career at first, is just as good and in some cases better. Orlando Cepeda hit 379 home runs to Allen's 351, but Cepeda was at bat nearly 1,600 more times. Similarly, Harmon Killebrew had 573 home runs in twenty-two seasons, but Allen still out-hit him, .292 to .256, won three slugging titles to Killebrew's one, and had more doubles and triples than Killebrew while batting about 1,800 fewer times.[5]

These statistics are certainly very respectable, especially since Allen played in the pitcher-friendly 1960s and '70s. Yet when his career numbers are viewed in the context of sabermetrics, he is among the very best players in baseball's golden era, if not in the history of the game itself.

In December 2014, Brian Kenny, host of "MLB Now" on the *MLB Network*, did a comprehensive analysis of Allen's adjusted on-base percentage plus slugging percentage (OPS+) and his offensive wins above replacement (WAR). Kenny found that Dick is one of the top twenty hitters in the history of baseball in terms of OPS+ and number one of all position players during 1964–74 in terms of WAR.[6] OPS+ offers a very good measure of a player's overall offensive production not only because it measures the ability of a player to get on base and to hit for power, but also because it adjusts his OPS score to reflect such variables as the dimensions of the park, run-scoring environment, or league in which he plays. For example, a 100 OPS+ is the league average, and each point up or down is one percentage point above or below that average. In other words, if a player had a ninety OPS+ the previous season, it means their OPS was 10% below the league average.

Although Allen played in one of the lowest run-scoring periods of the game, his 156 career OPS+ ties him for thirteenth highest in the Live Ball era and nineteenth all time if you go back to the 1800s:

Career OPS+ with rank in live ball era

Minimum 3,000 plate appearances

Dick Allen, Phillies, T-13th (156 OPS+)

Frank Thomas, Chicago White Sox, T-13th (156 OPS+)

Willie Mays, NY-SF Giants, T-13th (156 OPS+)

Hank Aaron, MIL-ATL Braves, T-16th (155 OPS+)

Joe DiMaggio, NY Yankees, T-16th (155 OPS+)

According to the OPS+ ranking, Allen, at bat for at bat, is comparable to some of the game's best hitters ever, especially when you consider that Mays and Aaron had over 5,000 more appearances at the plate.

The prime of Allen's career came between 1964 and 1974, when he hit .299 (fifth best in Major League Baseball) and compiled an on-base percentage (OBP) of .386 (fifth), 319 home runs (fifth), 3,005 total bases (fifth), and 775 walks (ninth). Only Aaron (391 home runs with 283 more plate appearances), Killebrew, Willie Stargell, and Willie McCovey had more home runs; only Billy Williams, Aaron, Lou Brock, and Pete Rose had more total bases. To be sure, Allen played fewer than 130 games in five of those eleven seasons, but his .940 OPS was second only to Aaron's .941 in the major leagues.

What's more, Allen was league leader in OPS+ three times (1966, '67, '72) and he was among the top three OPS+ leaders six times (1966–67, 1969, 1972–74). Thus, his 165 OPS+ during that eleven-year run was the best in the game, topping Hall of Famers Willie McCovey (161), Aaron (159), Frank Robinson (159), Willie Stargell (153), Roberto Clemente (151), Killebrew (148), and Mays (148).

But the metric that most clearly distinguishes Allen from his contemporaries is offensive WAR, which measures a player's overall contribution to a team in terms of wins and losses. Specifically, a player's WAR value is based on the number of additional wins his team has achieved above the number of expected team wins if that player was substituted by a replacement-level player—a player who may be added to the team for minimal cost and effort. To calculate the WAR of a position player like Allen, take their batting runs, base running runs, and fielding runs above average, add in a positional adjustment, a small adjustment for their league, and then add in replacement runs so that we are comparing their performance with the replacement level, rather than with that of the average player. After that, you simply take that sum and divide it by the runs per win value of that season to find the WAR. The simple equation looks something like this:

OPS+ Leaders per decade (>4500 PA)					
decade		player	decade		player
1880	1889	Roger Connor	1934	1943	Mel Ott
1881	1890	Dan Brouthers	1935	1944	Mel Ott
1882	1891	Dan Brouthers	1936	1945	Mel Ott
1883	1892	Dan Brouthers	1937	1946	Mel Ott
1884	1893	Dan Brouthers	1938	1947	Mel Ott
1885	1894	Dan Brouthers	1939	1948	Ted Williams
1886	1895	Dan Brouthers	1940	1949	Ted Williams
1887	1896	Dan Brouthers	1941	1950	Stan Musial
1888	1897	Billy Hamilton	1942	1951	Stan Musial
1889	1898	Ed Delahanty	1943	1952	Stan Musial
1890	1899	Ed Delahanty	1944	1953	Stan Musial
1891	1900	Ed Delahanty	1945	1954	Stan Musial
1892	1901	Ed Delahanty	1946	1955	Ted Williams
1893	1902	Ed Delahanty	1947	1956	Ted Williams
1894	1903	Ed Delahanty	1948	1957	Ted Williams
1865	1874	Ed Delahanty	1949	1958	Mickey Mantle
1896	1905	Nap Lajoie	1950	1959	Mickey Mantle
1897	1906	Nap Lajoie	1951	1960	Mickey Mantle
1898	1907	Nap Lajoie	1952	1961	Mickey Mantle
1899	1908	Honus Wagner	1953	1962	Mickey Mantle
1900	1909	Honus Wagner	1954	1963	Mickey Mantle
1901	1910	Nap Lajoie	1955	1964	Mickey Mantle
1902	1911	Honus Wagner	1956	1965	Mickey Mantle
1903	1912	Honus Wagner	1957	1966	Mickey Mantle
1904	1913	Ty Cobb	1958	1967	Mickey Mantle
1905	1914	Ty Cobb	1959	1968	Mickey Mantle
1906	1915	Ty Cobb	1960	1969	Frank Robinson
1907	1916	Ty Cobb	1961	1970	Frank Robinson
1908	1917	Ty Cobb	1962	1971	Hank Aaron
1909	1918	Ty Cobb	1963	1972	Dick Allen
1910	1919	Ty Cobb	1964	1973	Dick Allen
1911	1920	Ty Cobb	1965	1974	Willie McCovey
1912	1921	Ty Cobb	1966	1975	Willie McCovey
1913	1922	Ty Cobb	1967	1976	Willie McCovey
1914	1923	Rogers Hornsby	1968	1977	Willie McCovey
1915	1924	Babe Ruth	1969	1978	Willie Stargell
1916	1925	Babe Ruth	1970	1979	Willie Stargell
1917	1926	Babe Ruth	1971	1980	Willie Stargell
1918	1927	Babe Ruth	1972	1981	Reggie Jackson
1919	1928	Babe Ruth	1973	1982	Reggie Jackson
1920	1929	Babe Ruth	1974	1983	Mike Schmidt
1921	1930	Babe Ruth	1975	1984	Mike Schmidt
1922	1931	Babe Ruth	1976	1985	Mike Schmidt
1923	1932	Babe Ruth	1977	1986	Mike Schmidt
1924	1933	Babe Ruth	1978	1987	Mike Schmidt
1925	1934	Babe Ruth	1979	1988	Mike Schmidt
1926	1935	Babe Ruth	1980	1989	Mike Schmidt
1927	1936	Babe Ruth	1981	1990	Mike Schmidt
1928	1937	Lou Gehrig	1982	1991	Wade Boggs
1929	1938	Lou Gehrig	1983	1992	Rickey Henderson
1930	1939	Lou Gehrig	*decades*	15x	Barry Bonds
1931	1940	Lou Gehrig	*1993*	1x	Frank Thomas
1932	1941	Lou Gehrig	*to*	6x	Albert Pujols
1933	1942	Jimmy Foxx	*2015*	1x	Miguel Cabrera

Hall of Famers highlighted in green
not yet eligible in grey
among eligible players, only Barry Bonds and Dick Allen are not in Hall of Fame

#DickAllenHOF

OPS leaders by decade. *Chart by Drew Davis. Statistics courtesy of Baseballreference.com*

WAR = (Batting runs + Base running runs + Fielding runs + Positional adjustment + League adjustment + Replacement runs)/Runs per win

Allen's offensive WAR is 68.3, which ranks him number one of all position players 1964–74. The next closest player is Hank Aaron (63.7), followed by Frank Robinson (58.8), Carl Yastrezemski (56.1), and Joe Morgan (55.2), all of whom are members of Baseball's Hall of Fame:

Offensive WAR Leaders (1964–74)

1. Dick Allen, 68.3 WAR
2. Hank Aaron, 63.7 WAR
3. Frank Robinson, 58.8 WAR
4. Carl Yastrezemski, 56.1 WAR
5. Joe Morgan, 55.2 WAR

So why isn't Dick Allen in the Hall of Fame? Because the baseball writers who vote for immortality were unsure how to factor in Allen's unrealized potential and the controversy that surrounded him.

Before scientific weight training, muscle-building dietary supplements, and anabolic steroids, Allen boasted a powerful and muscular physique along the lines of Mickey Mantle and Jimmie Foxx. Many writers believed Allen had so much raw talent that he could have been an even greater player if he had placed a higher priority on his baseball career. They argue that Allen hit forty home runs just once during his fifteen-year career, but probably should have topped that mark half a dozen times. He might have even hit 600 home runs, possibly becoming the all time home run king in the era before steroids. Similarly, Allen drove in 100 runs three times during his career, but probably should have done that ten times or more. If he had achieved those milestones, according to the argument, Allen might have won several MVP awards and possibly a world championship or two. The detractors make some good points. But a Hall of Famer's candidacy is not based on what he *might* have done; it is based on his indisputable achievements. By that measure, Allen deserves to be in Cooperstown.

Ultimately, what has prevented Dick Allen from achieving baseball immortality is the controversy that surrounded him on and off the playing field during his MLB career. Bill James, a famed baseball historian and statistician, calls Allen the second most controversial player in baseball history behind only Rogers Hornsby, who was elected to the Hall of Fame in 1942. According to James, "Allen used racism as an explosive to blow his own teams apart." While the Wampum Walloper certainly instigated a fair share of controversy, the charge that he used "racism to blow his teams apart" is a gross exaggeration.

1966 National League home run leaders. *Courtesy of The Topps Company, Inc.*

Indeed, Allen was one of the most contentious players in baseball history, and he refused to change for anyone. He was a shy kid from a humble, rural community in western Pennsylvania, one that emphasized self-respect and a healthy cynicism of others. Strong willed and enormously talented in basketball and baseball, Allen, like many high school athletic prodigies of a later generation, did as he pleased. Only his mother could tell him to do otherwise. Even then, there were times her orders were challenged.

Sportswriters who later covered Allen's professional baseball career either ignored or failed to grasp that reality. That fact does not excuse his controversial behavior, but it does go a long way in explaining it.

Allen was also the first African American superstar in Phillies' history, and as such became an immediate target for Philadelphia's race-baiting sportswriters and contentious fans. In 1963, Allen, assigned to the Phillies' Triple A club in Little Rock, Arkansas, was forced to deal with considerable ridicule and racism. He was greeted with signs that read, "Nigger go home." Fans wrote messages on his windshield like

1966 National League RBI leaders. *Courtesy of The Topps Company, Inc.*

"Don't come back again, nigger." Allen, who was reserved by nature and kept to himself, was a troubled player living in a difficult environment.

Promoted to the Phillies in 1964, Allen was a young black ballplayer who was at a point in his life when he was struggling to establish an identity—not only as a professional athlete but also as a young African American man in a city that was hostile to blacks. Having been born and raised in an integrated rural community, the young slugger was not only thrust into a hostile urban environment where he was forced to grapple with racial discrimination, but had to do so in the high-visibility world of Major League Baseball. The well-publicized fight with his white teammate Frank Thomas in July 1965 only made his situation worse.

Manager Gene Mauch forbade Allen to tell the press his side of the story, so the sportswriters printed Thomas's version. In the process, they evoked the specter of racism and gave Allen an unwarranted reputation as a troublemaker. After that, he seemed to challenge management, the sportswriters, and the fans at each and every turn. In fact, Dick Allen was a *victim* of racism, not a purveyor of it.

1968 National League home run leaders. *Courtesy of The Topps Company, Inc.*

When the fans booed him, Allen took to scrawling words with his spikes in the dirt around first base. Once he returned their disapproval by printing, "Boo." When the fans showered him with racial epithets and threw coins and beer cans at him, Allen wore a batting helmet to play the outfield. He showed up late for games or not at all. Once he missed a team flight because he was late returning from the horse track. But he was also punished for the transgressions. Among the penalties were a twenty-eight-day-suspension, a $500-a-day fine, and finally a trade to the St. Louis Cardinals after the 1969 season.

Allen, who was tied to the Phillies by baseball's reserve clause, tried to force the organization to trade him. His controversial behavior was indicative of a player desperate to escape the kind of nightmarish psychological and emotional abuse that no person—black, white, Hispanic, or otherwise—should have to endure. But in the process, Allen's rebellious behavior reinforced the negative stereotype that the fans and media had imposed on him in the first place. If anything, the Phillies did not help matters.

The organization was at best naïve in their understanding of race relations. In an effort to distance the team from an infamous history of race relations, in 1963 owner Bob Carpenter used Allen to integrate the Phillies' Triple-A club in Little Rock, Arkansas. Richie, a sensitive person by nature, was subjected to racism as never before. To compensate, Carpenter, general manager John Quinn, and manager Gene Mauch created a double standard for Allen after he was promoted to the Phillies. Consciously at times and unwittingly at others, they indulged their young black superstar and his rebellious behavior because he was an *African American* player with tremendous talent. On the other hand, the Phillies' other black players—Johnny Briggs, Wes Covington, Grant Jackson, Fergie Jenkins, and Alex Johnson—were not given as much playing time or latitude. Nor were they always judged by merit, or treated the same as a white player of similar ability, though the organization claimed they were. As a result, Allen never really understood whom he could trust within the organization.

Nevertheless, he forced Philadelphia to come to terms with the racism that existed in the city by refusing to take the abuse that was doled out by the press, the fans, and at times the organization itself.

Traded to the St. Louis Cardinals for Curt Flood at the completion of the 1969 season, Dick forced the larger—still conservative—baseball establishment to confront issues of race, free expression, and contractual bargaining. Signed for only single seasons in St. Louis and Los Angeles, Allen had no say in where he played. He was exploited by both clubs as a rental player in hopes of getting to the postseason. At a time when the reserve clause was still in force and players signed contracts on an annual basis, Dick was literally owned by the Cardinals and Dodgers for as long as and on whatever terms those teams desired. He did have one advantage, though. The fight for free agency jacked up salaries tenfold, giving Allen the financial clout to speak his mind, which he did, for better and worse. In so doing, he became one of a handful of outspoken professional athletes, including Muhammad Ali, Joe Namath, and Oscar Robertson, who challenged the status quo, paving the way for many others whose behavior was even more offensive. While he felt more at home in Chicago and during his second tenure with the Phillies, Dick continued to speak his mind when he felt he or his closest teammates were underappreciated. There is something noble in having that kind of moral courage.

Eliminate the issue of race, and James still contends that Allen was a divisive force on those teams for which he played. But Craig Wright, a member of the Society for American Baseball Research, disproved that notion in 1995.[7] Wright interviewed Allen's former managers and coaches and discovered that none of those individuals had a problem with Dick. Gene Mauch, Allen's first manager, flatly rejected the notion that his young third baseman was a "clubhouse lawyer." When asked whether Allen's behavior ever had a negative influence on the Phillies teams of the mid- to late sixties, Mauch said, "Never. Dick's teammates always liked him. He didn't involve his teammates in his problems. When he was personally rebellious he didn't try to bring other players into it." The response was similar to one that Mauch gave sportswriters in 1966, when the press was trying to bait him. "Richie Allen walks to the beat of a different drummer," replied Mauch, suggesting his star player was more of an individual than a clubhouse lawyer.

James also points to the two one-year stints Allen spent in St. Louis and Los Angeles as evidence he was a troublemaker who divided the clubhouse. But neither the Cards' manager Red Schoendienst nor the Dodgers' manager Walt Alston saw Allen as a problem. Schoendienst insisted Allen was "great in our clubhouse." "He got along with everybody," he added. "Although he wasn't a rah-rah guy, he came to play, so his teammates respected him, and they liked him." Similarly, Walter Alston never complained about Allen. "Walt was a quiet guy," explained the Dodgers' third base coach Danny Ozark. "He didn't talk to a lot of players. If he didn't say anything,

1972 Major League Baseball home run leaders. *Courtesy of The Topps Company, Inc.*

1972 Major League Baseball RBI leaders. *Courtesy of The Topps Company, Inc.*

you assumed it was all right. I know he didn't say anything bad about Dick Allen, and I would have heard it if he did." Carol Beringer, another Dodger coach, confirmed Ozark's remark. "I don't remember any problems with Richie," said Beringer.

When the Dodgers traded Allen to the Chicago White Sox in 1972, Allen, aware of his reputation as a divisive force among teammates, did everything in his power to disprove it. "Dick was our leader, the captain, the manager on the field," said the White Sox manager Chuck Tanner. "He took care of the young kids, took them under his wing. And he played every game as if it was his last day on earth." Tanner also credited Allen with turning a mediocre White Sox squad into a "first division team" during his three years in Chicago.

Rich Gossage, a teammate and Hall of Famer, confirmed Tanner's view. "I've been around the game a long time, and Dick's the greatest player I've ever seen in my life," said Gossage:

> He's the smartest baseball man I've ever been around. Dick taught me how to pitch from a hitter's prospective and taught me how to play the game right. There's no telling the numbers this guy could have put up if all he worried about was stats. No question—the guy belongs in the Hall of Fame.[8]

Similarly, when Allen returned to Philadelphia in 1975, he provided the inspiration for a young group of Phillies who were struggling to win a division title. He took Mike Schmidt, another player who would become a Hall of Famer, under his wing, teaching the introverted young third baseman how to cope with the fickleness of Philadelphia's sportswriters and fans. "The baseball writers used to claim that Dick would divide the clubhouse along racial lines," recalled Schmidt when asked about Dick's influence on those young Phillies. "That was a lie. Dick was a wonderful teammate. He always helped the younger guys like me, Gary Maddox, and Bull [Greg Luzinski] with our hitting. He never divided any clubhouse. He just got guys thinking."[9]

1974 Major League Baseball home run leaders. *Courtesy of The Topps Company, Inc.*

It seems as though those baseball writers who claimed Allen was a "divisive figure" based their judgments on their own impressions, rather than substantive evidence. Or they might have simply been part of the era's white conservative baseball establishment. According to the Hall of Famer Willie Stargell, a contemporary of Allen's, those were the kinds of people who criticized the black power hitter. "Dick played the game in the most conservative era in baseball history," explained Stargell:

> It was a time of change and protest in the country and baseball reacted against all that. The owners saw it as a threat to the game. The sportswriters were reactionary too. They didn't like seeing a man of such extraordinary skills doing it his way. It made them nervous. In reality, Dick Allen was ahead of his time. His views and way of doing things would go unnoticed today.[10]

To be sure, when the boorish behavior of today's superstar athletes is considered, Allen's conduct hardly seems controversial. He certainly did not tarnish the integrity of Major League Baseball by betting on the game or using steroids to pad his statistics. Nor can his personal integrity be questioned. Not once in his career did Dick ever make offensive gestures or engage in a shouting match with hostile fans, turn away a struggling teammate, or fail to give his very best effort whenever he stepped on to a baseball diamond. Allen has spent the past two decades of his life as a goodwill ambassador for the Phillies, a part-time hitting instructor for the team, and a mentor to youngsters involved in the Reviving Baseball in Inner Cities program.

If we admire Allen, we should do so for those selfless contributions, as well as for his impressive playing career and his genuine attempt to push Major League Baseball past the moral conventions that once condoned racism. If, on the other hand, we fault Allen for his self-expression and independent ways, we should at least acknowledge that he was a product of a rural environment that encouraged those traits.

After that is done, it is difficult to deny that Dick Allen belongs in the Hall of Fame and that he is a baseball immortal in every sense of the term.

APPENDIX A:
DICK ALLEN'S MINOR LEAGUE CAREER STATISTICS

BORN	POSITIONS			HEIGHT	WEIGHT	BATTED	THREW
March 8, 1942, in Wampum, Pennsylvania	Shortstop	Second Base	Outfield	5' 11"	180 lb.	Right	Right

BATTING

YEAR	AGE	TEAM	LEAGUE	LEVEL	AFF	G	PA	AB	R	H	2B	3B	HR	RBI	SB/CS	BB	SO	BA	OBP	SLG	OPS	TB
1960	18	Elmira	NY-Penn	D	Phillies	88	384	320	56	90	19	10	8	42	6/1	57	75	.281	.389	.478	.868	153
1961	19	Magic Valley	Pioneer	C	Phillies	117	526	460	101	146	17	8	21	94	10/4	63	131	.317	.401	.526	.927	242
1962	20	Williamsport	Eastern	A	Phillies	132	584	511	97	168	32	10	20	109	11/0	69	106	.329	.409	.548	.957	280
1963	21	Arkansas	Internat'l	AAA	Phillies	145	592	544	93	157	19	12	33	97	3/1	42	110	.289	.341	.550	.891	299
TOTAL		4 SEASONS				482	2086	1835	347	561	87	40	82	342	30/6	231	422	.306	.384	.531	.915	974

KEY

G	Games played
AB	At bats
PA	Plate appearances
R	Runs scored
H	Hits
2B	Doubles
3B	Triples
HR	Home runs
RBI	Runs batted in
SB/CS	Stolen bases/Caught stealing
BB	Walks
SO	Strikeouts
BA	Batting average
OBP	On-base percentage
SLG	Slugging percentage
OPS	OBP + SLG
TB	Total bases

FIELDING

YEAR	AGE	TEAM	LEAGUE	LEVEL	AFF	POS	G	CH	PO	A	E	DP	Fld%	RF/G
1960	18	Elmira	NY-Penn	D	Phillies	SS	85	362	141	173	48	31	.867	3.69
1961	19	Magic Valley	Pioneer	C	Phillies	2B	116	576	258	291	27	67	.953	4.73
1962	20	Williamsport	Eastern	A	Phillies	2B	15	95	41	47	7	14	.926	5.87
1962	20	Williamsport	Eastern	A	Phillies	OF	116	236	214	12	10	2	.958	1.98
1963	21	Arkansas	Internat'l	AAA	Phillies	OF	141	265	246	8	11	1	.958	1.80
TOTAL		2 SEASONS				2B	131	671	299	338	34	81	.949	4.86
		2 SEASONS				OF	257	501	460	20	21	3	.958	1.97

KEY

POS.	Field position
G	Games played
Ch	Chances
PO	Put outs
E	Errors
DP	Double plays
Fld%	Fielding percentage
A	Assists
RF/G	Range factor per game (PO + A)/Games played

APPENDIX B:
DICK ALLEN'S MAJOR LEAGUE CAREER STATISTICS

BATTING

YEAR	AGE	TEAM	LEAGUE	G	PA	AB	R	H	2B	3B	HR	RBI	SB/CS	BB	SO	BA	OBP	SLG	OPS	OPS+	TB
1963	21	Phillies	NL	10	25	24	6	7	2	1	0	2	0/0	0	5	.292	.280	.458	.738	110	11
1964	22	Phillies	NL	162	709	632	125	201	38	13	29	91	3/4	67	138	.318	.382	.557	.939	162	352
1965*	23	Phillies	NL	161	707	619	93	187	31	14	20	85	15/2	74	150	.302	.375	.494	.870	145	306
1966*	24	Phillies	NL	141	599	524	112	166	25	10	40	110	10/6	68	136	.317	.396	.632	1.027	181	331
1967*	25	Phillies	NL	122	540	463	89	142	31	10	23	77	20/5	75	117	.307	.404	.566	.970	174	262
1968	26	Phillies	NL	152	605	521	87	137	17	9	33	90	7/7	74	161	.263	.352	.520	.872	160	271
1969	27	Phillies	NL	118	506	438	79	126	23	3	32	89	9/3	64	144	.288	.375	.573	.949	165	251
1970*	28	Cardinals	NL	122	533	459	88	128	17	5	34	101	5/4	71	118	.279	.377	.560	.937	146	257
1971	29	Dodgers	NL	155	649	549	82	162	24	1	23	90	8/1	93	113	.295	.395	.468	.863	151	257
1972*	30	Chisox	AL	148	609	506	90	156	28	5	37	113	19/8	99	126	.308	.420	.603	1.023	199	305
1973*	31	Chisox	AL	72	288	250	39	79	20	3	16	41	7/2	33	51	.316	.394	.612	1.006	176	153

YEAR	AGE	TEAM	LEAGUE	G	PA	AB	R	H	2B	3B	HR	RBI	SB/CS	BB	SO	BA	OBP	SLG	OPS	OPS+	TB
1974*	32	Chisox	AL	128	525	462	84	139	23	1	32	88	7/1	57	89	.301	.375	.563	.938	164	260
1975	33	Phillies	NL	119	481	416	54	97	21	3	12	62	11/2	58	109	.233	.327	.385	.712	94	160
1976	34	Phillies	NL	85	339	298	52	80	16	1	15	49	11/4	37	63	.268	.346	.480	.826	130	143
1977	35	Athletics	AL	54	200	171	19	41	4	0	5	31	1/3	24	36	.240	.330	.351	.681	89	60
TOTAL		15 YEARS		1749	7314	6332	1099	1848	320	79	351	1119	133/52	894	1556	.292	.378	.534	.912	156	3379

KEY

G	Games played
AB	At bats
PA	Plate appearances
R	Runs scored
H	Hits
2B	Doubles
3B	Triples
HR	Home runs
RBI	Runs batted in
SB/CS	Stolen bases/Caught stealing
BB	Walks
SO	Strikeouts
BA	Batting average
OBP	On-base percentage
SLG	Slugging percentage
OPS	OBP + SLG
TB	Total bases
OPS+	Adjusted to player's ballpark

*Selection to All-Star team

Bold numbers: League leader

FIELDING

YEAR	AGE	TEAM	LEAGUE	POS	G	CH	PO	A	E	DP	Fld%	RF/G
1963	21	Phillies	NL	LF	7	11	9	0	2	0	.818	1.29
				OF	7	12	10	0	2	0	.833	1.43
				3B	1	0	0	0	0	0	.000	0.00
1964	22	Phillies	NL	3B	162	520	154	325	41	30	.921	2.96
1965*	23	Phillies	NL	3B	160	460	129	305	26	29	.943	2.71
				SS	2	1	1	0	0	0	1.000	0.50
1966*	24	Phillies	NL	3B	91	270	81	180	9	15	.967	2.87
				LF	47	74	67	2	5	0	.932	1.47
				OF	47	72	65	2	5	0	.931	1.43
1967*	25	Phillies	NL	3B	121	379	95	249	35	23	.908	2.84
				2B	1	0	0	0	0	0	.000	0.00
				SS	1	0	0	0	0	0	.000	0.00
1968	26	Phillies	NL	LF	139	214	203	5	6	2	.972	1.50
				OF	139	219	208	5	6	0	.973	1.53
				3B	10	28	7	15	6	4	.786	2.20
				CF	1	0	0	0	0	0	.000	0.00
1969	27	Phillies	NL	1B	117	1094	1024	54	16	100	.985	9.21

YEAR	AGE	TEAM	LEAGUE	POS	G	CH	PO	A	E	DP	Fld%	RF/G
1970*	28	Cardinals	NL	1B	79	722	676	41	5	67	.933	9.08
				3B	38	105	27	67	11	3	.895	2.47
				LF	3	8	5	1	2	0	.750	2.00
				OF	3	8	5	1	2	0	.750	2.00
1971	29	Dodgers	NL	3B	67	184	36	133	15	12	.918	2.52
				LF	60	99	90	5	4	0	.960	1.58
				OF	60	97	88	5	4	0	.959	1.55
				1B	28	273	258	13	2	26	.993	9.68
1972*	30	Chisox	AL	1B	143	1308	1234	67	7	94	.995	9.10
				3B	2	3	1	2	0	0	1.000	1.50
1973*	31	Chisox	AL	1B	67	644	597	43	4	55	.994	9.55
				2B	2	7	4	3	0	0	1.000	3.50
				DH	1							
1974*	32	Chisox	AL	1B	125	1062	998	49	15	112	.986	8.38
				2B	1	2	0	1	1	0	.500	1.00
				DH	1							
1975	33	Phillies	NL	1B	113	988	900	70	18	79	.982	8.58
1976	34	Phillies	NL	1B	85	723	671	44	8	71	.989	8.41
1977	35	Athletics	AL	1B	50	433	389	37	7	36	.984	8.52
				DH	1							

YEAR	AGE	TEAM	LEAGUE	POS	G	CH	PO	A	E	DP	Fld%	RF/G
TOTAL		9 Seasons		1B	807	7247	6747	418	82	640	.989	8.88
		9 Seasons		3B	652	1949	530	1276	143	116	.927	2.77
		5 Seasons		OF	256	408	376	13	19	0	.953	1.52
		5 Seasons		LF	256	406	374	13	19	2	.953	1.51
		3 Seasons		2B	4	9	4	4	1	0	.889	2.00
		3 Seasons		DH	3							
		2 Seasons		SS	3	1	1	0	0	0	1.000	0.33
		1 Season		CF	1	0	0	0	0	0	.000	0.00
TOTAL		15 Seasons			1722	9614	7658	1711	245	756	.975	5.44

KEY

POS.	Field position
G	Games played
Ch	Chances
PO	Put outs
E	Errors
DP	Double plays
Fld%	Fielding percentage
A	Assists
RF/G	Range factor per game (PO + A)/Games played

*Selection to All-Star team

APPENDIX C:
DICK ALLEN'S HONORS AND CAREER AND SINGLE-SEASON RANKINGS

HIGHLIGHTS & AWARDS
National League Rookie of the Year Award: 1964
American League Most Valuable Player Award: 1972
7-time All Star: 1965-1967, 1970, 1972-1974
2-time American League Home Run Champion: 1972, 1974
American League RBI Champion: 1972
3-time Slugging % Leader: 1966 (NL), 1972, 1974 (AL)
3-time Adjusted OPS+ Leader: 1966, 1967 (NL), 1972 (AL)
2-time On-Base % Leader: 1967 (NL), 1972 (AL)
WAR Position Player Leader: 1972 (AL)
Total Bases Leader: 1964 (NL)
2-time Runs Created Leader: 1966 (NL), 1972 (AL)
3-time Extra Base Hits Leader: 1964, 1966 (NL), 1972 (AL)
Bases on Balls Leader: 1972 (AL)
20-Home Run Seasons: 10 (1964-1972 & 1974)
30-Home Run Seasons: 6 (1966, 1968-1970, 1972 & 1974)
40-Home Run Seasons: 1 (1966)
100 RBI Seasons: 3 (1966, 1970 & 1972)
100 Runs Scored Seasons: 2 (1964 & 1966)
200 Hits Seasons: 1 (1964)

HALL OF FAME VOTING (75% of vote needed for induction)		
1983	Baseball Writers	3.7%
1985	Baseball Writers	7.1%
1986	Baseball Writers	9.6%
1987	Baseball Writers	13.3%
1988	Baseball Writers	12.2%
1989	Baseball Writers	7.8%
1990	Baseball Writers	13.1%
1991	Baseball Writers	13.3%
1992	BaseballWriters	16.0%
1993	Baseball Writers	16.5%
1994	Baseball Writers	14.5%
1995	Baseball Writers	15.7%
1996	Baseball Writers	18.9%
1997	Baseball Writers	16.7%
2014	Veterans Com.	68.7%

ALL-TIME RANKINGS		
Home runs	92nd	(351)
RBI	196th	(1,119)
Batting average	336th	(.292)
On-base percentage	183rd	(.378)
Slugging average	41st	(.534)
OPS	55th	(.912)

MVP Award Voting		
1964	Phillies	7th
1965	Phillies	28th
1966	Phillies	4th
1972	White Sox	1st
1973	White Sox	35th
1974	White Sox	23rd

BATTING AVERAGE		
1964 NL	.318	(5th)
1965 NL	.302	(9th)
1966 NL	.317	(4th)
1967 NL	.307	(7th)
1972 AL	.308	(3rd)
1974 AL	.301	(10th)
Career:	**.292**	**(336th all-time)**

Wins Above Replacement (WAR)		
1964	National League	8.8 (3rd)
1966	National League	7.5 (8th)
1972	American League	8.6 (3rd)
Career:	58.7 (192nd all-time)	

WAR Position Players	
1964 NL	8.8 (3rd)
1965 NL	6.4 (7th)
1966 NL	7.5 (5th)
1967 NL	5.3 (10th)
1971 NL	5.4 (9th)
1972 AL	8.6 (1st)
Career:	58.7 (125th all-time)

Offensive WAR	
1964 NL	8.8 (2nd)
1965 NL	7.2 (4th)
1966 NL	8.3 (1st)
1967 NL	6.9 (4th)
1968 NL	5.4 (6th)
1971 NL	6.3 (4th)
1972 AL	8.8 (1st)
1974 AL	4.8 (7th)
Career:	69.9 (61st all-time)

ON-BASE PERCENTAGE	
1964 NL	.382 (7th)
1965 NL	.375 (9th)
1966 NL	.396 (3rd)
1967 NL	.404 (1st)
1971 NL	.395 (6th)
1972 AL	.420 (1st)
1974 AL	.375 (9th)
Career:	.378 (183rd all-time)

Adjusted OPS+	
1964 NL	162 (3rd)
1965 NL	145 (7th)
1966 NL	181 (1st)
1967 NL	174 (1st)
1968 NL	160 (2nd)
1969 NL	165 (6th)
1970 NL	146 (8th)
1971 NL	151 (5th)
1972 AL	199 (1st)
1974 AL	164 (2nd)
Career:	156 (20th all-time)

SLUGGING PERCENTAGE	
1964 NL	.557 (3rd)
1966 NL	.632 (1st)
1967 NL	.566 (2nd)
1968 NL	.520 (2nd)
1969 NL	.573 (3rd)
1970 NL	.560 (8th)
1972 AL	.603 (1st)
1974 AL	.563 (1st)
Career:	.534 (41st all-time)

GAMES PLAYED	
1964 NL	162 (2nd)
1965 NL	161 (6th)

AT BATS	
1964 NL	632 (6th)
1965 NL	619 (8th)

PLATE APPEARANCES	
1964 NL	709 (2nd)
1965 NL	707 (7th)

On-Base + Slugging % (OPS)	
1964 NL	.939 (5th)
1965 NL	.870 (7th)
1966 NL	1.027 (1st)
1967 NL	.970 (1st)
1968 NL	.872 (2nd)
1969 NL	.949 (5th)
1970 NL	.937 (8th)
1971 NL	.863 (10th)
1972 AL	1.023 (1st)
1974 AL	.938 (1st)
Career:	.912 (52nd all-time)

RUNS SCORED	
1964 NL	125 (1st)
1965 NL	93 (10th)
1966 NL	112 (3rd)
1968 NL	87 (6th)
1972 AL	90 (4th)
1974 AL	84 (7th)
Career:	1,099 (249th)

RUNS CREATED	
1964 NL	135 (2nd)
1965 NL	119 (6th)
1966 NL	131 (1st)
1967 NL	109 (6th)
1968 NL	97 (8th)
1971 NL	102 (9th)
1972 AL	131 (1st)
1974 AL	96 (7th)
Career:	**1,292 (153rd all-time)**

HITS	
1964 NL	201 (3rd)
1965 NL	187 (6th)
1972 AL	156 (8th)

DOUBLES	
1964 NL	38 (4th)
1965 NL	31 (8th)
1967 NL	31 (8th)
1972 AL	28 (6th)

TRIPLES	
1964 NL	13 (1st)
1965 NL	14 (2nd)
1966 NL	10 (4th)
1967 NL	10 (5th)
1968 NL	9 (4th)
1972 AL	5 (10th)

HOME RUNS	
1964 NL	29 (7th)
1966 NL	40 (2nd)
1967 NL	23 (10th)
1968 NL	33 (2nd)
1969 NL	32 (6th)
1970 NL	34 (7th)
1972 AL	37 (1st)
1974 AL	32 (1st)
Career:	**351 (92nd all-time)**

EXTRA BASE HITS	
1964 NL	80 (1st)
1965 NL	65 (9th)
1966 NL	75 (1st)
1967 NL	64 (4th)
1968 NL	59 (4th)
1969 NL	58 (10th)
1972 AL	70 (1st)
1974 AL	56 (4th)
Career:	**750 (150th all-time)**

TOTAL BASES	
1964 NL	352 (1st)
1965 NL	306 (9th)
1966 NL	331 (3rd)
1968 NL	271 (7th)
1972 AL	305 (2nd)
1974 AL	260 (7th)
Career:	**3,379 (195th all-time)**

RUNS BATTED IN	
1966 NL	110 (3rd)
1968 NL	90 (5th)
1972 AL	113 (1st)
1974 AL	88 (7th)
Career:	**1,119 (197th)**

BASES ON BALLS	
1964 NL	67 (7th)
1965 NL	74 (9th)
1966 NL	68 (9th)
1967 NL	75 (5th)
1968 NL	74 (4th)
1971 NL	93 (4th)
1972 AL	99 (1st)
Career:	**894 (173rd all-time)**

INTENTIONAL BASES ON BALLS	
1964 NL	13 (5th)
1966 NL	13 (5th)
1967 NL	18 (8th)
1968 NL	15 (8th)
1970 NL	16 (3rd)
1971 NL	13 (9th)
1972 AL	16 (3rd)
Career:	**138 (61st all-time)**

AT BAT PER HOME RUN	
1964 NL	21.8 (9th)
1966 NL	13.1 (1st)
1967 NL	20.1 (6th)
1968 NL	15.8 (2nd)
1969 NL	13.7 (3rd)
1970 NL	13.5 (3rd)
1972 AL	13.7 (1st)
1974 AL	14.4 (1st)
Career:	**18.0 (77th all-time)**

STRIKEOUTS	
1964 NL	138 (1st)
1965 NL	150 (1st)
1966 NL	136 (3rd)
1967 NL	117 (2nd)
1968 NL	161 (2nd)
1969 NL	144 (3rd)
1971 NL	113 (10th)
1972 AL	126 (3rd)
1975 NL	109 (5th)
Career:	**1,556 (45th all-time)**

STOLEN BASES	
1965 NL	15 (9th)
1967 NL	20 (8th)

NOTES

Preface

1. For game details see Ray Kelly, "37110 Watch Allen Slam Phils to a Split with Giants," *Philadelphia Evening Bulletin*, July 9, 1965. For fan treatment of Allen and quote see Dick Allen and Tim Whitaker, *Crash: The Life and Times of Dick Allen* (New York: Ticknor & Fields, 1989), 58–59.

2. Joseph S. Clark Jr., "Rally and Relapse, 1946–1968," in *Philadelphia: A 300-Year History*, ed. Russell F. Weigley (New York: W.W. Norton, 1981), 662–679; Bruce Kuklick, *To Every Thing a Season: Shibe Park and Urban Philadelphia, 1909–1976* (Princeton, NJ: Princeton University Press, 1991), 154–156.

3. Rich Westcott and Frank Bilovsky, *The Phillies Encyclopedia*, 3rd ed. (Philadelphia: Temple University Press, 2004), 125.

4. Allen and Whitaker, *Crash*, 58.

5. Allen and Whitaker, *Crash*, 69.

6. Bill Conlin, "Richie Is Beautiful, He Don't Give a Damn for Nobody," *Jock Magazine,* January 1970, 88–94.

7. For most controversial columns see: Larry Merchant, "Two Games and an Apology at Richie Allen Dell," *Philadelphia Daily News*, July 8, 1965; Larry Merchant, "'Psst, Larry . . . I Heard A Story," *Philadelphia Daily News*, July 9, 1965; Larry Merchant, "Allen v. Thomas, Round 10," *Philadelphia Daily News*, July 12, 1965; Stan Hochman, "Sleepy-time Superstar," *Philadelphia Daily News*, July 10, 1967; Stan Hochman, "AWOL Allen: 'I'd Be Different on Another Club,'" *Philadelphia Daily News*, March 9, 1968; Stan Hochman, "Even Allen's 'Manager' Wishes He'd Grow Up," *Philadelphia Daily News*, March 12, 1968; Bill Conlin, "Allen Answered to Boos: 'I Think I Might Like to Be Traded,'" *Philadelphia Daily News*, August 18, 1967; Bill Conlin, "After the Big Fine, More Pampering?," *Philadelphia Daily News*, March 9, 1968; Bill Conlin, "What If Allen Were White?" *Philadelphia Daily News*, July 3, 1969; and Conlin, "Richie Is Beautiful," 88–94.

8. Dan Epstein, *Big Hair and Plastic Grass: A Funky Ride through Baseball and America in the Swinging '70s* (New York: Thomas Dunne Books, 2010), 2–4.

9. Allen and Whitaker, *Crash*; William C. Kashatus, *September Swoon: Richie Allen, the 1964 Phillies, and Racial Integration* (University Park: Penn State University Press, 2004); and Mitchell Nathanson, *God Almighty Hisself: The Life and Legacy of Dick Allen* (Philadelphia: University of Pennsylvania Press, 2016).

10. Gene Collier, "Allen's Book Like Career: It Could Have Been Better," *Philadelphia Inquirer*, April 5, 1989; and Stan Hochman, "A Book on Allen Should Do More Than Blame Writers," *Philadelphia Daily News*, April 3, 1989.

11. For book reviews of *September Swoon* in the popular press see: Allen Barra, "The Best Player Eligible for the Hall of Fame," *Wall Street Journal*, July 28, 2005; Tony Reid, "'September Swoon' Offers Picture of Change," *The Washington Post*, March 21, 2004; David Plaut, "Your Summer Baseball Reading List: 'September Swoon,' " *Baseball Weekly/ USA TODAY*, June 23–29, 2004, 47; Jon Caroulis, "Book Relieves Pain of Phillies 1964 Collapse," *Baseball America*, April 26–May 9, 2004, 46; Bruce Seeman, "Regrets? Allen Had a Few with Phillies," *Charlotte Observer* (Charlotte, NC), May 2, 2004; and Bill O'Driscoll, "Book Review: September Swoon," *Pittsburgh City Paper*, August 5, 2004. For reviews from scholarly journals, see: Paul Blairon, "Sacrificial Lamb," *California Literary Review*, April 24, 2007; Art Rust Jr., "Book Review: September Swoon," *Black Issues*, July–August 2004; Derek Catsam, "Book Review: September Swoon," *Virginia Quarterly Review*, July 1, 2004; Neil Lanctot, "September Swoon," *Pennsylvania Magazine of History and Biography* (April 2005): 242; and "The Dave Moore Award," *Elysian Field Quarterly: The Baseball Review* (Winter 2005): 3.

12. Allen has refused all book interviews since 2003, when I did my second and final interview for *September Swoon*. He did agree to record his experiences for History Making Productions, a Philadelphia-based film production company, in 2012. Allen appears in two films: *Promise for a Better City, 1944–1964* and *The Fight, 1965–1978*. The films are part of a much larger, ongoing work titled "Philadelphia: The Great Experiment," which attempts to capture the city's history on film. But he is guarded, offering nothing more than what he had already said in his 1989 autobiography.

13. Nathanson, *God Almighty Hisself*, 335–338.

Chapter 1: Wampum

1. Joseph F. Lowry, "Whoever Heard of Wampum, Pa.?" *The Sunday Bulletin Magazine*, June 21, 1964, 4.

2. For the description of Wampum, the residents, and community values, see interviews by the author with Dick Allen, West Chester, Pennsylvania, August 15, 2003; Hank Allen, Upper Marlboro, Maryland, April 9, 2016; Guy Demaio, New Castle, Pennsylvania, March 28, 2016; and Jim Santelli, Ellwood City, Pennsylvania, March 29, 2016.

3. Loretta Jefferson, "The Rhodes Story: Genealogy and History of the Rhodes-Whitmire Family" (unpublished manuscript, 1998), 3, 12–13. The six children of James Rhodes and Sallie Whitmire were Louise, Javan, two infant sons who died shortly after birth, Era, and Cora.

4. Jefferson, "The Rhodes Story," 14; and Sonny King, interview with the author, Wampum, Pennsylvania, June 1, 2016.

5. See Jefferson, "The Rhodes Story," 6–7; Hank Allen, interview; and Era Allen quoted in Myron Cope, "What, Then, Is Wrong With Richie Allen?" *Sport Magazine*, May 1966, 85. Helen Craine, the eldest daughter, died of pneumonia at fourteen (see Hank Allen, interview). Initially, President Franklin D. Roosevelt's New Deal programs of the 1930s were not directed at women because their roles were typically relegated to housewife and mother. But First Lady Eleanor Roosevelt soon promoted the idea of a women's division in the new Federal Emergency Relief Administration (FERA). She sponsored a White House Conference on the "Emergency Needs of Women" in November 1933. Shortly after, a new program, the Civil Works Administration (CWA), included women. By the end of 1933, nationwide about 300,000 needy women were at work on CWA jobs, including canning, running school lunchrooms, sewing, and weaving. In 1935, a new and much larger work program, the Works Progress Administration (WPA), was created. At its peak in 1936, about a half million women were on what were called "made work" jobs that were categorized as "socially useful." Needy families benefited from the clothing, household goods, and mattresses made on the Clothing and Production Projects. According to Hank Allen, Era was a seamstress for the CWA and WPA programs. See Martha H. Swain, "Women's Work Relief in the Great Depression," Mississippi History Now, www.mshistory.k12.ms.us/articles/251/womens-work-relief-in-the-great-depression; and Hank Allen, interview.

6. "Era C. Allen, 88, mother of ex-Phillie Dick Allen," *New Castle News*, April 25, 1995; Hank Allen, interview; and Allen and Whitaker, *Crash*, 49.

7. Allen and Whitaker, *Crash*, 48–51; Hank Allen, interview; and Ron Allen, interview with the author, Youngstown, Ohio, April 8, 2016.

8. Allen Barra, "An Embarrassment of Richies," *Philadelphia Magazine* 38 (August 1995): 53.

9. Allen and Whitaker, *Crash*, 37; Cope, "What, Then, Is Wrong With Richie Allen?," 36; and Lowery, "Whoever Heard of Wampum, Pa.?" 5. Various accounts maintain that Dick injured his left eye in different ways, but according to his brother Hank, the initial injury was the result of an exploding spring from a screen door. Hank also maintained that Dick reinjured the same eye on at least two more occasions (see Hank Allen, interview).

10. Dick Allen quoted in Cope, "What, Then, Is Wrong With Richie Allen?," 84; and Dick Allen quoted in Charles Moritz, "Dick Allen," *Current Biography Yearbook*, 1973 (New York: H. W. Wilson, 1973), 4. Allen would later admit that in spite of Wampum's racial tolerance, he learned that "there were things you just didn't do, like dating a white girl" (see Allen and Whitaker, *Crash*, 42). Dick's brothers Hank and Ronnie stated that they learned pretty quickly how to navigate race relations in the town. They also admitted that sometimes they felt they were accepted by white residents only because they were gifted athletes (Hank Allen, interview; and Ron Allen, interview).

11. Dick Allen quoted in Roy Blount Jr., "Swinging in a Groove of His Own. When Dick Allen Crashed, So Did the White Sox," *Sports Illustrated* 39, no. 11 (September 10, 1973): 104–114.

12. Allen and Whitaker, *Crash*, 39.

13. Era Allen quoted in William Leggett, "The Rookie From Wampum, Pa.," *Sports Illustrated* 20, no. 16 (April 20, 1964): 29; and Sandy Grady, "Allen's 2 Heroes: His Mom and Ernie Banks," *Philadelphia Evening Bulletin*, April 26, 1964.

14. Walter Kubinski quoted in Lowery, "Whoever Heard of Wampum?" 5.

15. Santelli, interview.

16. Kubinski quoted in Lowery, "Whoever Heard of Wampum, Pa.?," 5.

17. Hank Allen, interview; and Ron Allen, interview.

18. Allen quoted in George Kiseda, "Allen Ignores Fans; Catcalls," *Philadelphia Evening Bulletin*, July 8, 1965; Allen quoted in Grady, "Allen's 2 Heroes"; and Dick Allen, interview with the author, West Chester, Pennsylvania, April 21, 2001.

19. Era Allen quoted in Lowry, "Whoever Heard of Wampum, Pa.?," 5.

20. Era Allen quoted in Lowry, "Whoever Heard of Wampum, Pa.?," 4.

21. Era Allen quoted in Grady, "What, Then, Is Wrong With Richie Allen?," 85.

22. Allen and Whitaker, *Crash*, 36.

23. Hank Allen, interview.

24. L. Butler Hennon quoted in Cope, "What, Then, Is Wrong with Richie Allen?," 36.

25. Hennon quoted in Grady, "Allen's 2 Heroes."

26. Dick Allen, interview, 2001.

27. Hank Allen, interview; Ron Allen, interview; and Dick Allen quoted in Bob Broeg, "'I'm No Angel, But I'll Play Ball,' Says Allen," *St. Louis Post-Dispatch*, March 13, 1970.

28. Richard Allen Jr. in "Dick Allen & the Misleading 'Paternal Abandonment Script,'" National Parents Organization, www. nationalparentsorganization.org/blog/1160-dick-allen-the-mis, accessed March 6, 2016.

29. Wendell Allen quoted in Lowery, "Whoever Heard of Wampum, Pa.?," 5.

30. Jeff Bales Jr., "Wampum High School Gymnasium," LawrenceCountyMemoirs.com, accessed March 14, 2016.

31. Hank Allen, interview.

32. Bales Jr., "Wampum High School Gymnasium." Some of Hennon's unusual practice techniques were subsequently adopted by the Soviet Union's Olympic basketball team.

33. Santelli, interview.

34. Bob Melder, "Wampum Wins, Defeats Avonworth By Margin of 25 Points," *New Castle News*, March 11, 1958.

35. Bob Melder, "Wampum Captures WPIAL Championship," *New Castle News*, March 14, 1958.

36. Bob Melder, "Wampum Humiliates Renovo. Harold Allen Turns in 22 Points for Indians," *New Castle News*, March 19, 1958.

37. Bob Melder, "Never-Say-Die Indians Defeat Fredonia, 63-60," *New Castle News*, March 26, 1958.

38. Bob Melder, "State Title Breeze For Wampum," *New Castle News*, March 29, 1958.

39. Bob Melder, "Snowden Bumps Wampum from WPIAL," *New Castle News*, March 4, 1959.

40. "Sleepy Tops Scorers. Indians Own 20-2 Mark," *New Castle News*, February 24, 1959.

41. Santelli, interview.

42. "Rich Allen Section 20 Point Leader," *New Castle News*, March 16, 1960; and Thad Burowski, "Sleepy Allen Leads Indians to '20' Title Playoff," *New Castle News*, February 24, 1960.

43. Santelli, interview.

44. Larry Craven quoted in Lowry, "Whoever Heard of Wampum, Pa.?," 5.

45. Hennon quoted in Bob Smizik, "Somebody Still Likes Rich Allen," *Pittsburgh Press*, July 1, 1969

46. Bob Melder, "They Beat Us Up Physically: Milanovich," *New Castle News*, March 5, 1960.

47. Bob Melder, "Indians Coast Into WPIAL Final," *New Castle News*, March 10, 1960; and Bob Melder, "Wampum Has Easy Time in WPIAL Final," *New Castle News*, March 15, 1960.

48. Bob Vosburg, "Indians Roll To West Regional Game," *New Castle News*, March 19, 1960; Bob Melder, "West Middlesex Bows Out, 51-37; Montrose Next Foe," *New Castle News*, March 23, 1960; and Bob Vosburg, "Wampum Defeats Dogged Montrose Meteors, 57-51, in Uphill Struggle For PIAA Crown," *New Castle News*, March 26, 1960. Wampum High School's status as a basketball powerhouse came to an end in the 1961–62 school year with the decision to merge into the newly reorganized Ellwood City Area School District. Afterward, students from Wampum and Chewton began attending Lincoln Junior-Senior High School in Ellwood. Although Hennon went on to coach the Lincoln varsity basketball team at the Class A level, he never again realized the success he had achieved at Wampum. In March 1994, the small gymnasium where the Indians played was rededicated as the "L. B. Hennon Recreation Center" and is still used by the public today

49. "Rich Allen Section 20 Point Leader"; Allen and Whitaker, *Crash*, 36; and Ron Allen, interview.

50. Hennon quoted in Lou Skursenski, "Richard Allen Chosen MVP in Section 20," *New Castle News*, March 22, 1960; and Hennon quoted in Smizik, "Somebody Still Likes Rich Allen."

51. Bukowski quoted in Skursenski, "Richard Allen Chosen MVP."

52. Santelli, interview.

53. Demaio, interview.

54. Demaio, interview.

55. Demaio, interview.

56. Demaio, interview.

57. King, interview.

58. Ogden quoted in Sandy Grady, "The Old Allen John Ogden Remembers," *Philadelphia Evening Bulletin*, September 9, 1969.

59. Grady, "The Old Allen John Ogden Remembers"; Davis O. Barker, "Baseball's Greatest Sacrifice," www.baseballalmanac.com., accessed March 14, 2016; and Bill Weiss and Marshall Wright, "Baseball's Top 100 Teams: 1922 Baltimore Orioles," www.milb.com, accessed March 14, 2016. Ogden led the International League the next three years in wins and innings pitched. In 1920, he went 27-9 (3.25) with 321 innings pitched, and in 1921, he had the best year of his career: 31-9 (2.30) with 318 innings pitched. During the 1921 season, Ogden won eighteen consecutive victories. In nine of the games, he gave up five or fewer hits. Both the thirty-one victories and eighteen consecutive wins were twentieth-century league records at the time, but were surpassed two years later by his teammate Rube Parnham, with thirty-three wins, twenty in a row. Ogden remained with the Orioles through 1927, pitching for six of the seven consecutive championship teams. He topped the twenty-game victory mark in six of his eight years with Baltimore and led the league in wins one more time with a 24-15 record in 1926. He was purchased by the St. Louis Browns before the 1928 season for $12,500 and two players. Ogden went 14-15 (4.15) in 1928, then dropped to 4-8 (4.94) in 1929. He was out of baseball in 1930, returning to pitch for Cincinnati in 1931–32, with little success. His major league totals were 25-34 with a 4.24 ERA. He went back to the International League in 1933 with Rochester and finished the season with Baltimore. His minor league record was 213-103 (3.36), all in the International League. He holds the league record for career victories.

60. Ogden quoted in Grady, "The Old Allen John Ogden Remembers." The baseball historian Bill Jenkinson, an authority on home run history, claims that "based upon the record of batsmen without the benefit of performance enhancing drugs, Dick Allen is the single mightiest hitter that Major League Baseball has produced in the last half century." See "Dick Allen: Hall of Fame Power Hitter," Dickallen15.com, accessed March 14, 2016.

61. Kashatus, *September Swoon*, 46–47.

62. Era Allen quoted in Grady, "Allen's 2 Heroes"; Allen and Whitaker, *Crash*, 47–48; and Hank Allen, interview.

63. Hank Allen, interview.

64. Era Allen quoted in Grady, "Allen's 2 Heroes."

65. Dick Allen, interview, 2003.

66. Grady, "The Old Allen John Ogden Remembers."

67. Dick Allen, interview, 2001.

68. Allen and Whitaker, *Crash*, 47–48.

69. Cope, "What, Then, Is Wrong With Richie Allen?," 85.

Chapter 2: Baptism by Fire

1. Jackie Robinson, *I Never Had It Made* (New York: Putnam, 1972), 71–76.

2. David Falkner, *Great Time Coming: The Life of Jackie Robinson from Baseball to Birmingham* (New York: Simon & Schuster, 1995), 163–164; Tom McGrath, "Color Me Badd," *The Fan,* September 1996, 39; and William C. Kashatus, *Jackie & Campy: The Untold Story of Their Rocky Relationship and the Breaking of Baseball's Color Line* (Lincoln: University of Nebraska Press, 2014), 95–101.

3. Ed Linn, "The Tragedy of the Phillies," *Sport Magazine* 36 (March 1965): 23–26; and "Obituary of John Kennedy, Former Phillies Shortstop, 71," *Philadelphia Inquirer*, April 30, 1998. Among the early black prospects who signed with the Phillies but never made it to the major leagues with the team were pitcher Jim Mason and shortstop Teddy Washington. While Kennedy was the first African American promoted to the big leagues by the Phillies, his time there was brief. After going hitless in five regular-season games, Kennedy was sent down to the minors, never to be heard from again. See *Philadelphia Inquirer*, May 6, 1957.

4. Michael Sokolove, "Nice Is Not Enough," *Philadelphia Inquirer Magazine,* March 30, 1997, 21; and McGrath, "Color Me Badd," 39.

5. For the urban history of Philadelphia see Russell F. Weigley, *Philadelphia: A 300-Year History* (New York: W. W. Norton, 1982), 704–727; and John Bauman, Norman P. Hummon, and Edward K. Muller, "Public Housing, Isolation and the Urban Underclass: Philadelphia's Richard Allen Homes, 1941–1965," in *African Americans in Pennsylvania: Shifting Historical Perspectives*, ed. Joe William Trotter Jr. and Eric Ledell Smith (Harrisburg: Pennsylvania Historical and Museum Commission & Pennsylvania State University Press, 1997), 443–468. For an analysis of the social problems confronting Philadelphia in the 1960s see James A. Michener, *The Quality of Life* (Philadelphia: Girard Company, 1970).

6. "Mayor in the Middle: Philadelphia's James Tate," *New York Times*, August 31, 1964

7. Weigley, *Philadelphia*, 661–663; and S. A. Paolantonio, *Frank Rizzo: The Last Big Man in Bog City America* (Philadelphia: Camino Books, 1993).

8. Westcott and Bilovsky, *Phillies Encyclopedia*, 68–75.

9. Kuklick, *To Every Thing A Season*, 148–149.

10. Robert R. M. Carpenter Jr. quoted in Westcott and Bilovsky, *Phillies Encyclopedia*, 377.

11. Ed Richter, *View from the Dugout: A Season with Baseball's Amazing Gene Mauch* (Philadelphia: Chilton Books, 1964); and Westcott and Bilovsky, *Phillies Encyclopedia*, 452–454.

12. Mauch quoted in Ray Kelly, "Mauch Cracks Down on Phillies," *Philadelphia Evening Bulletin*, May 12, 1960.

13. See "Robert M. Carpenter Papers, Philadelphia Baseball Club – National League," manuscript box no. 1: Player Development Papers, 1957–1964, Manuscript Collection, Hagley Library, Wilmington, Delaware (hereafter "Carpenter Papers"). Approximately twenty players were on the roster of each team in the Phillies' minor league system during 1957–64. Those teams were Buffalo (AAA), Indianapolis (AAA), Chatanooga (AA), Ashville (A), Williamsport (A), Des Moines (B), Bakersfield (C), Tampa (D), Elmira (D), and Johnson City (D).

14. See "Player Signings, 1958–1964," Carpenter Papers.

15. See "Player Signings, 1958–1964," Carpenter Papers.

16. Westcott and Bilovsky, *Phillies Encyclopedia*, 490–491. It is important to note that John Kennedy was not the first minority player signed by the Phillies. That distinction belongs to Chico Fernandez, who was acquired from the Brooklyn Dodgers in spring 1957 to fill the team's need at shortstop. Fernandez was the Phillies' regular shortstop for two years, hitting .260 in 1957 and .230 in 1958 before losing the starting job. See Westcott and Bilovsky, *Phillies Encyclopedia*, 234–235.

17. Hank Allen, interview.

18. Dick Allen, interview, 2003.

19. For Allen's minor league statistics see "Dick Allen, Minor League Baseball Statistics," http://www.baseball-reference.com/register/player.cgi?id=allen-002ric, accessed March 2, 2016.

20. Ogden quoted in Dick Allen, interview, 2003; and Peter Bonventre, "Dick Allen: 'Still My Own Man,'" *Newsweek*, August 21, 1972, 83.

21. "Allen's Minor League Statistics"; and Cope, "What, Then, Is Wrong With Richie Allen?," 85.

22. Barbara Moore Allen, interview with the author, Williamsport, Pennsylvania, April 6, 2016; and Richard Allen Jr., interview with the author, Williamsport, Pennsylvania, November 10, 2015.

23. Dick Allen, interview, 2003.

24. Gayle Ronan Sims, "'Pete' Cera, 86; Worked for Phillies," obituary, *Philadelphia Inquirer*, February 26, 2004.

25. James P. Quigel Jr. and Louis E. Hunsinger Jr., *Gateway to the Majors: Williamsport and Minor League Baseball* (University Park: Pennsylvania State University Press, 2001), 134–136.

26. "Allen's Minor League Hitting Statistics."

27. Allen and Whitaker, *Crash*, 11.

28. "Williamsport Grays are 1962 Eastern League Champions," *Williamsport Grit*, September 2, 1962.

29. Allen and Whitaker, *Crash*, 14; and Carl Nesfield, "New Team, New Town, New Richie?" *Black Sports*, July 1971, 31.

30. Allen and Whitaker, *Crash*, 13–15.

31. Allen and Whitaker, *Crash*, 17.

32. Bob Razer, "The Black Traveler: Dick Allen and Little Rock Baseball, 1963," *Pulaski County Historical Review* 61 (Spring 2013): 2–10; and Leggett, "The Rookie From Wampum, Pa.," 29.

33. Razer, "The Black Traveler," 7–9.

34. Amis Guthridge to Ray Winder, Little Rock, Arkansas, October 13, 1962, letter quoted in Bob Razor, "Dick Allen," *The Encyclopedia of Arkansas History & Culture* (Little Rock: Central Arkansas Library System, 2014). www.encyclopediaofArkansas.net, accessed March 23, 2016.

35. Razor, "Dick Allen."

36. Orville Henry, *Arkansas Gazette*, April 21, 1963.

37. Allen and Whitaker, *Crash*, 11.

38. Bailey quoted in Razer, "The Black Traveler," 7–9.

39. Allen and Whitaker, *Crash*, 11.

40. Bailey quoted in Razer, "The Black Traveler," 7–9.

41. Allen and Whitaker, *Crash*, 13–14.

42. Allen and Whitaker, *Crash*, 20; and Matthew Frye Jacobson, "'Richie' Allen, Whitey's Ways, and Me: A Political Education," in *In the Game: Race, Identity, and Sports in the Twentieth Century*, ed. Amy Bass (New York: Palgrave, 2005), 19–46; and William C. Rhoden, "Weighing the Complexity of a Hall Candidate, and His Times," *New York Times*, December 7, 2014.

43. Dick Allen, interview, 2003.

44. Coy Craine quoted in Allen and Whitaker, *Crash*, 17–18.

45. Barbara Allen quoted in Allen and Whitaker, *Crash*, 18.

46. Barbara Moore Allen, interview.

47. Frank Lucchesi, interview with the author, Colleyville, Texas, January 26, 2014.

48. Dick Allen, interview, 2003.

49. Robert R. M. "Ruly" Carpenter III, interview with the author, Wilmington, Delaware, April 5, 2016

50. "Allen's Minor League Statistics."

51. Dick Allen, interview, 2003.

52. Westcott and Bilovsky, *Phillies Encyclopedia*, 79.

53. Dick Allen quoted in Allen Lewis, "Phils May Transplant Speedy Gardener Allen at Hot Corner," *Sporting News*, October 26, 1963.

54. Allen and Whitaker, *Crash*, 15.

Chapter 3: Rookie of the Year

1. Westcott and Bilovsky, *Phillies Encyclopedia*, 77.

2. Mauch quoted in Ray Kelly, "Mauch Set to Deal at Winter Confab," *Philadelphia Bulletin*, November 26, 1963; and Mauch quoted in Lewis, "Phils May Transplant Speedy Gardener Allen at Hot Corner."

3. Mauch to Allen, quoted in William Leggett, "The Rise and Fall of the Phillies," *Sports Illustrated*, March 1, 1965, 58; and Leggett, "The Rookie From Wampum, Pa.," 29.

4. Richie Allen quoted in Ray Kelly, "Phils Rich Allen 'Loves' Chance to Play Third Base," *Philadelphia Bulletin*, January 12, 1964.

5. Hoak quoted in Larry Merchant, "Hoak's Vow: 'I'm Going to Play,'" *Philadelphia Daily News*, March 26, 1964.

6. Allen quoted in Stan Hochman, "Hoak's Eyes Pinned on Allen," *Philadelphia Daily News*, March 9, 1964.

7. Hoak quoted in Merchant, "Hoak's Vow."

8. The baseball historian Bill Jenkinson compiled logs of all Allen's career home runs, as well as his daily offensive performance for every game he played, beginning in 1963 with the Arkansas Travelers and ending on May 17, 1977, his last MLB game with the Oakland A's. Hereafter, the home run log is referred to as "Jenkinson, HR log" and the daily offensive performance log is referred to as "Jenkinson, DOP log."

9. Bill Jenkinson, interview with the author, Paoli, PA, March 17, 2016.

10. Stan Hochman, "There's Only One Richie Allen," *Philadelphia Daily News*, April 20, 1964.

11. William A. Cook, *Summer of '64: A Pennant Lost* (Jefferson, NC: McFarland, 2002), 44–45.

12. Johnny Callison with John Sletten, *The Johnny Callison Story* (New York: Vantage, 1991), 104.

13. Callison with Sletten, *Johnny Callison Story*, 104.

14. Claude E. Harrison Jr., "Phils Have Pride and Richie Allen," *Philadelphia Tribune*, May 19, 1964.

15. Mauch quoted in Allen Lewis, "Phils Get Rich with Wampum Whiz," *Sporting News*, May 23, 1964.

16. Claude E. Harrison Jr.,"Phils' Allen to be Cited in Pittsburgh," *Philadelphia Tribune*, May 16, 1964.

17. Cook, *Summer of '64*, 55.

18. Frank Dolson, *Jim Bunning: Baseball and Beyond* (Philadelphia: Temple University Press, 1998), 58–59.

19. Dolson, *Jim Bunning*, 59.

20. Westcott and Bilovsky, *Phillies Encyclopedia*, 143.

21. Bunning quoted in Stan Hochman, "Bunning On the Ball in Real All Star Performance," *Philadelphia Daily News*, April 25, 1964.

22. Westcott and Bilovsky, *Phillies Encyclopedia*, 256–257.

23. Cook, *Summer of '64*, 67–68.

24. For the complete roster of the 1964 Phillies, see Westcott and Bilovsky, *Phillies Encyclopedia*, 80–81.

25. Dennis Bennett, interview with the author, Klamath Falls, OR: January 15, 2012.

26. Tony Taylor, interview with the author, Philadelphia, August 14, 2015.

27. Tony Gonzalez, interview with the author, Burlington, NJ, April 14, 2002.

28. Clay Dalrymple, interview with the author, Gold Beach, OR, April 10, 2016.

29. Westcott and Bilovsky, *Phillies Encyclopedia*, 441–442. For summary of Bunning's perfect game victory, see Dolson, *Jim Bunning*, 288–289.

30. Johnny Callison, interview with the author, Glenside, PA, July 19, 2001; Callison with Sletten, *Johnny Callison Story*, 106–107; and Cook, *Summer of '64*, 120–122.

31. Dalrymple, interview.

32. Larry Merchant, "Something Special," *Philadelphia Daily News*, July 13, 1964.

33. Era Allen quoted in Sandy Grady, "Mom Had Quick Hands Too—on Son's Seat," *Sporting News*, May 23, 1964.

34. Richie Allen quoted in Grady, "Mom Had Quick Hands Too."

35. Grant Jackson, interview with the author, Scranton, PA, June 8, 2002.

36. Johnny Briggs, interview with the author, West Chester, PA, April 21, 2001.

37. Allen and Whitaker, *Crash*, 105–106.

38. Bennett, interview. Johnny Briggs, Johnny Callison, Clay Dalrymple, and Tony Taylor all confirmed Bennet's remark on Allen being the first to protect Phillies hurlers after a knockdown pitch.

39. Claude E. Harrison Jr., "Another Allen, Ron, Signed by Phillies," *Philadelphia Tribune*, June 20, 1964. Ron Allen was a "bonus baby" who signed for $30,000. Initially, Ron Allen deferred to his mother and accepted a basketball scholarship to Youngstown State University instead of signing with the Phillies. But after he completed his junior year of college, Era Allen granted her permission after securing from her son a promise that he would complete his college education (see Ron Allen, interview).

40. Steve Wulf, "Year of the Blue Snow," *Sports Illustrated*, September 25, 1989, 84.

41. Leggett, "Rise and Fall of the Phillies," 59.

42. Leggett, "Rise and Fall of the Phillies," 59.

43. Allen Lewis, "Frank Thomas," in *The Ballplayers: Baseball's Ultimate Biographical Reference*, ed. Mike Shatzkin (New York: William Morrow, 1990), 1080–1082.

44. Dolson, *Jim Bunning*, 67.

45. Cook, *Summer of '64*, 174.

46. Ray Kelly, "Phils Obtain Cubs' Shantz on Waivers," *Philadelphia Bulletin*, August 16, 1964.

47. Cook, *Summer of '64*, 186–187.

48. Clark, "Rally and Relapse," 676.

49. Cook, *Summer of '64*, 191.

50. Clark, "Rally and Relapse," 676; and Kuklick, *To Every Thing A Season*, 155–156.

51. North Philadelphia resident named "R" quoted in Gerald Early, "Baseball and African American Life," in *Baseball: An Illustrated History*, ed. Geoffrey Ward and Ken Burns. (New York: Alfred Knopf, 1994), 417.

52. Dick Allen, interview, 2003.

53. Through the 1968 season, both first-place teams automatically went to the World Series, the only postseason play of that time.

54. Cook, *Summer of '64*, 215.

55. Cook, *Summer of '64*, 216–217; and Leggett, "Rise and Fall of the Phillies," 60.

56. Leggett, "Rise and Fall of the Phillies," 60; B. G. Kelly, "The Boys of Bummer," *Inside Sports*, October 1994, 77.

57. Allen and Whitaker, *Crash*, 56.

58. Dave Anderson, "1964: The Phillies Phlop" in *Pennant Races* (New York: Doubleday, 1994), 266; and Leggett, "Rise and Fall of the Phillies," 61.

59. Leggett, "Rise and Fall of the Phillies," 62.

60. Allen and Whitaker, *Crash*, 54–55

61. Anderson, "1964: The Phillies Phlop," 272–273.

62. Westcott and Bilovsky, *Phillies' Encyclopedia*, 125–126.

63. Ray Kelly, "Allen Sets Whiff Mark," *Philadelphia Evening Bulletin*, September 30, 1964.

64. Westcott and Bilovsky, *Phillies Encyclopedia*, 125–126.

65. Mauch quoted in Westcott and Bilovsky, *Phillies Encyclopedia*, 125.

Chapter 4: Boo!

1. Westcott and Bilovsky, *Phillies Encyclopedia*, 81.

2. Allen and Whitaker, *Crash*, 4.

3. Briggs, interview; Allen Lewis, "Briggs Came to Play and Phils Are Glad They Gave Him a Break," *Philadelphia Evening Bulletin*, July 31, 1965; and Allen Lewis, "Phils Eye Briggs as Stu's Successor," *Sporting News*, October 30, 1965.

4. Allen and Whitaker, *Crash*, 5–6.

5. Allen and Whitaker, *Crash*, 7; and Ruben Amaro Sr., interview with the author, Scranton, PA, August 11, 1999.

6. Johnny Callison, interview with the author, West Chester, PA, April 21, 2001.

7. Ray Kelly, "Reds Snap Phils' 6-Game Streak, 10-8," *Philadelphia Evening Bulletin*, July 4, 1965.

8. Allen and Whitaker, *Crash*, 8–9; and George Kiseda, "Allen Ignores Fans' Catcalls," *Philadelphia Evening Bulletin*, July 8, 1965.

9. Mauch quoted in David Wolf, "Let's Everybody Boo Rich Allen!" *Life Magazine*, August 1969, 51.

10. Thomas quoted in Allen Lewis, "Thomas Says He Regrets Fight, Calls Waiver Unfair," *Philadelphia Inquirer*, July 5, 1965.

11. Callison, interview.

12. Mauch quoted in Craig R. Wright, "Another View of Dick Allen," *SABR Baseball Research Journal* 25 (1995): 4.

13. Allen and Whitaker, *Crash*, 58–59; and Conlin, "Richie Is Beautiful," 91.

14. Allen and Whitaker, *Crash*, 69.

15. For the most controversial columns, see Larry Merchant, "Two Games and an Apology at Richie Allen Dell," *Philadelphia Daily News*, July 8, 1965; Larry Merchant, "'Psst, Larry . . . I Heard A Story," *Philadelphia Daily News*, July 9, 1965; Larry Merchant, "Allen v. Thomas, Round 10," *Philadelphia Daily News*, July 12, 1965; Stan Hochman, "Sleepy-time Superstar," *Philadelphia Daily News*, July 10, 1967; Stan Hochman, "AWOL Allen: 'I'd Be Different on Another Club,'" *Philadelphia Daily News*, March 9, 1968; Stan Hochman, "Even Allen's 'Manager' Wishes He'd Grow Up," *Philadelphia Daily News*, March 12, 1968; Bill Conlin, "Allen Answered to Boos: 'I Think I Might Like to Be Traded,'" *Philadelphia Daily News*, August 18, 1967; Bill Conlin, "After the Big Fine, More Pampering?" *Philadelphia Daily News*, March 9, 1968; Bill Conlin, "What If Allen Were White?" *Philadelphia Daily News*, July 3, 1969; and Conlin, "Richie Is Beautiful," 88–94.

16. Taylor, interview.

17. Hennon quoted in Bob Smizik, "Somebody Still Likes Rich Allen," *Pittsburgh Press*, July 1, 1969.

18. See Lois Wark, ed., *Millennium Philadelphia: The Last 100 Years* (Philadelphia: Camino Press, 1999), 219; and William Bennett, John Dilulio, and John P. Walters, *Body Count: Moral Poverty . . . and How to Win America's War Against Crime and Drugs* (New York: Simon & Schuster, 1996), 41.

19. Clark, "Rally and Relapse," 662–679; and Kuklick, *To Every Thing a Season*, 154–156.

20. Allen and Whitaker, *Crash*, 58.

21. Barbara Moore Allen, interview.

22. *Philadelphia Bulletin*, July 9, 1965.

23. *Philadelphia Inquirer*, August 20, 1966.

24. *Philadelphia Inquirer*, June 7, 1967.

25. Jenkinson, HR log; Jenkinson, DOP log.

26. Taylor, interview; and Jenkinson, HR log.

27. Taylor, interview; and Jenkinson, HR log.

28. Taylor, interview; and Jenkinson, HR log.

29. Tom Seaver and Willie Stargell quoted in *Baseball Digest* (January 1975): 36.

30. Westcott and Bilovsky, *Phillies Encyclopedia*, 81.

31. Westcott and Bilovsky, *Phillies Encyclopedia*, 126.

32. Ray Kelly, "Hard-Riding Rich Eludes Pitcher Posse," *Sporting News*, December 31, 1966, 27.

33. Allen quoted in Conlin, "Richie Is Beautiful," 91; and Allen and Whitaker, *Crash*, 8.

34. Allen and Whitaker, *Crash*, 65; and Wright, "Another View of Dick Allen," 5.

35. Era Allen quoted in Chris Perry, "Richie Allen's Mother Says She Raised a Good Son," *Philadelphia Tribune*, August 28, 1965; and Era Allen quoted in Smizik, "Somebody Still Likes Rich Allen."

36. Allen and Whitaker, *Crash*, 70–73.

37. Conlin, "Richie Is Beautiful," 91–92.

38. Frank Bilovsky, "Phils Fire Mauch in Coast-to-Coast Call," *Philadelphia Sunday Bulletin*, June 16, 1968.

39. Allen Lewis, "Lots of 'Ifs' in Mauch Sizeup of Phils," *Sporting News*, February 17, 1968.

40. John Quinn quoted in Allen Lewis, "Allen Rift Called 'Factor' in Mauch's Firing," *Sporting News*, June 29, 1968.

41. Gene Mauch quoted in Allen Lewis "Mauch Absolves Phillies in Firing Snafu," *Philadelphia Inquirer*, July 6, 1968.

42. Stan Hochman, "Mauch Fired, Phils Tried to Trade Allen," *Philadelphia Daily News*, June 17, 1968.

43. Arthur Daley, "Sports of the Times," *New York Times*, June 25, 1968.

44. Dalrymple, interview.

45. Barra, "An Embarrassment of Richies," 53.

46. Allen quoted in Wolf, "Let's Boo Allen," 52.

47. Bob Skinner quoted in Allen Lewis, "Many Pilots Would Like Rich—I'm One of 'Em—Skinner," *Sporting News*, June 29, 1968.

48. Claude E. Harrison, "Allen Celebrates Being a New Father by Getting on Base 9 Times," *Philadelphia Tribune*, June 22, 1968.

49. Howie Bedell, interview with the author, Pottstown, PA, March 20, 2016.

50. Bedell, interview.

51. Allen Lewis, "Phils End Drysale's Scoreless Inning Streak in 5-3 Loss," *Philadelphia Inquirer*, June 9, 1968.

52. Westcott and Bilovsky, *Phillies Encyclopedia*, 126.

53. Westcott and Bilovsky, *Phillies Encyclopedia*, 83.

54. Bob Carpenter quoted in Allen Lewis, "Carpenter Planning Shakeup of Phillies," *Sporting News*, October 19, 1968.

55. Allen Lewis, "Phils Put Callison, Rojas and Allen on the Trading Block," *Sporting News*, October 26, 1968.

56. Allen and Whitaker, *Crash*, 43.

57. Carl "Stump" Merrill, interview with the author, Harpswell, ME, May 4, 2016.

58. Allen quoted in "Richie Allen Not All Bad Boy," *New York Times*, May 18, 1969.

59. Allen and Rojas quoted in Wolf, "Let's Boo Rich Allen," 53.

60. Stan Hochman, "Allen's Latest Vacation Might Be His Last," *Philadelphia Daily News*, June 25, 1969.

61. Conlin, "Richie Is Beautiful," 93–94.

62. Exchange between President Nixon and Grant Jackson, quoted in Conlin, "Richie Is Beautiful," 88.

63. Leonard Sheeter, "Richie Allen A Hip Hitter," *Sport Magazine*, no. 44 (July 1967): 67; and Leonard Sheeter, "Baseball's Most Feared Power Hitter," *Sport Magazine*, no. 50 (July 1970): 45.

64. Lacy J. Banks, "Dick Allen a Regular Brother," *Ebony Magazine*, no. 25 (July 1970): 88

65. Dick Allen quoted in George Kiseda, "Rich Wants to be Alone in Clubhouse," *Philadelphia Evening Bulletin*, July 30, 1969.

66. Bob Skinner quoted in Bill Conlin, "Phillies' Ugliest Tug-of-War," *Philadelphia Daily News*, July 26, 1969.

67. Hisle and Jackson quoted in Conlin, "What If Allen Were White?"

68. Butler Hennon quoted in Smizik, "Somebody Still Likes Rich Allen."

69. Ray Kelly quoted in Cope, "What, Then, Is Wrong With Richie Allen?"

70. Skinner quoted in Allen Lewis, "Skinner Quits—Had His Fill of Richie," *Philadelphia Inquirer*, August 8, 1969; and Sandy Grady, "Skinner Quits: 'Had No Support,'" *Philadelphia Evening Bulletin*, August 7, 1969.

71. Carpenter quoted in Ray Kelly, "Carpenter Backs Son and Quinn," *Philadelphia Evening Bulletin*, August 7, 1969.

72. Dick Allen quoted in Sandy Padwe, "Inside the Richie Allen Mystery," *Grand Slam*, February 12, 1970, 16.

73. George Myatt quoted in Conlin, "Richie Is Beautiful," 93.

74. Ray Kelly, "Myatt Takes Control, Loosens Reins," *Philadelphia Evening Bulletin*, August 8, 1969; and Conlin, "Richie Is Beautiful," 93.

75. "Allen's Footwork Out of Step to Phils," *Sporting News*, August 23, 1969; Allen and Whitaker, *Crash*, 78; and Wolf, "Let's Boo Allen," 51–53.

76. "Phils Trade Allen to St. Louis, Phila. Gets Hoerner and Browne—Flood Plans to Retire as Player," *New York Times*, October 9, 1969.

77. Brad Snyder, *A Well-Paid Slave: Curt Flood's Fight for Free Agency in Professional Sports* (New York: Plume, 2007).

78. Allen quoted in William Mead, *Explosive Sixties: Baseball's Decade of Expansion* (Alexandria, VA: Redefinition, 1989), 101.

79. Allen quoted in *St. Louis Post-Dispatch*, October 11, 1969.

80. Barbara Allen quoted in Padwe, "Inside the Richie Allen Mystery."

Chapter 5: Interlude

1. Dick Allen quoted in Bob Broeg, "'I'm No Angel,'"; and Allen and Whitaker, *Crash*, 123–124.

2. Epstein, *Big Hair and Plastic Grass*, 36–37, 58–59.

3. Epstein, *Big Hair and Plastic Grass*, 171–172, 179.

4. For Flood's challenge of the reserve clause see Snyder, *A Well-Paid Slave*; and Alan Barra, "How Curt Flood Changed Baseball and Killed His Career in the Process," *Atlantic Monthly*, July 12, 2011, http://www.theatlantic.com/entertainment/archive/2011/07/how-curt-flood-changed-baseball-and-killed-his-career-in-the-process/241783/, accessed March 18, 2016. When he refused to report, the Phillies traded Flood to the Washington Senators. After losing his court battle, Flood played just thirteen games for the Senators before retiring in 1971. Although unsuccessful, his historic challenge paved the way for federal arbitration of salary demands, which MLB agreed to in 1973. Two years later, an arbitrator effectively reversed the court's 1972 verdict, throwing out the reserve clause and opening the door for the modern free agency that exists today.

5. "Steve Carlton's Major League Pitching Statistics," Baseballreference.com, accessed March 18, 2016.

6. Carlton and Busch quoted in William Leggett, "A Bird in Hand and a Burning Busch," *Sports Illustrated*, March 23, 1970, 18–22. Carlton would eventually sign with the Cardinals for $40,000. After posting a 20-9 record that season Carlton demanded a huge raise. Fed up, Busch traded him to the Phillies for Rick Wise, who was also embroiled in a salary dispute. The deal far exceeded Carlton's wildest dreams. During the next fourteen years Carlton won 240 games and four Cy Young awards (1972, '77, '80, '82), establishing himself as one of the greatest left-handers in the game. The Phillies also paid him handsomely. Over that same fouteen-year period, Carlton earned over $11 million in salary and bonuses, and was one of the highest paid pitchers in the 1980s. See Steve Bucci and Dave Brown, *Drinking Coffee with a Fork: The Story of Steve Carlton and the '72 Phillies* (Philadelphia: Camino Books, 2011); and Westcott and Bilovsky, *Phillies Encyclopedia*, 146–148.

7. Broeg, "'I'm No Angel.'"

8. Leggett, "Bird in Hand and a Burning Busch," 22. In 1969, the National and American leagues were divided into eastern and western divisions of six teams each to accommodate expansion. Each league held a best-of-five League Championship Series to decide the pennant. The American League was divided purely along geographic lines, but when it came time to assign divisions in the National League, the Chicago Cubs and St. Louis Cardinals insisted on being placed in the same division with the New York Mets and Philadelphia Phillies on the basis that more games with eastern teams would create a more lucrative schedule. Thus, Atlanta and Cincinnati were placed in the National League Western division. This alignment also addressed concerns that putting the league's three strongest clubs—St. Louis, San Francisco, and the Cubs—in the west would result in divisional inequity.

9. Broeg, "'I'm No Angel.'" Allen severed the ulnar nerve in his right hand in 1967, when he was pushing his car and his hand broke through the headlight. In 1966, he suffered a shoulder separation. Both injuries left him with bursitis, diminishing the quality of his field play, especially in colder weather.

10. Neal Russo, "When Richard the Stone Heart Almost Wept," *Sporting News*, April 25, 1970, 5.

11. Allen and Whitaker, *Crash*, 125–126.

12. Jenkinson, HR log.

13. Neal Russo, "Richie Could Need Big September to Top Mize," *St. Louis Post-Dispatch*, August 21, 1970.

14. Nesfield, "New Team, New Town, New Richie?," 63.

15. Neal Russo, "Cards Give Fast Shuffle to Allen," *Sporting News*, October 17, 1970, 5.

16. Richard Allen Jr., interview.

17. Barbara Moore Allen, interview.

18. Rick Allen, interview with the author, Jeannette, PA, April 25, 2016.

19. Barbara Moore Allen, interview.

20. Richard Allen Jr., interview.

21. Barbara Moore Allen, interview.

22. Richard Allen Jr., interview.

23. Jose Cardenal, interview with the author, Hazleton, PA, December 15, 2015.

24. Allen and Whitaker, *Crash*, 129.

25. George Kiseda, "Allen's Blast Sinks Phils," *Philadelphia Evening Bulletin*, September 9, 1970.

26. Allen and Whitaker, *Crash*, 130.

27. "Cardinals Sacrifice Richie Allen's Homerun Power to Shore up Team's No. 1 Headache in '70-Defense," *Jefferson City Post Tribune* (Missouri), October 6, 1970.

28. Los Angeles Dodgers, "Press release: Dodgers trade Ted Sizemore and Bob Stinson to the Cardinals for heavy-hitting Rich Allen," October 5, 1970.

29. Frank Dolson, "A Golden Glove For Richie Allen," *Philadelphia Inquirer*, March 31, 1970.

30. Campanis quoted in Leggett, "Bird in Hand and a Burning Busch," 21.

31. Moritz, "Dick Allen," 5.

32. Dick Allen quoted in Russo, "Cards Give Fast Shuffle to Allen."

33. Ron Allen, interview.

34. Dick Allen quoted in Russo, "Cards Give Fast Shuffle to Allen."

35. Ed Levitt, "The New Dodgers," *Oakland Tribune*, May 16, 1971, 53.

36. Dick Allen quoted in Nesfield, "New Team, New Town, New Richie?" 63.

37. Tommy Hutton, interview with the author, Palm Beach Gardens, FL, April 8, 2016.

38. Anonymous sportswriter and Dick Allen quoted in Nesfield, "New Team, New Town, New Richie?," 63.

39. Moritz, "Dick Allen," 6.

40. Dick Allen quoted in Nesfield, "New Team, New Town, New Richie?," 63.

41. Jim Barniak, "Allen Restores Some Tradition," *Philadelphia Evening Bulletin*, June 9, 1971.

42. Wes Parker quoted in Nesfield, "New Team, New Town, New Richie?," 70.

43. Bobby Valentine quoted in Blount, "Swinging in a Groove of His Own," 133.

44. Nesfield, "New Team, New Town, New Richie?," 70; and "Willie Crawford's Major League Hitting Statistics," Baseballreference.com.

45. "Dick Allen's MLB Hitting Statistics," Baseballreference.com.

46. Danny Ozark quoted in Wright, "Another View of Dick Allen," 12.

47. Allen and Whitaker, *Crash*, 134.

48. Carol Beringer quoted in Wright, "Another View of Dick Allen," 8–9.

49. "Allen Tells White Sox to Trade Him," *Philadelphia Evening Bulletin*, March 15, 1972.

50. Larry Merchant, "Allen Continues to Produce on His Terms," *New York Post*, March 30, 1972.

51. Allen and Whitaker, *Crash*, 136.

Chapter 6: Most Valuable Player

1. "Allen Tells White Sox to Trade Him."

2. Dick Allen quoted in Mike Rathet, "Will Richie Allen Destroy the Cardinals?" *Sport Magazine*, April 1970, 21, 78.

3. Edgar Munzel, "Allen's Mom Prime Mover in Chisox Surge," *Sporting News*, August 26, 1972.

4. Tanner quoted in Allen and Whitaker, *Crash*, 141–142.

5. Tanner quoted in Jim Barniak, "White Sox Lean on Allen's Shoulders," *Philadelphia Evening Bulletin*, April 28, 1978.

6. Era Allen quoted in Munzel, "Allen's Mom Prime Mover in Chisox Surge."

7. William Leggett, "Happy Days Are Here Again," *Sports Illustrated*, August 28, 1972, 18–21.

8. Richard Lindberg, *The White Sox Encyclopedia* (Philadelphia: Temple University Press, 1997), 373–374; and Epstein, *Big Hair and Plastic Grass*, 104–110.

9. Leggett, "Happy Days Are Here Again," 19.

10. John Helyar, *The Lords of the Realm: The Real History of Baseball* (New York: Ballantine, 1995), 116–129, 184.

11. George Langford, "Sox Whitewash Rangers, Allen Hits Pair of Doubles in Debut," *Chicago Tribune*, April 19, 1972.

12. Rich "Goose" Gossage, interview with the author, Colorado Springs, CO, April 15, 2016.

13. Jenkinson, DOP log.

14. Tanner quoted in Allen and Whitaker, *Crash*, 142–143.

15. Tanner quoted in Moritz, "Dick Allen," 6.

16. William Barry Furlong, "Dick Allen: Chicago Colossus," in *Baseball Stars of 1973*, ed. Ray Robinson (New York: Pyramid Books, 1973), 27.

17. Mark Stewart, Mike Kennedy, and Ron Jaffe, "Dick Allen: Crash Course," JockBio.com, accessed March 15, 2016; and Jenkinson, HR log.

18. Dick Allen quoted in Sandy Padwe, "MVP Dick Allen's Payoff," *Grand Slam*, September 1973, 14.

19. For Allen's 1972 All-Star Game performance see Jenkinson, DOP log. The 1972 All-Star Game was played on July 25 at Atlanta's Fulton County Stadium. The National League won 4-3 in ten innings. It would mark the start of an eleven-game winning streak for the NL, the longest winning streak by either league in the exhibitions' history. See John Thorn, ed., *Total Baseball*, 5th ed. (New York: Viking Press, 1997), 253.

20. Stewart, Kennedy, and Jaffe, "Dick Allen: Crash Course"; and Jenkinson, HR log.

21. Leggett, "Happy Days Are Here Again," 19.

22. William Leggett, "No Holes in These Sox to Mend," *Sports Illustrated* 38, no. 10 (March 12, 1973): 26–27. Melton, trying to remove his small son from a garage roof, fell off a ladder and aggravated an old disc injury. He played with increasing pain until June, when he was finally forced from the lineup for treatment.

23. Reggie Jackson quoted in Louis Robinson, "The Importance of Being Dick Allen," *Black Sports*, August 1972, 196.

24. Dick Allen quoted in Epstein, *Big Hair and Plastic Grass*, 69.

25. "1972 Chicago White Sox Pitching Statistics," Baseballreference.com, accessed March 22, 2016.

26. "1972 Chicago White Sox Hitting Statistics," Baseballreference.com, accessed March 22, 2016; and George Vass, "A New Murderers' Row?," *Baseball Digest*, August 1973, 24–26.

27. Bill Melton, interview with the author, Chicago, Illinois, April 5, 2016.

28. Gossage, interview. See also "Dick Allen's Pitching Advice to Goose Gossage," *New York Times*, July 26, 2008; and Kevin Kernan, "Goose and the Candor," *New York Post*, July 27, 2008.

29. Dick Allen quoted in Padwe, "MVP Dick Allen's Payoff," 104.

30. Stewart, Kennedy, and Jaffe, "Dick Allen: Crash Course"; and Jenkinson, HR log.

31. Melton, interview.

32. Gossage, interview.

33. Joseph Durso, "Dick Allen, in Landslide, Is Voted American League's Most Valuable," *New York Times*, November 16, 1972; and Arthur Daley, "The Most Valuable Nonconformist," *New York Times*, November 16, 1972. Rod Carew of the Minnesota Twins captured the American League batting title in 1972 with a .318 batting average. Lou Piniella of the Kansas City Royals finished second at .312, and Allen third with a .308 average. See "1972 American League Batting Leaders," Baseballreference.com, accessed April 1, 2016.

34. Hemond quoted in Durso, "Dick Allen, in Landslide."

35. David Fletcher, "Dick Allen—Best Player of His Generation Not in Hall of Fame," December 1, 2014, info@chicagobaseballmuseum.org, accessed January 27, 2016. WEAW, an Evanston, Illinois–based FM station, also carried the White Sox in 1971–72. It had a high-frequency signal broadcasting off the John Hancock Center, but at that time most cars did not have FM radios.

36. Dick Allen quoted in "'You Made Me a Human Being,' MVP Allen Tells Chisox Fans," *Sporting News*, December 2, 1972.

37. United Press International, "'Born Leader' Allen Now Highest Paid," *Philadelphia Daily News*, February 28, 1973; and Moritz, "Dick Allen," 6.

38. Leggett, "No Holes to Mend in These Sox," 26–27.

39. Epstein, *Big Hair and Plastic Grass*, 85.

40. Murray Chass, "Allen Reports to Spring Training Early," *New York Times*, March 14, 1973.

41. Allen quoted in Edgar Munzel, "'DH Rule Could Ruin Baseball,' Warns Allen," *Sporting News*, March 23, 1973, 7.

42. Melton, interview.

43. Dick Allen quoted in Blount, "Swinging in a Groove of His Own," 107.

44. Blount, "Swinging in a Groove of His Own," 107.

45. Dick Allen quoted in Blount, "Swinging in a Groove of His Own," 107.

46. Dick Allen quoted in Padwe, "MVP Dick Allen's Payoff," 14.

47. Blount, "Swinging in a Groove of His Own," 106.

48. Melton, interview.

49. Dick Allen quoted in Blount, "Swinging in a Groove of His Own," 106.

50. Hank Allen, interview. Hank enjoyed an extremely successful minor league career. In 1962, when he played for the Phillies' Class C Magic Valley Pioneers, he earned the Triple Crown, leading the Pioneer League with a .346 batting average, thirty-seven home runs, and 140 RBIs. Traded to the Washington Senators' organization in 1965, Hank Allen led the Pacific Coast League the following year with 288 total bases while playing for the Hawaii Islanders. Hank was promoted to the Washington Senators at the end of that season, but his major league career was not as successful. He appeared in a total of 352 games for Washington and Milwaukee over the next four years, batting .241 with just six home runs and fifty-seven RBIs. Retiring from baseball after the 1970 season,

Hank returned to the majors in September 1972 at the invitation of Chisox manager Chuck Tanner. The following season he appeared in twenty-eight games for the White Sox. Used as a defensive replacement, Hank played first, second, left field, and right field, and even caught one game on August 17, 1973, against the Cleveland Indians at Comiskey. Released by Chicago at the end of the season, he tried to catch on in the Pacific Coast League with Hawaii in '74, but after seventeen games he retired for good.

51. Dick Allen quoted in Blount, "Swinging in a Groove of His Own," 106.

52. Bill Jenkinson, *Baseball's Ultimate Power: Ranking the All-Time Greatest Distance Home Run Hitters* (Guilford, CT: Lyons Press, 2010), 167–168.

53. Robinson, "Importance of Being Dick Allen," 200; and Bonventre, "Dick Allen: 'Still My Own Man,'" 84.

54. Epstein, *Big Hair and Plastic Grass*, 89–90.

55. Bill Furlong, "Dick Allen: Money Guy in Chi," in *Baseball Stars of 1974*, ed. Ray Robinson (New York: Pyramid Books, 1974), 27.

56. Blount, "Swinging in a Groove of His Own," 112–114.

57. Hemond quoted in Jerome Holtzman, "Allen Shirked Duty, Medic Charges," *Sporting News*, March 2, 1974.

58. Dick Allen quoted in Stan Hochman, "Horses Gentle on Allen's Mind," *Philadelphia Daily News*, November 12, 1974.

59. Allen and Whitaker, *Crash*, 149.

60. See George Langford, "Dick Allen Shows Up Early for Sox Training Camp," *Chicago Tribune*, February 24, 1974; George Langford, "Sour Bite for Chuck in Allen 'Citric' Debut," *Chicago Tribune*, March 23, 1974; and George Langford, "Allen Makes Line-up . . . But Not Ballpark," *Chicago Tribune*, April 2, 1974.

61. Epstein, *Big Hair and Plastic Grass*, 126.

62. Jenkinson, DOP log.

63. Jerome Holtzman, "Well-Paid Allen Just Goes Through Motions," *Sporting News*, June 8, 1974.

64. Will Grimsley, "Dick Allen: An Enigma Reports to Camp," *Los Angeles Times*, March 19, 1974; George Langford, "Sox Sink Again; Allen 'Main Leak,'" *Chicago Tribune*, April 15, 1974; and George Langford, "Sox Lose 2-1; Allen Tardy, Santo Starts at 1st Base," *Chicago Tribune*, June 15, 1974.

65. A. S. Doc Young, "Allen Still Rapped by Writers, Fans," *Chicago Defender*, July 20, 1974; and A. S. Doc Young, "Aw C'mon, Now . . . ! *Chicago Defender*, August 1, 1974.

66. Tanner quoted in Phil Elderkin, "Dick Allen a Manager? Tanner Says He'd Be A Great One!" *Christian Science Monitor*, June 5, 1974.

67. Melton, interview.

68. Fletcher, "Dick Allen—Best Player of His Generation Not in Hall of Fame."

69. Allen and Whitaker, *Crash*, 150–151.

70. Jenkinson, *Baseball's Ultimate Power*, 168, 220.

71. Jenkinson, HR log.

72. Jim Barniak, "Allen Keeps All-Stars Guessing," *Philadelphia Evening Bulletin*, July 24, 1974; and Stan Hochman, "Allen's Late Show Rerun Has All-Star Cast," *Philadelphia Daily News*, July 24, 1974.

73. Dick Allen, interview, 2001; and Bruce Markusen, "Cooperstown Confidential: Dick Allen," *Hardball Times*, December 18, 2009, http://www.hardballtimes.com/cooperstown-confidential-dick-allen/, accessed March 3, 2016.

74. Dick Allen quoted in Richard Dozer, "Allen Bids Adieu to Chisox Fame and Fortune," *Sporting News*, September 28, 1974.

75. Melton, interview.

76. Gossage, interview.

77. "Allen's Major League Hitting Statistics."

78. Kevin Hurley, interview with the author, Chicago, IL, June 2, 2016.

79. Jerome Holtzman, "Chisox Glad to be Rid of Allen," *Sporting News*, October 12, 1974.

80. Richard Dozer, "Has Allen Retired? No, Not Officially," *Sporting News*, November 2, 1974. Fueling Allen's departure from the White Sox was an offer from a Japanese baseball team for $2 million a season, much more than the top MLB players were earning at the time.

81. Glenn Schwartz, "Atlanta Un-retires Allen from Chisox," *San Francisco Examiner*, December 3, 1974.

Chapter 7: Return to Philly

1. "Philadelphia Negotiating for Allen," *Philadelphia Inquirer*, February 17, 1975. See also Frank Hyland, "Braves Jump Out of the Frying Pan and Into the Fire," *Atlanta Journal*, December 5, 1974; and Wayne Minshew, "Braves Obtain Allen—But Will He Play?" *Sporting News*, December 21, 1974.

2. William C. Kashatus, *Almost a Dynasty: The Rise and Fall of the 1980 Phillies* (Philadelphia: University of Pennsylvania Press, 2008), 31–47, 74–77.

3. Westcott and Bilovsky, *Phillies Encyclopedia*, 252.

4. "Phils Get Tug McGraw from Mets," *Philadelphia Daily News*, December 3, 1974; and Tug McGraw with Don Yaeger, *Ya Gotta Believe! My Roller Coaster Life as a Screwball Pitcher and Part-time Father, and My Hope-Filled Fight Against Brain Cancer* (New York: New American Library, 2004), 134–137.

5. "Phils send Brett to Bucs for Dave Cash," *Philadelphia Daily News*, October 18, 1973; and Kashatus, *Almost a Dynasty*, 91–92.

6. Allen and Whitaker, *Crash*, 153.

7. For leaks on Allen's interest in returning to Philadelphia, see Allen Lewis, "Phils Secretly Trying to Lure Dick Allen Off the Farm," *Philadelphia Inquirer*, February 4, 1975; Bill Lyon, "Phils Believe They Can Win It All . . . With Dick Allen," *Philadelphia Inquirer*, February 11, 1975; Allen Lewis, "Montanez Ready to Vacate First for Allen," *Philadelphia Inquirer*, March 3, 1975; and Bill Conlin, "Can Allen Answer Trade Riddle?," *Philadelphia Daily News*, May 5, 1975.

8. Allen and Whitaker, *Crash*, 154.

9. Frank Dolson, *The Philadelphia Story: A City of Winners* (South Bend, IN: Icarus, 1981), 194.

10. "Phils Sign Allen, Give Up Essian," *Philadelphia Daily News*, May 7, 1975; "Dick Allen Comes Back to the Phillies," *Philadelphia Evening Bulletin*, May 7, 1974; and Bill Verigan, "Braves Give Up Allen for 3 Phil Farmhands, $," *New York Daily News*, May 8, 1975.

11. Allen quoted in Stan Hochman, "Dick Allen: 'I'm No Messiah,'" *Philadelphia Daily News*, May 8, 1975.

12. Barry Rosenberg, "Two for the See-Saw: Mike Schmidt and Dick Allen," *Philadelphia Magazine*, September 1975, 130–144.

13. Dick Allen, interview, 2001.

14. Bill Conlin, "Danny Ozark's Five Simple Rules for Dick Allen," *Philadelphia Daily News*, May 8, 1975.

15. Ozark quoted in Dolson, *Philadelphia Story*, 194.

16. Hutton, interview.

17. Dick Allen, interview, 2001.

18. Mark Carfagno, interview with the author, South Philadelphia, March 24, 2016.

19. Frank Dolson, "The Boos Turn to Cheers for Richie Allen," *Philadelphia Inquirer*, May 15, 1975; Ellen Karasik, "Richie's Back . . . to 3 Standing Ovations," *Philadelphia Inquirer*, May 15, 1975; and Stan Hochman, "Allen Starts New Love Affair," *Philadelphia Daily News*, May 15, 1975.

20. "Phils Beat Giants, 1-0, in Extras," *Philadelphia Daily News*, May 27, 1975; Rosenberg, "Two for the See-Saw," 138; and Allen Lewis, "Allen Can't Escape the Aura of Being a Man of Miracles," *Philadelphia Inquirer*, May 23, 1975.

21. Rosenberg, "Two for the See-Saw," 131–132.

22. Ruly Carpenter quoted in Rosenberg, "Two for the See-Saw," 135.

23. Ruly Carpenter, interview.

24. Rich Westcott, *Veterans Stadium* (Philadelphia: Temple University Press, 2005), 114, 135–143; and Epstein, *Big Hair and Plastic Grass*, 46–57.

25. Dick Allen, interview, 2001. For the effects of a torn Achilles on MLB power hitters see Jeff Passan, "Ryan Howard Feels Kinship with Achilles Survivors," Grapefruit League 2012, Yahoo! Sports, March 2, 2012; and "Baseball Injuries Part 2: Hitters," Premier Orthopaedics, www.premier-ortho.com/baseball-injuries-part-2-hitters/, accessed March 31, 2016.

26. Ray Kelley, "Allen Clouts Pair, Carlton Blanks LA," *Philadelphia Bulletin*, June 8, 1975.

27. "Allen Hits 9th Homer to Lead Phils over Pads, 6-5," *Philadelphia Daily News*, August 23, 1975.

28. Ralph Bernstein, "Bowa: Stiff Arm, Failure to Adjust to Allen Blamed for Errors of His Ways," *Philadelphia Inquirer*, September 5, 1975.

29. Westcott and Bilovsky, *Phillies Encyclopedia*, 88.

30. Allen Lewis, "Allen's Future? 'I Gotta Play,'" *Philadelphia Inquirer*, September 13, 1975.

31. Westcott and Bilovsky, *Phillies Encyclopedia*, 88–89.

32. Dick Allen quoted in Ray Kelly, "'I Owe Phillies,' Says Allen After Dismal Season," *Sporting News*, October 11, 1975.

33. Ray Kelly, "Dick Allen Fanning Less and Enjoying It Much More," *Philadelphia Evening Bulletin*, April 4, 1976; and Bill Conlin, "Allen's 'Father' Dies," *Philadelphia Daily News*, March 29, 1976.

34. Hutton, interview.

35. Allen Lewis, "Allen's Pride is Hurt: Bats 7th," *Philadelphia Inquirer*, May 19, 1976.

36. Mike Schmidt, interview with the author, Jupiter, FL, February 15, 2016.

37. Allen and Whitaker, *Crash*, 161.

38. Larry Eldridge, "Mike Schmidt Would Rather Be Consistent," *Baseball Digest*, September 1976, 68–71.

39. Allen and Whitaker, *Crash*, 161–162.

40. Rich Ashburn, "Schmidt Misplaced in Line-up," *Philadelphia Bulletin*, April 14, 1976.

41. Dick Allen quoted in Hochman, *King of Swing*, 62.

42. Allen Lewis, "Schmidt Hits 4 HRs as Cubs Bow, 18-16," *Philadelphia Inquirer*, April 18, 1976.

43. Schmidt, interview.

44. Larry Christenson, interview with the author, Malvern, PA, April 13, 2016.

45. Allen Lewis, "Allen Clouts 2: Phils Win 12–4," *Philadelphia Inquirer*, June 26, 1976.

46. Allen and Whitaker, *Crash*, 163.

47. Bruce Keidan, "Today's the BIG Day that Allen Comes Back," *Philadelphia Inquirer*, August 10, 1976.

48. Bill Conlin, "Anatomy of a Slump," *Philadelphia Daily News*, September 13, 1976; and Stan Hochman, "Is Anxiety Key to Phils' Slump?" *Philadelphia Daily News*, September 7, 1976.

49. Allen and Whitaker, *Crash*, 163.

50. Schmidt, interview.

51. Ruly Carpenter, interview.

52. Christenson, interview.

53. Allen Lewis, "Phils Win, Take Division Title," *Philadelphia Inquirer*, September 27, 1976.

54. Bruce Keidan, "Allen Declines to Join in Phils' Fun," *Philadelphia Inquirer*, September 27, 1976; and Allen and Whitaker, *Crash*, 166.

55. See Bill Conlin, “Phils Do Their Flying Without Dick Allen,” *Philadelphia Daily News*, September 27, 1976.

56. See Bill Conlin, “Dissension Brewing on Phillies,” *Philadelphia Daily News*, September 29, 1976; and Bill Conlin, “Phils Feuding over Allen’s Flight?” *Philadelphia Daily News*, September 30, 1976.

57. Dave Cash, interview, with the author Utica, NY, January 23, 2015.

58. Garry Maddox quoted in Keidan, “Allen Declines to Join in Phils’ Fun.”

59. For Schmidt, Cash, Maddox, and Allen as Christian athletes, see Mike Schmidt, “Something More,” *Guideposts*, July 1987, 3; and Schmidt, interview.

60. For more on the Christian athlete movement in baseball see Phil Elderkin, “Religion and Baseball,” *Christian Science Monitor*, August 2, 1977; Dave Brannon and Joe Pellegrino, *Safe at Home: Winning Players Talk About Baseball and Their Faith* (Chicago: Moodly Press, 1992); and Steve Hubbard, *Faith in Sports: Athletes and Their Religion On and Off the Field* (New York: Doubleday, 1998).

61. Schmidt, interview.

62. Tug McGraw, quoted in Chuck Slater, "Phils Weigh Dropping Allen for Playoffs, World Series." *New York Daily News*. October 1, 1976.

63. Maddox quoted in Slater, “Phils Weigh Dropping Allen for Playoffs, World Series.”

64. Tug McGraw, interview with the author, Media, PA, September 8, 2002.

65. Allen and Whitaker, *Crash*, 164.

66. Ruly Carpenter, interview.

67. Dick Allen quoted in Bill Conlin, “If Taylor Sits Out, So Will Allen,” *Philadelphia Daily News*, September 25, 1976.

68. Ozark quoted in Slater, “Phils Weigh Dropping Allen.”

69. Bruce Keidan, “Allen to Play, Taylor to Coach: Owner Settles Dispute,” *Philadelphia Inquirer*, October 1, 1976.

70. Taylor, interview.

71. Westcott and Bilovsky, *Phillies Encyclopedia*, 481–482.

72. Westcott and Bilovsky, *Phillies Encyclopedia*, 88–89.

73. "Only Finley Shows Interest in Dick Allen," *Los Angeles Times*, November 13, 1976; "Allen Agrees to Contract with A's," *Philadelphia Inquirer*, March 11, 1977; and "Allen Joins A's," *Philadelphia Daily News*, March 11, 1977.

74. G. Michael Green and Roger D. Lanius, *Charlie Finley: The Outrageous Story of Baseball's Super Showman* (New York: Walker Books, 2010), 159–162; Epstein, *Big Hair and Plastic Grass*, 107–108, 172–173.

75. Bruce Markusen, *A Baseball Dynasty: Charlie Finley's Swingin' A's* (Haworth, NJ: St. Johann Press, 2002); Epstein, *Big Hair and Plastic Grass*, 76.

76. Eddie Jeffries, "Allen's Drumbeat Comes to an End," *New Pittsburgh Courier*, August 6, 1977; Dave Anderson, "Lolich, Allen Spring Eternal," *New York Times*, March 11, 1978; and "Dick Allen is Cut from A's Roster," *Los Angeles Times*, March 29, 1978. Allen played his final game for the A's on June 19, 1977.

Chapter 8: Reconciliation

1. Red Smith, "Dick's Designated Runners," *New York Times*, December 29, 1974. After the 1974 MLB season, when Allen thought of retiring, he returned to Perkasie and tended to his two prized race horses: "Getting Ready," a maiden, and "Pisces' Dream," a high-priced gelding he bought at the Kentucky sales. "Pisces' Dream" ran in a five-horse race in the sixth at Keystone Racetrack on November 11, 1974, and finished fifth, beaten a head and a neck for third. See Hochman, "Horses Gentle on Allen's Mind."

2. Franz Lidz, "What Ever Happened To . . . Dick Allen," *Sports Illustrated*, July 19, 1993, 86.

3. Hank Allen, interview.

4. Hank Allen, interview.

5. George Vecsey, "Racing's Big League Trainer," *New York Times*, May 19, 1985; and Neil Milbert, "Still Dealing With Thoroughbreds. Dick Allen's Brother Hank Finds Success as Trainer After Baseball Career," *Chicago Tribune*, July 12, 1987; Joe DeVino, "Laurel Park: Blessed Soul and trainer Hank Allen back in stakes for Maryland Racing Media," *Daily Racing Form*, February 21, 2013.

6. Eddie Smith quoted in Red Smith, "Dick's Designated Runners."

7. Dick Allen quoted in Hochman, "Horses Gentle on Allen's Mind."

8. Ted Silary, "Another Dick Allen is Working in Phils' Infield," *Philadelphia Daily News*, June 26, 1986.

9. Richard Allen Jr., interview.

10. Mark Stewart, Mike Kennedy, and Ron Jaffe, "Dick Allen: Crash Course," JockBio.com, accessed March 15, 2016.

11. Mark Kram, "'She Was Special' 'Everyone Loved Her' Family, Friends Mourn Loss Dick Allen's Daughter, Terri," *Philadelphia Daily News*, June 12, 1991; and M. Floyd Hall, "Ex-Phillie's Daughter Dies In Maryland," *Morning Call* (Allentown, PA), June 7, 1991.

12. Kram, "'She Was Special.'" To honor Terri Allen's memory, Howard University established a scholarship in the broadcast journalism department in her name. The scholarship was awarded annually "to the student who has the same energetic hope for the future as Terri possessed."

13. Barbara Allen quoted in Hall, "Ex-Phillie's Daughter Slain in Maryland."

14. Richard Allen Jr., interview.

15. Richard Allen Jr., interview.

16. Frank Dolson, "The Fans Still Love Dick Allen," *Philadelphia Inquirer*, January 6, 1985; and Glen Duffy, "Where's Dick Allen?" *Philadelphia Magazine*, April 1987, 160, 209–210.

17. Rich D'Ambrosio, "Dick Allen," in *The Year of the Blue Snow: The 1964 Philadelphia Phillies*, ed. Mel Marmer and Bill Nowlin (Cleveland, OH: Society of American Baseball Research, 2013), 15; and Lidz, "What Ever Happened To . . . Dick Allen."

18. Dick Allen quoted in Lidz, "What Ever Happened To . . . Dick Allen."

19. Stan Hochman, "Allen Feels Good to Be Returning," *Philadelphia Daily News*, March 2, 1994; Frank Dolson, "The Good Memories Return with Allen," *Philadelphia Inquirer*, March 3, 1994.

20. Jeremy Treatman, "Phillies' RBI Program a Hit," Liberty City Press, September 1, 2015, www.libertycitypress.com/play-article/1028-phillies-rbi-program-is-a-hit.html, accessed April 3, 2016.

21. Dick Allen quoted in Sandy Padwe, "Chicago Finds the Secret for Success," *Black Sports*, May 1973, 21.

22. Stewart, Kennedy, and Jaffe, "Dick Allen: Crash Course."

23. Frank Fitzpatrick, "Enshrined or Not, Allen Has Clout," *Philadelphia Inquirer*, July 18, 2010; and Ted Silary, "Allen, Phils in Lovefest," *Philadelphia Daily News*, August 7, 1999.

24. Demaio, interview.

25. Santelli, interview.

26. Fitzpatrick, "Enshrined or Not, Allen Has Clout"; "After 38 Years, White Sox Savior Dick Allen Finally Gets His Due," *Chicago Sun-Times*, June 11, 2012.

27. Carfagno, interview.

28. Mike Tollin, interview with the author, Los Angeles, CA, February 22, 2016.

29. Phil Sheridan, "Polarizing, captivating. A film on Dick Allen is in the works," *Philadelphia Inquirer*, August 8, 2010; and Fitzpatrick, "Enshrined or Not, Allen Has Clout."

30. Tollin, interview.

31. Bedell, interview.

32. Phone conversation with author, Wampum, PA, March 25, 2016.

Chapter 9: Hall of Famer in Waiting

1. Ryan Lawrence, "Dick Allen Misses Hall of Fame by One Vote," *Philadelphia Daily News*, December 10, 2014; Dan Epstein, "Baseball's Hall of Fame Gets It Wrong Again," *Rolling Stone*, December 8, 2014; and National Baseball Hall of Fame, "Eras Committees," www.baseball.org, accessed January 25, 2017.

2. "Dick Allen's Major League Career Batting Statistics," www.baseballreference.com, accessed March 25, 2016; and Westcott and Bilovsky, *Phillies Encyclopedia*, 125–126.

3. Jenkinson, *Baseball's Ultimate Power*, 195, 237.

4. "Allen's Major League Career Batting Statistics."

5. Allen Barra, "The Best Player Eligible for the Hall of Fame," *Wall Street Journal*, July 28, 2006.

6. Brian Kenny, "Dick Allen Is a Hall of Famer," Sports on Earth, December 5, 2014, www.sportsonearth.com/article/103259248/dick-allen-hall-of-fame-golden-era, accessed March 25, 2016. Kenney did a more detailed presentation of Allen's career batting statistics on a December 4, 2016, segment of "MLB Now."

7. Wright, "Another View of Dick Allen," 2–14. Quotations from Gene Mauch, Red Schoendienst, Carol Beringer, and Chuck Tanner were taken from Wright's essay.

8. Gossage, interview.

9. Schmidt, interview.

10. Willie Stargell quoted in Allen and Whitaker, *Crash*, 185.

BIBLIOGRAPHY

Allen, Dick, and Tim Whitaker. *Crash: The Life and Times of Dick Allen*. New York: Ticknor & Fields, 1989.

Blount, Roy Jr. "Swinging in a Groove of His Own. When Dick Allen Crashed, So Did the White Sox." *Sports Illustrated* 39, no. 11 (September 10, 1973): 104–114.

Bonventre, Peter. "Dick Allen: 'Still My Own Man,'" *Newsweek*, August 21, 1972, 83–84.

Bunning, Jim. *The Jim Bunning Story*. Philadelphia: Chilton Books, 1965.

Callison, Johnny with John Sletten. *The Johnny Callison Story*. New York: Vantage Press, 1991.

Conlin, Bill. "Richie Is Beautiful, He Don't Give a Damn for Nobody." *Jock Magazine,* January 1970, 88–94.

Cope, Myron. "What, Then, Is Wrong With Richie Allen?" *Sport Magazine*, May 1966, 36, 84–86.

Duffy, Glen. "Where's Dick Allen?" *Philadelphia Magazine*, April 1987, 153–160, 209–210.

Epstein, Dan. *Big Hair and Plastic Grass: A Funky Ride through Baseball and America in the Swinging '70s*. New York: Thomas Dunn Books, 2010.

Jacobson, Matthew Frye. "'Richie' Allen, Whitey's Ways and Me: A Political Education." In *In the Game: Race, Identity, and Sports in the Twentieth Century*, edited by Amy Bass, 19–46. New York: Palgrave, 2005.

Jenkinson, Bill. *Baseball's Ultimate Power: Ranking the All-Time Greatest Distance Home Run Hitters*. Guilford, CT: Lyons Press, 2010.

Kashatus, William C. *Almost a Dynasty: The Rise and Fall of the 1980 Phillies.* Philadelphia: University of Pennsylvania Press, 2008.

Kashatus, William C. *September Swoon: Richie Allen, the '64 Phillies, and Racial Integration*. University Park: Pennsylvania State University Press, 2004.

Kuklick, Bruce. *To Every Thing a Season: Shibe Park and Urban Philadelphia, 1909–1976*. Princeton, NJ: Princeton University Press, 1991.

Leggett, William. "A Bird in Hand and a Burning Busch," *Sports Illustrated* 32, no. 12 (March 23, 1970): 18–22.

Leggett, William. "Happy Days Are Here Again," *Sports Illustrated* 37, no. 9 (August 28, 1972): 18–21.
Leggett, William. "No Holes to Mend in These Sox. As Spring Training Opens, Dick Allen Is Rich and Ready," *Sports Illustrated* 38, no. 10 (March 12, 1973): 26–27.
Leggett, William. "The Rookie From Wampum, PA," *Sports Illustrated* 20, no. 16 (April 20, 1964): 28–29.
Lowry, Joseph F. "Whoever Heard of Wampum, Pa.?" *The Sunday Bulletin Magazine*, June 21, 1964, 4–5.
Nathanson, Mitchell. *God Almighty Hisself. The Life and Legacy of Dick Allen.* Philadelphia: University of Pennsylvania Press, 2016.
Nesfield, Carl. "New Team, New Town, New Richie?" *Black Sports*, July 1971, 30–31, 62–63, 70.
Padwe, Sandy. "Chicago Finds the Secret for Success," *Black Sports*, May 1973, 18–23.
Padwe, Sandy. "MVP Dick Allen's Payoff," *Grand Slam*, September 1973, 12–14, 104.
Razer, Bob. "The Black Traveler: Dick Allen and Little Rock Baseball, 1963." *Pulaski County Historical Review* 61 (Spring 2013): 2–10.
Rhoden, William C. "Weighing the Complexity of a Hall Candidate, and His Times." *New York Times*, December 7, 2014.
Rosenberg, Barry. "Two for the See-Saw: Mike Schmidt and Dick Allen." *Philadelphia Magazine*, September 1975, 130–144.
Westcott, Rich, and Frank Bilovsky. *The Phillies Encyclopedia*. 3rd ed. Philadelphia: Temple University Press, 2004.
Wolf, David. "Let's Everybody Boo Rich Allen!" *Life Magazine*, August 1969, 50–53.
Wright, Craig R. "Another View of Dick Allen." *SABR Baseball Research Journal* 24 (1995): 2–14.
Wulf, Steve. "Year of the Blue Snow." *Sports Illustrated*, September 25, 1989, 76–86.

ACKNOWLEDGMENTS

On May 5, 2004, I received a letter from Dick Allen thanking me for writing *September Swoon*, a book that addressed his early career with the Philadelphia Phillies. He told me my work was "a much more accurate appraisal of [his] career than [that of] any sportswriter who covered it," and that I was "right on the mark" with most of my conclusions. At the same time, Dick confessed the book was "very painful for [him] to read" and that he would rather "forget the past and move on with [his] life."

I was grateful he took the time to write the letter, since most professional athletes would not extend the same courtesy. But I was also saddened that my book brought back such painful memories. While I do not feel my ability as a writer was validated by that letter, or see myself as an apologist for Dick, he has become a friend since then. Thus, I am extremely grateful for his blessing to do another book on his career.

Although Dick declined my request to be interviewed for this work, I certainly understand his reasons for doing so. Besides, I already possessed an additional three hours of audio tape from earlier interviews that dealt with his career between 1970 and 1977 that I did not use in *Swoon*. Thus, I was confident I could offer wholly new material if I decided to write a second book on Dick.

As a baseball historian, I have always tried to go beyond the newspaper and magazine accounts, as well as book treatments, of any ballplayer on whose career I have chosen to write. What matters most to me is that I capture the human integrity of my subject. To do that, I have a responsibility to address their professional and personal lives, identify the virtues and shortcomings in them, and then draw insightful conclusions about their impact on the national pastime. When the subject is as complex as Dick Allen, these responsibilities become especially challenging. I am extremely grateful to Dick's son, Richard Allen Jr.; Howie Bedell; Mark "Frog" Carfagno; Mike Schmidt; and Mike Tollin for providing important contacts, supporting the book project unconditionally, and troubleshooting when necessary. These five individuals have also been instrumental in spearheading the campaign to get Allen inducted into the National Baseball Hall of Fame. It is fitting that this book is dedicated to them, and to the memory of Dick's mother, Era, who was the greatest love and inspiration of his life.

Since Dick declined the opportunity to do another interview, I am grateful to his family members, teammates, and close friends for sharing with me their insights into his personality and career. In addition to Richard Jr., Howie, Frog, Schmitty, and Mike, I am grateful to Barbara, Hank, Rick, and Ron Allen; Jose Cardenal; Ruly Carpenter; Dave Cash; Clay Dalrymple; Larry Christenson; Guy Demaio; Rich "Goose" Gossage; Tommy Hutton; Bill Jenkinson; Sonny King; Frank Lucchesi; Bill Melton; Carl "Stump" Merrill; Jim Santelli; and Tony Taylor for their willingness to be interviewed.

Special thanks is also due to Sheila Sager of Penn State University Press and Zoe Gould of the University of Pennsylvania Press for permission to reprint sections of my earlier books; Joseph Kapenstein for his extensive collection of newspaper articles on Allen's career; the baseball historian Bill Jenkinson for sharing Dick's home run and daily offensive performance logs that he researched over the past few decades, and for his endorsement of the book; Bob Grim of the Chicago White Sox for providing access to photographs and contact information for former Chisox players; Mike Schmidt for writing the foreword and for his endorsement; and Tony Taylor for his endorsement.

Other folks were invaluable in providing artwork and photographs, especially artists Drew Davis, Rob Larsen, Kate and Nancy Linnett, Dick Perez, and Gregory Sgambato; Rick Allen, steward of the Allen family photograph collection; Mark Carfagno and Cassie Duffy, Mandalay Sports Media; David Fletcher, Chicago Baseball Museum; Bob Grim, Chicago White Sox; Dave Montgomery, Philadelphia Phillies Baseball Club; Steve Mucha, Bernard Oravec, and Karen Kennedy of the *Williamsport Sun-Gazette*; and Heather Greenberg and Alexis Melisi of the Topps Company, Inc., all of whom waived fees to reprint artwork or photos in the book. Others were helpful locating iconic images of Dick Allen and/or assisting in the paperwork to purchase and gaining permission to reprint them. For this, I am grateful to Stephanie Bayless, Butler Center, Central Arkansas Library System, Little Rock; Brenda Galloway-Wright, Temple University Libraries; John Horne, National Baseball Hall of Fame and Library; Lou Hunsinger of the Williamsport Crosscutters Baseball Club; Jessica Stremmel, YGS Group; and Dalen Touza, Getty Images.

Special thanks is also due to Nancy and Peter Schiffer, as well as Ted Kutt and Ian Robertson of Schiffer Publishing. They were a pleasure to work with and took a chance on publishing my work. I only hope the final product—and sales—meet with their approbation.

Finally, I am grateful for the unconditional support and inspiration of my parents, William and Balbina; my wife, Jackie; and my sons Tim, Peter, and Ben. Few men admit to having heroes. I thank the good Lord for having been born, married, and being a father to mine. Words cannot adequately express the love and admiration I have for them.